Stitches to Riches?

DIRECTIONS IN DEVELOPMENT
Poverty

Stitches to Riches?

Apparel Employment, Trade, and Economic Development in South Asia

Gladys Lopez-Acevedo and Raymond Robertson, Editors

WORLD BANK GROUP

Contents

Tables

Acknowledgments

This report was written by a team led by Gladys Lopez-Acevedo (Lead Economist, SARCE) and Raymond Robertson (Professor, Texas A&M) and consisting of (in alphabetic order) Ritika D'Souza (Consultant, SARCE), Stacey Frederick (Consultant, SARCE), Atisha Kumar (Consultant, SARCE), and Yevgeniya Savchenko (Economist, GPVDR). Substantive analytical contributions were made by Diego Cardozo (chapter 4), Benjamin Goldman (chapter 3), Jyotinder Kaur (chapter 4), Amir Sadeghi (chapter 4), and Cornelia Staritz (chapter 2). The team is grateful to Laura Wallace (Consultant, SARCE) for skillful editing of the report and compiling the appendix, Michael Alwan for formatting, Anna Socrates for editing of background papers, and Neelam Chowdhry for team assistance support.

The team benefited from the insightful advice of our peer reviewers, David Gould (Lead Economist, ECACE), Sanjay Kathuria (Lead Economist, T&C), Vincent Palmade (Lead Economist, T&C), and Binayak Sen (Research Director, Bangladesh Institute of Development Studies). We are also grateful to colleagues from the World Bank for their comments and contributions at various stages in the process of developing the study, notably Vincent Arthur Floreani (WBG Analyst, IFC), Bilgehan Gokcen (Consultant, ECADE), Markus Kitzmuller (Economist, SARCE), Yue Li (Senior Economist, SARCE), Denis Medvedev (Senior Economist, T&C), Anna O'Donnell (Social Development Specialist, GSURR), and Ayesha Raheem.

The cover illustration for this report was conceptualized and executed by Harshad Marathe. The World Bank Group's Publishing and Knowledge Division managed the editorial services, design, production, and printing of the book. The World Bank Group's General Services Department printed the book.

The team acknowledges the generous support for the preparation of this book through the MTDF TF071865 trust fund. This report was sponsored by the Office of the Chief Economist South Asia (SARCE) of the World Bank under the leadership of Martin Rama (Chief Economist, SARCE).

About the Editors and Contributors

Editors

Gladys Lopez-Acevedo is a lead economist at the World Bank in the Chief Economist's Office for the South Asia Region (SARCE) working in the areas of welfare, gender, conflict, and jobs. Gladys was a senior economist in the World Bank Central Vice Presidency Poverty Reduction and Economic Management (PREM) unit and in the Latin America Region at the World Bank, managing a portfolio on evaluation, fragility, and poverty. Her research interests include poverty, labor markets, and evaluation, and she has published extensively in these areas in academic and policy journals. She is a fellow in leading global knowledge institutions such as the Latin America Economic Association (LACEA) and the International Initiative for Impact Evaluation. Prior to joining the World Bank, she held high-level positions in the Government of Mexico, including adviser to the vice minister of finance and deputy director in the Ministry of Economy. Gladys has been an associate professor at the Instituto Tecnológico Autónomo de México (ITAM) and a research fellow at the University of Virginia. She holds a BA in economics from ITAM and a PhD in economics from the University of Virginia.

Raymond Robertson holds the Helen and Roy Ryu Chair in Economics and Government in the Department of International Affairs at the Bush School of Government and Public Service at Texas A&M University. Robertson is also a research fellow at the Institute for the Study of Labor in Bonn, currently chairs the U.S. Department of Labor's National Advisory Committee for Labor Provisions of the U.S. Free Trade Agreements, and is a member of the Center for Global Development's advisory board.

Contributors

Ritika D'Souza is an analyst at the World Bank's Office of the Chief Economist for the South Asia Region (SARCE). Her current research covers welfare, nutrition, education, gender, and jobs. Previously, she worked on impact evaluations of agriculture, food security, and nutrition projects in Rwanda and Nepal with the World Bank's Development Impact Evaluation (DIME) group. She received a master's in public administration from the School of International and Public Affairs, Columbia University.

Stacey Frederick is a research scientist at Duke University's Center on Globalization, Governance & Competitiveness (Duke CGGC). She received her BS in textile management and her PhD in textile technology management at North Carolina State University. Her research involves using value chain analysis to identify economic, social, and environmental upgrading opportunities for countries and firms in a variety of industries. Within textiles and apparel, she has analyzed issues for numerous nongovernmental organizations and country governments ranging from employment generation to trade policy impacts in several countries and regions, including Africa, Asia, and North and South America.

Atisha Kumar is the research director at the JustJobs Network in New Delhi. She received a master's in public administration in international development from the Harvard Kennedy School. Her research focuses on the political economy of trade and labor economics. Previously, she worked on the South Asia competitiveness flagship report for the World Bank.

Yevgeniya Savchenko is an economist in the Poverty and Equity Practice in the Latin America and the Caribbean Region at the World Bank, leading the poverty program in the Caribbean. She works on issues related to poverty, labor markets, skills development, and competitiveness. Prior to joining the group, she worked in the South Asia Region, the Europe and Central Asia Region, and the World Bank Institute. She holds an MS in economics from the University of Illinois at Urbana-Champaign and a PhD in economics from Georgetown University, where she taught econometrics and statistics.

Abbreviations

AEPC	Apparel Export Promotion Council
AITUC	All India Trade Union Congress
APTMA	All Pakistan Textile Mill Association
APTUF	All Pakistan Trade Union Federation
ASEAN	Association of Southeast Asian Nations
ASEAN-4	Indonesia, Malaysia, the Philippines, and Thailand
ASI	Annual Survey of Industries
BBS	Bangladesh Bureau of Statistics
BCWS	Bangladesh Centre for Workers' Solidarity
BEPZA	Bangladesh Export Processing Zones Authority
BGIWF	Bangladesh Garment & Industrial Workers Federation
BGMEA	Bangladesh Garment Manufacturers and Exporters Association
BIGUF	Bangladesh Independent Garment Workers Union Federation
BKMEA	Bangladesh Knitwear Manufacturers and Exporters Association
BOI	Board of Investment
BTMA	Bangladesh Textile Mills Association
CAGR	compound annual growth rate
CIAE	Confederation of Indian Apparel Exporters
CITI	Confederation of Indian Textile Industry
CMAI	Clothing Manufacturers Association of India
COMTRADE	United Nations Trade Statistics Database
CSR	corporate social responsibility
EDB	Engineering Development Board
ENOE	Encuesta Nacional de Ocupación y Empleo
EPB	Export Promotion Bureau
EPZ	export processing zone
EU	European Union

EU-15	Refers to the 15 member states of the European Union (EU) as of December 31, 2003, before the new member states joined the EU: Austria, Belgium, Denmark, Finland, France, Germany, Greece, Ireland, Italy, Luxembourg, the Netherlands, Portugal, Spain, Sweden, and the United Kingdom.
EUROSTAT	European Commission Database
FDI	foreign direct investment
FIIA	Foreign Investment Implementation Authority
FIPB	Foreign Investment Promotion Board
FOB	free on board
FTA	free trade agreement
FTZWU	Free Trade Zone Workers' Union (Sri Lanka)
GAFWU	Garment and Fashion Workers' Union (India)
GATWU	Garment and Textile Workers' Union
GDP	gross domestic product
GSP	generalized system of preferences
HIES	Household Income and Expenditure Survey
HMS	Hind Mazdoor Sabha (India)
HS	Harmonized System
HTS	Harmonized Tariff System
INTUC	India National Trade Union Congress
ISIC	International Standard Industrial Classification
JAAF	Joint Apparel Association Forum
JSS	Jathika Sevaka Sangamaya (Sri Lanka)
JV	joint venture
KSA	Kurt Salmon Associates
LDC	least-developed country
LFP	labor force participation
LFS	Labor Force Survey
LPI	Logistics Performance Index
MEM	Mazdoor Ekta Manch (India)
MFA	Multifibre Arrangement
MFN	most-favored nation
MGEM	Multiplicative General Error Model
MMF	manmade fiber
MoC	Ministry of Commerce
MoCI	Ministry of Commerce & Industry
MoI	Ministry of Industry
MoIC	Ministry of Industry and Commerce

MoIP	Ministry of Industry and Production
MoT	Ministry of Textile Industry
MoTJ	Ministry of Textile & Jute
NBR	National Board of Revenue
NGO	nongovernmental organization
NGWF	National Garment Workers' Federation
NSS	National Sample Survey
NTC	National Tariff Commission
NTPA	National Tripartite Plan of Action
NTUF	National Trade Union Federation (Pakistan)
NWC	National Workers Congress (Sri Lanka)
OHS	occupational health and safety
OTEXA	Office of Textiles and Apparel of the U.S. Department of Commerce
P	price
PNTLGGWF	Pakistan National Textile Leather Garments & General Workers' Federation
PRGMEA	Pakistan Readymade Garment Manufacturer & Exporter Association
PTEA	Pakistan Textile Exporters' Association
Q	quantity
ROW	rest of the world
SAFTA	South Asian Free Trade Area
SAR	sample South Asian countries: Bangladesh, India, Pakistan, and Sri Lanka
SEAB	Southeast Asian Benchmark Countries: Cambodia, Indonesia, and Vietnam
SIA	Secretariat for Industrial Assistance
SITP	Scheme for Integrated Textile Parks (India)
SLR	Sri Lanka rupees
SME	square meter equivalence
SMEDA	Small & Medium Enterprises Development Authority
SMI	Survey of Manufacturing Industries
SSA	Sub-Saharan Africa
SUR	seemingly unrelated regression
TDAP	Trade Development Authority of Pakistan
TEXMIN	Ministry of Textiles, India
Tk	Taka (Bangladesh)
TPP	Trans-Pacific Partnership

TUFS	Technology Upgradation Funds Scheme
UAE	United Arab Emirates
UN	United Nations
UNCTAD	United Nations Conference on Trade and Development
UNIDO	United Nations Industrial Development Organization
U.S.	United States
US$	United States dollar

Overview

Key Messages

- South Asia must create good-quality jobs for a rapidly expanding young population and bring more women into the labor force.
- The apparel sector in South Asia is labor intensive, employs more women on average than other manufacturing sectors, and provides jobs that allow for the acquisition of skills.
- Apparel already constitutes approximately 40 percent of manufacturing employment. And, given that much of apparel production continues to be labor intensive, the potential to create more and better jobs is immense.
- Despite these development benefits, the sector has not reached its full potential because of inefficiencies that affect its competitiveness.
- As a creator of jobs that are "good for development" and an illustration of the distortions that stifle productivity in light manufacturing in South Asia, this sector merits careful analysis.

Focusing on Jobs for Development

As developing countries explore ways to boost living standards and reduce poverty, they are increasingly focusing on policy options to create jobs that are "good for development." For South Asia, this is a high priority, given that it must absorb nearly 1 million individuals who will enter the workforce every month for the next three decades, and that it continues to have a stubbornly low rate (30 percent) of female labor force participation. This job focus offers huge payoffs. As the *World Development Report 2013: Jobs* (World Bank 2013b) reminds us, the value of a job to society can far exceed its value to the individual jobholder. Job opportunities tilted toward the poor may have greater impacts on poverty reduction. Jobs for women may influence resource allocations at the household level and benefit their children. Jobs connected to world markets may lead to knowledge spillovers and make workers more productive (World Bank 2013b). And jobs that make these significant contributions to society are good jobs for development.

Export-oriented apparel production—long a key industry in South Asia—displays characteristics of good jobs for development. Apparel work is highly female intensive, with women's share of total apparel employment being much higher than women's share of the national labor force in nearly every country in the region. As apparel exports increase, the rising demand for female labor pulls women from agriculture and other informal sectors. Women employed in the formal sector tend to have fewer children, reducing population growth; and several studies have found that women are more likely to dedicate their income to the health and education of children (World Bank 2015). Finally, apparel exports pay women higher wages than they could earn elsewhere (Lopez Acevedo and Robertson 2012).

Already Bangladesh, India, Pakistan, and Sri Lanka (the "SAR [South Asia] group" highlighted in this report) have made substantial investments in world apparel trade—which is considered a gateway to globalized manufacturing exports. In 2012, apparel represented 83 percent of Bangladeshi exports, 45 percent of Sri Lankan exports, 19 percent of Pakistani exports, and 5 percent of Indian exports. The share of female employment in apparel in South Asia is higher than in other manufacturing industries, ranging from 5 percent in Pakistan to 71 percent in Sri Lanka. Plus, recent elections in India and Pakistan have featured energetic debates on the role of the apparel sector in development. At the same time, however, recent industrial disasters have attracted global attention, raising questions about whether some countries can overcome significant challenges in health, safety, and labor relations.

China now dominates global apparel trade, but that may change in the years ahead. Between 2000 and 2012, its share of global apparel exports increased from 25 percent to 41 percent. However, as China continues to develop, it is likely to either move up the value chain into higher-value goods (and out of apparel) or be subject to production shifts in response to its higher wages (box O.1). A 2013 survey of leading global buyers in the United States and the European Union (EU) found that 72 percent of respondents planned to decrease their share of sourcing from China over the next five years (2012–2016). In addition, rising prices in China are encouraging investors to seek out apparel firms in countries like Cambodia and Vietnam. There is also evidence that China is looking to shift production to higher value added industries like electronics. Although China remains the world's largest apparel exporter, apparel as a share of its total exports in 2012 accounted for only 7.1 percent—about half of the 15.6 percent in 1990. The potential decrease in Chinese exports presents a huge opportunity for South Asian countries—which currently account for 12 percent of global apparel exports—prompting a lot of debate about how best to position the region and generate good jobs.

The recently completed Trans Pacific Partnership (TPP)—a trade agreement between 12 Pacific Rim countries including the United States—will also likely have far-reaching impacts for key sectors in South Asia, including apparel. A reduction in tariff and nontariff barriers could lead to trade diversion for South Asia, including in the textiles and apparel sector. Petri, Plummer, and

---

Box O.1 Moving up the Global Value Chain in Apparel

Global value chains, which include the full range of activities required to bring a product from its conception to its end use, can be driven by producers or buyers. Apparel is a classic example of a buyer-driven chain. It is characterized by decentralized, globally dispersed production networks and coordinated by lead firms that control the highest-value activities related to retailing, marketing, branding, and design. The buyers outsource most of the manufacturing process to a global network of suppliers—for apparel, this is typically to low-income countries.

The main segments of the supply chain include apparel manufacturing, textile components (yarn and fabric) and trim, and fiber production. The top three globally traded apparel product categories by export value include trousers, knit shirts, and sweaters/sweatshirts, which together account for 46 percent of traded apparel. Given the relevance of these products, a country needs to be a key player in these categories to account for a sizeable share of the global industry. It also must have the capability to produce products that are growing in terms of global market share such as fashion products and fiber type and, of course, to diversify markets.

As the competition in the global apparel sector continues to intensify (buyers' consolidation process), successful manufacturers will need not only to offer lower costs but also to introduce new processes, work organization, and technology—all of which improve operational performance and productivity. They can do so through vertical or horizontal upgrading. One example would be setting up backward manufacturing links, especially to the textile industry. Another would be shifting to more sophisticated products with higher unit prices. Yet another would be increasing the range of functions or shifting or changing the mix of activities to higher-value tasks.

Zhai (2011) find that India could experience trade diversion losses of about 0.2 percent of its gross domestic product (GDP) under an Asia-Pacific Free Trade area. Under the new agreement, TPP members such as Vietnam will enjoy duty-free access to the United States, but South Asian countries will continue to pay import duties, thus making South Asian apparel costlier. South Asia would also lose out in the textiles sector. One of the provisions of the TPP is the "Yarn Forward Rule," which makes it mandatory for apparel producers to source yarn, fabric, and other inputs from TPP partner countries to get duty preferences. Vietnam currently imports yarns and fabric from India as an input into its final apparel. Under the new provision, imports from member countries are expected to rise at a greater rate than from nonmembers (CUTS International 2015). Thus, Vietnam may no longer import fabric from India to avoid losing out on significant preferences.

This report is aimed at better informing that debate by demystifying the global and South Asian apparel markets, estimating the potential gains in exports and jobs (including for women), and identifying policies that can unleash South Asia's export and job potential. Our sample South Asian countries—the SAR group of Bangladesh, India, Pakistan, and Sri Lanka—are the largest apparel exporters. Our sample Southeast Asian benchmark countries (hereafter the "SEAB group") are Cambodia, Indonesia, and Vietnam. Given that the extent to which these countries will be able to create more jobs will depend on the individual decisions of their firms and workers, we concentrate on how changes in the global market (like rising apparel prices in China) could affect exports, wages, and employment in the apparel sector in other countries.

Analytical Framework

Our analytical framework centers on the production function of a typical firm, where output (y) is a function of technology (A), capital (K), and labor (L). This approach is particularly useful in our study for three reasons. First, output is modeled as the production sold in international markets, which is greatly affected by the kinds of conditions that motivate our study. Second, the production function represents an implicit demand for labor. As is well known, the demand for labor is a derived demand that is directly affected by changes in output markets. Third, the familiar technology term A often represents those factors in the production function that are not easily quantifiable. In our analysis, we acknowledge these qualitative aspects that affect both the outputs and the inputs with a careful discussion of the economic and policy environment, which is often lacking in purely quantitative studies.

To illustrate how the report is structured, consider figure O.1, which shows the production function in the center with two key relationships: (i) the output market and how changes in the international market affect the demand for the firm's product (left-hand side); and (ii) the input market (right-hand side). The input market is affected by the demand for output, the structure of the

Figure O.1 Overarching Framework for *Stitches to Riches*

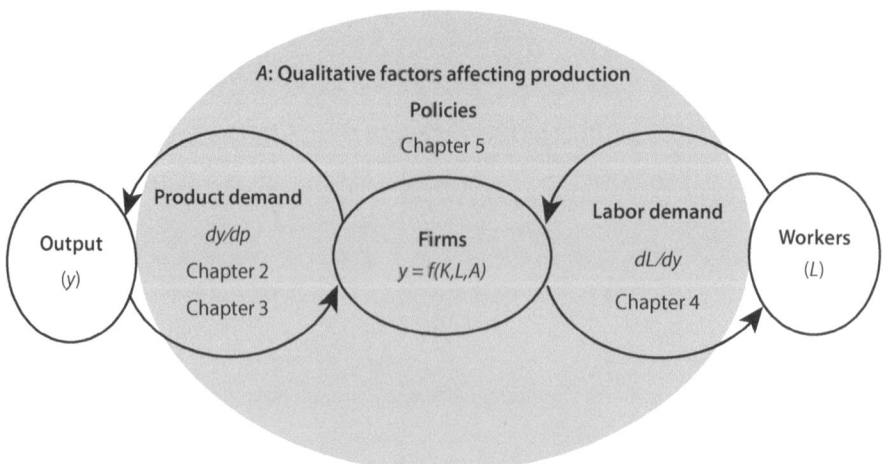

Note: A = technology; K = capital; L = labor; y = output.

production function, and the supply of inputs. Surrounding the core production function (represented by the areas above and below the production function and its implied output and input relationships) are the qualitative dimensions.

Our study follows this structure closely. We begin at the left of figure O.1 with an analysis of what shapes global demand for apparel. Chapter 2 presents the benchmarking analysis that characterizes the global apparel market and identifies the factors that buyers care about when making their sourcing decisions. Then chapter 3 presents empirical estimates of how much exports from our focus countries might change given rising apparel prices in China. And, because the changes in the output market have implications for labor demand, we can then (in chapter 4) move on to the input market. Here we explicitly and empirically model both firm-level labor demand and labor supply to estimate how local employment would be affected by the change in global export markets. We then move to the policy areas that affect A (in chapter 5) to analyze the policy environment and, drawing on the analysis of the previous three chapters, present some policy implications. We also use the calculations from chapters 2, 3, and 4 to estimate potential employment gains for the SAR group from higher demand for apparel exports, assuming that current policies and conditions remain constant.

Our empirical estimates of the potential for South Asia to increase apparel exports and employment do not take into account the impact of the TPP. However, given the predicted adverse impacts of the TPP for South Asia, our estimates are likely conservative. In reality, the potential upside in terms of exports and employment from the sector would likely be higher once the TPP is in place.

The main message of this report is that it is important for South Asian economies to address existing impediments and to facilitate growth in apparel to foster the creation of good jobs for development. If they fail to do so—and fail to do so quickly—they risk losing out on a huge opportunity to create good jobs for development given China's rising apparel prices. In addition, the successful manufacturers will be those who can introduce new processes, work organization, and technology and who can respond to the fast-changing apparel industry demands—not just those who offer low costs.

South Asia's Potential to Expand Apparel Exports

As South Asian countries look for ways to step up their apparel exports, it is important to establish how they fare compared to global competitors. Our analysis in chapter 2 on global benchmarking finds that, in terms of value and global market share, countries in the SAR group have steadily increased their share of global apparel trade above the world average and greater than China's but lower than that of the SEAB group. At the country level, however, some have done a lot better than others—with export growth rising in Bangladesh (the top performer), and to a lesser extent in Pakistan, while slowing in India and Sri Lanka.

In terms of product categories, most competitors are adequately producing and selling basic items that match global trends in current demand in
these areas. However, India and Sri Lanka concentrate on higher-value
exports in relatively smaller runs, focusing on value addition and more complex and differentiated items, something all the SAR group countries will
need to think about as they try to hold on to their competitive edge
(box O.1). As for fiber type, the SAR group is heavily focused on cotton-
based apparel products (75 percent of apparel exports), which fits current
demand, although this is well above the world average (46 percent). And
such a large deviation from the world average—which reflects the growing
role of manmade fiber (MMF) exports—will pose problems for satisfying
future demand and product diversity.

Regarding end markets, apparel exports from the SAR group are concentrated on the EU-15, accounting for 52 percent, followed by the United States
at 25 percent. Exports from the SEAB group are also focused on the EU and
the United States; but, whereas the SAR group exports more to the EU market,
the SEAB group is more concentrated on the United States. Looking ahead, the
SAR group needs to accelerate the diversification process in light of the fact
that China has more diversified export markets than the SAR or SEAB group
countries.

Given the significant variation in export patterns, this report also sought to
find out how apparel buyers' preferences fit in. Our analysis shows that the
SEAB group and China are outperforming the SAR group in terms of overall
apparel export performance, product diversity, and non-cost-related factors
important to global buyers (table O.1). SAR group countries—with the exception of Sri Lanka—generally appear to be cost competitive in apparel but fare less
well on other factors important to global buyers such as quality, lead times,
reliability, and social compliance.

Much of the pressure on social compliance comes from corporate social
responsibility (CSR) campaigns by nongovernmental organizations, compliance-
conscious consumers, and, more recently, the higher number of disasters in
apparel factories (box O.2). We know that working conditions in apparel manufacturing establishments in many developing countries are characterized by low
wages, long hours, high temperatures, excessive noise, poor air quality, unsanitary
environments, and abuse (both verbal and physical). Yet we lack consistent and
quantitative evidence that is comparable across countries and that would help
inform the policy debate. Further complicating matters is the fact that apparel is
not only labor intensive but also one of the easiest manufacturing sectors for
women to enter because it requires only basic skills (and thus relatively low levels of education) and typically does not involve working with machines. In addition, the apparel sector offers a promising and realistic entry point for women
into the formal labor force, thanks to a high wage premium compared to agriculture. Plus, in developing countries, working conditions often depend on what the
country can afford—such as providing reliable electricity—and sometimes just
getting a job is a life-changing event for an individual.

Table O.1 Room for SAR to Diversify Products and Better Meet Buyers' Preferences
(Global Benchmarking Analysis)

Key results	Bangladesh	India	Pakistan	Sri Lanka
Increasing market share	Largest increase in global market share within SAR	Exports increase but at a lower rate than the world average	Exports increase at a higher rate than the world average	Exports increase but at a lower rate than the world average
Product diversity and availability is a key concern	Lack of MMF-based products	Lack of MMF-based products Limited MMF availability Barriers to MMF textile imports	Lack of MMF-based products Limited MMF availability Barriers to MMF textile imports	Lack of diversity across product categories outside of intimate apparel and activewear
All SAR group countries have substantially diversified their end markets away from the dominant EU-15 (and to a lesser extent United States), but compared to China there is still room to diversify.				
Mostly strong performance on factors buyers care about	Cost competitive Compliance is an issue	Cost competitive Non-cost issues present a hurdle	Cost competitive Reliability Compliance	Not cost competitive
Limited foreign investment and participation in global production networks				

Source: World Bank (see chapter 2 of this report).
Note: EU-15 = Austria, Belgium, Denmark, Finland, France, Germany, Greece, Ireland, Italy, Luxembourg, Netherlands, Portugal, Spain, Sweden, and the United Kingdom; MMF = manmade fiber.

Box O.2 Growing International Concern about South Asian Working Conditions

Bangladesh. Wages and working conditions have long been a source of concern in the apparel sector, as evidenced by the frequent strikes and labor unrest following the collapse of the Rana Plaza factory in April 2013 (which killed more than 1,000 people) and other incidents such as the fire at Tazreen Fashions in November 2012 (which killed 112 workers). In response, the industry—in collaboration with the government, foreign buyers, and development partners— has agreed on several policy measures to improve factory safety and social compliance. However, negotiating collective bargaining agreements is still very difficult. Female workers in particular lack voice and representation in the country's weak industrial relations system. And regulatory capacity is generally weak because of underfunded, understaffed, and under-requipped labor ministries, inspectors, and courts.

India. Workers in the formal sector generally enjoy better working conditions and wages than those in the informal sector, where compliance is limited and actually most apparel workers are employed. Overtime seems to be a serious problem, (AEPC 2013b) child labor has been a recurring issue (although not at first-tier apparel factories), and there are reports of discrimination against pregnant women and of sexual harassment. In the rapidly expanding apparel cluster in Tirupur (Tamil Nadu), migrant workers face discrimination under a scheme known as Sumangali. In response, the Ministry of Textiles and the Apparel Export Promotion Council have launched a certification scheme to raise awareness in apparel export value chains (AEPC 2013b), and in 2011 India joined the multistakeholder Ethical Trading Initiative (ETI website).

box continues next page

Box O.2 Growing International Concern about South Asian Working Conditions *(continued)*

Pakistan. Working conditions are better in the formal industry than in the large cottage sector; but short-term or temporary contracts are widely used, particularly for women (ILO 2010b), and the factory fire in Karachi in September 2012 highlighted poor safety standards. However, the granting of Generalized System of Preferences (GSP) Plus status by the European Union in 2013 is seen as a way to promote Pakistan as a compliant producer. Another key concern is political (Global Apparel Buyers 2014). Many buyers avoid Pakistan because of the security situation and hence entrepreneurs have to travel to Dubai to meet them, which complicates sourcing (National Stakeholders 2014).

Sri Lanka. Working conditions are generally better than in the other South Asian countries (National Stakeholders 2014). To improve the international and local image of the apparel industry, the Joint Apparel Association Forum (JAAF) established the "Garment without Guilt" initiative in 2006—which includes a certification program—as part of the Five-Year Strategy following the end of the Multifibre Arrangement (MFA). Compliance and political stability are strong areas for Sri Lanka, and the country has attracted partnerships with ethically oriented buyers, including M&S, Nike, and Victoria's Secret (Global Apparel Buyers 2014; National Stakeholders 2014).

Source: World Bank (see chapter 2 of this report).

So how much would an SAR group country's apparel exports increase for a given increase in Chinese apparel prices? Chapter 3 tries to answer this by computing the responsiveness of apparel exports to prices in China, what economists call the "elasticity of substitution." These estimates are then compared with the elasticity of substitution for the potential competitors. The target markets are the two largest apparel buyers, the United States and the EU. Our results suggest that a 10 percent increase in Chinese apparel prices will result in a 13–25 percent (depending on country) rise in South Asian countries' apparel exports to the United States (table O.2), although this is below the 37–51 percent increase in Southeast Asian countries. This underscores that apparel producers face intense international competition in the sense that apparel production is very responsive to price changes. It also suggests SEAB group countries (such as Vietnam and Cambodia) stand to gain much more than the SAR group countries. This becomes even more relevant because the apparel industry is undergoing a consolidation process with global buyers looking for fewer places and firms for outsourcing (box O.1).

How Higher Exports Would Affect SAR's Labor Market

In the next section of this report, we move on to examine what would occur at the firm and worker level if South Asia is able to capture a larger share of the apparel market. Chapter 4 notes that, because apparel exports represent a major share of total exports in most SAR countries and because exports represent a

Table O.2 Some SAR Countries Will Capture More Global Market Share Than Others

Key results	Bangladesh		India		Pakistan		Sri Lanka	
Export elastic-ity: effect of a 10% rise in Chinese prices on exports	U.S. exports	EU exports	U.S. exports	EU Exports	U.S. exports	EU exports	U.S. exports	EU exports
	13.58%	Change not statisti-cally signifi-cant	14.62%	18.95%	25.31%	Change not statisti-cally signifi-cant	Less than 1%	22.49%

Source: World Bank (see chapter 3 of this report).
Note: EU = European Union.

major share of their apparel production—in Bangladesh, 75 percent of apparel output is exported—one could expect that labor demand in the apparel sector would be mainly driven by exports.

On the demand side, we explore how much the expansion in the textile and apparel sector would increase labor demand in the region—that is, how many new jobs firms would create in response to higher exports. Our main results show that a 1 percent increase in apparel output (which is used as a proxy for exports) is associated with a 0.3–0.4 percent increase in employment (for both men and women) in Bangladesh, Pakistan, and Sri Lanka. India's values are lower, at a 0.14 percent increase in demand for male workers and a 0.08 percent increase in demand for female workers. These results suggest that the sector has a larger potential for job generation in response to an increase in exports than do other industries, especially for women (table O.3).

On the supply side, we investigate how more jobs or higher wages would reshape the labor pool. In other words, to what extent (the labor supply "elas-ticity") higher expected labor income would draw more women into the labor force. Our results show that female labor, especially low-skilled labor, is very responsive to higher wages. A 1 percent increase in the expected wage increases the likelihood of women joining the labor force by between 16 per-cent in Pakistan and 89 percent in Sri Lanka. We also find that a wage pre-mium exists in the apparel sector compared to agriculture that ranges from 8 to 27 percent, depending on the country—a premium that is even higher when only women are considered. However, this premium has stopped rising in all SAR countries besides Bangladesh with the end of the Multifibre Arrangement (MFA) in 2005.

South Asia's Potential to Create Jobs

In the final section of this report, we pull together the analysis in the previous chapters to ask how many new jobs the increased demand will translate into. Keep in mind that we have assumed that higher Chinese prices will boost the demand for apparel from South Asia and that firms in South Asia will respond by creating jobs. We have also assumed that more jobs will enhance welfare (as opposed to simply leaving the level of welfare unchanged) because workers will be drawn from either the informal sector or agriculture, both of which pay lower wages than apparel exporting firms. In other words, apparel exporters face a relatively elastic supply curve, especially in the short run because there is a large pool of temporary workers.

We calculate the potential job creation in chapter 5 by combining two elasticity estimates: (i) the responsiveness of South Asian apparel exports to an increase in Chinese prices (from chapter 3); and (ii) the responsiveness of employment to an increase in apparel output (from chapter 4) for both males and females in the U.S. and EU markets. Together, they give us the elasticity of employment to prices.

For the U.S. market, we find that a 10 percent increase in Chinese apparel prices would increase apparel employment in Pakistan for males by 8.93 percent— by far the biggest winner—followed by Bangladesh (4.22 percent) and India (3.32 percent) (table O.3, panels a and b). The gains for Sri Lanka are less than 1 percent, but it is important to keep in mind that the estimates in table O.3 panels a and b are for exports to the United States only. The story is much the same for females. In India, the gains in employment for females are small (2.51 percent) due to the small employment estimate for India, which may reflect rigidities in the labor market that make employment not very responsive to changes in output. Overall, because apparel hires relatively more females to begin with, the expected total number of women working in apparel would increase more than the number of men working in apparel.

For the EU market, the most striking result is the large difference in the prediction for Sri Lanka, whose elasticity is very high (table O.3, panels c and d). The results suggest that a 10 percent increase in Chinese apparel prices would increase Sri Lankan male apparel employment by 8.55 percent, followed by India (4.30 percent); but Bangladesh and Pakistan would experience small decreases because their trade estimates do not suggest that they are close substitutes for Chinese apparel products in the EU market. For females, the results are qualitatively similar in that female employment in Sri Lanka now would appear to increase by 7.87 percent, while the other countries are predicted to have a small change. Again, the exception might be India. If China's prices to Europe increase by 10 percent, India could have a 3.26 percent increase in female employment. Therefore, an increase in demand could draw many new workers into apparel.

Although the estimates for the U.S. and EU markets—which together account for about half of global apparel imports—are not necessarily small, they are smaller than those predicted for Southeast Asia countries. We do not have the employment elasticities for the latter group of countries, but using the mean of the estimates from the South Asian countries above suggests that the gains would be even higher in Southeast Asia. One possible reason for the different expected job effects arises from the fact that the trade elasticities of these two regions may differ.

Table O.3 For U.S Market, Pakistan and Bangladesh Are the Big Winners, Whereas Sri Lanka Wins for the EU

Panel a: Male employment responses for exports to United States

Country	Elasticity of exports to prices (ε_{xp})	Elasticity of jobs to exports (ε_{Ex})	Elasticity of jobs to prices $\left(\dfrac{\%\Delta Employment}{\%\Delta Prices}\right)$
Bangladesh	1.358*	0.311***	0.422
India	1.462*	0.227	0.332
Pakistan	2.531*	0.353***	0.893
Sri Lanka	0.024	0.380***	0.009

Panel b: Female employment responses for exports to United States

Country	ε_{xp}	ε_{ex}	$\dfrac{\%\Delta Employment}{\%\Delta Prices}$
Bangladesh	1.358*	0.323***	0.439
India	1.462*	0.172***	0.251
Pakistan	2.531*	0.336***	0.850
Sri Lanka	0.024	0.350***	0.008

Panel c: Male employment responses for exports to Europe

Country	ε_{xp}	ε_{ex}	$\dfrac{\%\Delta Employment}{\%\Delta Prices}$
Bangladesh	−0.238	0.311***	−0.074
India	1.895*	0.227***	0.430
Pakistan	−0.060	0.353***	−0.021
Sri Lanka	2.249*	0.380***	0.855

Panel d: Female employment responses for exports to Europe

Country	ε_{xp}	ε_{ex}	$\dfrac{\%\Delta Employment}{\%\Delta Prices}$
Bangladesh	−0.238	0.323***	−0.077
India	1.895*	0.172***	0.326
Pakistan	−0.060	0.336***	−0.020
Sri Lanka	2.249*	0.350***	0.787

Source: World Bank (see chapters 3, 4, and 5 of this report).
Note: z-statistics in parentheses, *** $p<0.01$, ** $p<0.05$, * $p<0.1$. The elasticities reported here are for a 1 percent increase in prices of Chinese apparel.

Thoughts on a New Strategic Approach

South Asia has put in place a number of policies to support the textile and apparel sector; but, as identified in the benchmark analysis in chapter 2, there is still significant room for improvement in a number of key areas—product concentration, quality, input availability, lead times, reliability, and compliance—that are relevant to boost exports and create good jobs for development. This matters greatly because our report finds that, under the status quo (that is, even without reforming these areas), South Asia exhibits significant potential to capture displaced apparel production as a result of rising costs in China. Indeed, our estimates suggest that a 10 percent increase in China's prices would boost

South Asian exports between 13 and 25 percent, although the gain would be even bigger for Southeast Asia (between 37 and 51 percent).

These higher exports, in turn, would potentially translate into more good jobs for development. Moreover, female workers are expected to benefit the most—including through higher expected wages than in agriculture, which would have positive ripple effects for both the overall economies and individual households. Indeed, this report estimates that a 10 percent rise in Chinese wages could be associated with an increase of up to 9 percent in male and female employment in the South Asian countries. Individual estimates vary by country, gender, and trading partner—with Pakistan and Bangladesh winning the biggest gains for the U.S. market and Sri Lanka doing the best in the EU markets. This also underscores the unique situation and policies in place in each country.

Thus, it is important for South Asian economies to design and implement policies to improve competitiveness in apparel. Most South Asian countries would benefit significantly from easing barriers to the import of inputs and facilitating market access and foreign investment. In chapter 5, we identify emerging reform priorities and provide policy options for the four South Asia countries, which highlight the following common themes: increasing market access, removing barriers to access to MMF, and attracting more foreign investment.

Bangladesh

Bangladesh's apparel firms produce large quantities of apparel at low costs, due largely to its low wage rates. Firms mostly specialize in low-value and mid-market price segment apparel and have not penetrated the high-end apparel segments. Along almost every apparel product category, the benchmarking highlights that Bangladesh has the lowest prices. However, it performs poorly in the areas of compliance, quality, and reliability—which are important in attracting foreign investment. Bangladesh also stands to gain greatly in terms of jobs from additional apparel exports—a 10 percent increase in Chinese prices to the United States would lead to an increase of over 4 percent each in male and female employment.

Bangladesh has many policy options to increase exports. Policy makers could attract more foreign investment through additional incentives and transparency to ensure access to buyers and additional capital. They could ensure that policies to improve compliance are enforced (such as better safety conditions in export processing zones [EPZs]), which will help make Bangladesh a more attractive destination for foreign investors. And they could reduce the import barriers faced by firms in importing MMFs to improve quality and produce more higher–value added apparel.

India

Apparel firms in India are disproportionately concentrated in the informal sector and tend to be small. Further, firms mainly produce cotton garments and have not made inroads into the market for synthetic apparel. As the benchmarking revealed, India currently has midrange unit values but low productivity, product diversity, and lead times. Our elasticity estimates reveal that a 10 percent increase in Chinese prices to the EU can increase male employment by 4.3 percent and female employment by 3.26 percent.

As for policy options for product diversity, policy makers could reduce tariffs and import barriers to ease access to MMFs—such as more transparency for duty drawback schemes and bonded warehouses, and removing antidumping duties on MMFs. They could also lower excise taxes or provide other incentives to develop a domestic MMF industry. To improve productivity, they could help firms enter the formal sector and take advantage of economies of scale with less complex labor policies. They could also promote foreign investment for apparel by adopting clear and transparent policies on foreign ownership (already in place for textiles) and within EPZs. Plus, India could diversify markets by taking advantage of market access to emerging markets. Given that almost all apparel and textile firms are domestically owned, India is in a better position to expand exports to markets—other than the United States and Europe—that already have established production networks and sourcing relationships with East Asian and Southeast Asian firms. Finally, better roads will shorten lead times.

Pakistan

Pakistan has a fast-growing apparel sector that accounts for 19 percent of its exports, and firms are competitive with global exporters in terms of prices. Yet, despite low prices in most apparel product categories, Pakistan lags competitors in reliability, and political stability is still an issue. It also remains highly concentrated in cotton products. Fortunately, Pakistan stands to gain many jobs from the apparel sector. A 10 percent increase in Chinese prices to the United States would increase male employment by 8.93 percent and female employment by 8.5 percent.

For policy makers, one way to increase product diversity and move away from cotton-based apparel is to reduce barriers on imports to ease access to MMFs. They could attract global buyers and investors by adopting policies to reduce red tape and increase transparency. They could diversify markets, taking advantage of market access to emerging markets. And they could shorten lead times by improving road infrastructure to facilitate access to ports for exporting firms.

Sri Lanka

Sri Lankan apparel prices are higher than those of competitors in most product categories, and its product portfolio is largely made up of higher-value, niche products. Average literacy in Sri Lanka is higher than in other South Asian countries, and a more skilled workforce also allows them to produce more sophisticated apparel products. Sri Lanka stands to gain significantly from increasing its apparel exports, particularly to the EU market. Elasticity estimates highlight that a 10 percent increase in Chinese apparel prices could increase Sri Lankan male employment by 8.55 percent and female employment by 7.87 percent.

Sri Lanka could benefit from policies to diversify its export markets, attract additional foreign investment, and capitalize on its skills advantage by producing new, more sophisticated products. To help firms diversify end markets and export destinations for existing products, policy makers might consider more trade agreements with potential partners—foreign investment remains at 2 percent of GDP, even five years after the end of armed conflict. Also helpful might be adopting clear investment policies to portray stability and attract additional investment. To capitalize on Sri Lanka's skills advantage, firms could expand into new products such as formal wear and high-end outerwear that require higher skills. Finally, policy makers could position Sri Lanka as a regional apparel and textile trade hub, taking advantage of infrastructure and location.

South Asia must create good quality jobs for a rapidly expanding young population and bring more women into the labor force. The apparel sector in South Asia is labor intensive, employs more women on average than other manufacturing sectors, and provides jobs that allow for the acquisition of skills. Despite these development benefits, the sector has not reached its full potential because of inefficiencies that affect its competitiveness. The main message of this report is that it is important for South Asian economies to address existing impediments and facilitate growth in apparel to foster the creation of good jobs for development. If they fail to do so—and fail to do so quickly—they risk losing out on a huge opportunity to create good jobs for development given China's rising apparel prices. In addition, the successful manufacturers will be those who can introduce new processes, work organization, and technology and can respond to the fast changing apparel industry demands—not just those who offer low costs.

Bibliography

Alfridi, Farzana, Abhiroop Mukhopadhyay, and Soham Sahoo. 2012. "Female Labour Force Participation and Child Education in India: The Effect of the National Rural Employment Guarantee Scheme." IZA working paper 6593. Institute for the Study of Labor, Bonn.

Anderson, James E., and Eric van Wincoop. 2003. "Gravity and Gravitas: A Solution to the Border Puzzle." *American Economic Review* 93 (1): 170–92.

Bhattacharya, Debapriya, and Mustafizur Rahman. 2001. "Female Employment under Export Propelled Industrialization: Prospects for Internalizing Global Opportunities in the Apparel Sector in Bangladesh." Occasional Paper 10, United Nations Research Institute for Social Development (UNRISD).

CUTS International. 2015. *Mega Regional Trade Agreements and the Indian Economy: An Analysis of Potential Challenges and Opportunities.* Geneva: CUTS International.

Fukunishi, Takahiro, and Tatsufumi Yamagata, eds. 2014. *The Garment Industry in Low-Income Countries: An Entry Point of Industrialization.* IDE-JETRO. Basingstoke, UK: Palgrave Macmillian.

Gereffi, Gary, and Stacey Frederick. 2010. "The Global Apparel Value Chain, Trade, and the Crisis: Challenges and Opportunities for Developing Countries." In *Global Value Chains in a Postcrisis World: A Development Perspective*, edited by Olivier Cattaneo, Gary Gereffi, and Cornelia Staritz, 157–208. Washington, DC: World Bank.

Global Apparel Buyers. 2014. *Interviews with Global Apparel Buyers.* Interviewer: S. Frederick.

Greenaway, David, Aruneema Mahabir, and Chris Milner. 2008. "Has China Displaced Other Asian Countries' Exports?" *China Economic Review* 19: 152–69.

Jensen, Robert. 2012. "Do Labor Market Opportunities Affect Young Women's Work and Family Decisions? Experimental Evidence from India." *Quarterly Journal of Economics* 127 (2): 753–92.

Jordan, L. S., B. Kamphuis, and S. P. Setia. 2014. *A New Agenda: Improving the Competitiveness of the Textiles and Apparel Value Chain in India.* Washington, DC: World Bank.

Kee, Hiau Looi. 2014. "Non-tariff Barriers in South Asian Countries and Its Trade Impact." Mimeo, World Bank, Washington, DC.

Klasen, S., and J. Pieters. 2012. "Push or Pull? Drivers of Female Labor Force Participation during India's Economic Boom." IZA Discussion Paper 6395, Institute for the Study of Labor, Bonn.

Kumar, R., and G. Krishna. 2015. "Macroeconomic Update: TPP: Trans-Pacific Partnership." Centre for Policy Research, New Delhi, November.

Lopez-Acevedo, Gladys, and Raymond Robertson, eds. 2012. *Sewing Success? Employment, Wages, and Poverty Following the End of the Multi-fibre Arrangement.* Washington, DC: World Bank.

Luke, N., and K. Munshi. 2011. "Women as Agents of Change: Female Income and Mobility in India." *Journal of Development Economics* 94 (1): 1–17.

Nabi, I., and H. Naveed. 2013. "Garments as a Driver of Economic Growth: Insights from Pakistan Case Studies." Draft, IGC, Pakistan.

National Stakeholders. 2014. *Interviews with National Industry Stakeholders.* Interviewer: C. Staritz.

Petri, Peter A., Michael G. Plummer, and Fan Zhai. 2011. "The Trans-Pacific Partnership and Asia-Pacific Integration: A Quantitative Assessment." Economic Series 119, East-West Institute, Honolulu, HI, October.

Ramaswamy, K. V., and G. Gereffi. 1998. "India's Apparel Sector in the Global Economy: Catching Up or Falling Behind." *Economic and Political Weekly* 33 (3): 122–30.

Sivasankaran, Anitha. 2014. "Work and Women's Marriage, Fertility and Empowerment: Evidence from Textile Mill Employment." Harvard University Job Market Paper, Harvard University, Cambridge, MA.

Tewari, M. 2005. "Post-MFA Adjustments in India's Textile and Apparel Industry: Emerging Issues and Trends." Working Paper 167, Indian Council for Research on International Economic Relations, New Delhi.

World Bank. 2013a. *Bangladesh Diagnostic Trade Integration Study.* Volume 3: *Sector Studies.* Washington, DC: World Bank.

———. 2013b. *World Development Report 2013: Jobs.* Washington, DC: World Bank.

———. 2014. "Gender Equality and Shared Prosperity in South Asia—What Will It Take?" Mimeo, World Bank, Washington, DC.

———. 2015. *Interwoven: How the Better Work Program Improves Job and Life Quality in the Apparel Sector.* Washington, DC: World Bank.

## CHAPTER 1

Setting the Stage

Key Messages

- South Asia needs to create jobs in labor-intensive industries where it enjoys a comparative advantage—such as apparel—to employ its burgeoning youth and attract more women into the workforce.
- But the region now has to compete in an environment of increased competition (post-2005 phaseout of the Multifibre Arrangement), with market incentives (rather than quotas) prevailing and buyers consolidating sources.
- Even so, with apparel wages rising in China, South Asia can create an enormous amount of jobs, especially if it increases market access, eases import barriers, and facilitates foreign investment.

South Asia's Jobs Challenge

South Asia is in the midst of a demographic transition. For the next three decades, the growth of the region's working-age population will far outpace the growth of dependents. Approximately 1 million individuals will enter the workforce every month. This large, economically active population can increase the region's capacity to save and make crucial investments in physical capital, job training, and technological advancement.

But, for South Asia to realize these dividends, it must ensure that its working-age population is productively employed. This means that the region must create jobs in industries where the region's vast, albeit unskilled workforce (with an average six years of schooling) constitutes a comparative advantage (Lin 2011; World Bank 2013). As one of the most prominent labor-intensive industries in developing countries, apparel manufacturing is a prime contender. With about 4.7 million workers in the formal sector (and several million more informally employed), apparel, along with textiles,

The author, Ritika D'Souza, is grateful for comments provided by the core team of the study—in particular, Raymond Robertson for the analytical framework.

already constitutes 40 percent of manufacturing employment. And, given that much of apparel production continues to be labor intensive, the potential to create more and better jobs is immense.

The potential gains do not end there. As the *World Development Report 2013: Jobs* reminds us, the value of a job to society can far exceed its value to the individual jobholder. Job opportunities tilted toward the poor may have greater impacts on poverty reduction. Jobs for women may influence resource allocations at the household level and benefit their children. Jobs connected to world markets may lead to knowledge spillovers and make workers more productive (World Bank 2013). Jobs that make these significant contributions to society are good jobs for development.

Jobs in the apparel sector display many of these characteristics. With relatively low skill requirements, apparel manufacturing presents the poor with job opportunities. International evidence confirms that apparel is the sector poor laborers find most attractive when they transition out of agriculture (see chapter 4) and that employment in apparel has contributed significantly to poverty reduction (Nicita and Razzaz 2003; Yamagata 2006). The sector has also demonstrated a unique ability to attract female workers, which is vital for a region with one of the lowest female labor force participation rates in the world. Increasing the number of employed women in South Asia could lead to increased total factor productivity (Loko and Diouf 2009) and higher gross domestic product (GDP) growth rates (Lawson 2008). Equally important are the social spillovers, with studies linking women's employment to a greater role in economic decision making (Anderson and Eswaran 2009), marriage and fertility decisions (Sivasankaran 2014), and higher school attendance rates for their children (Afridi, Mukhopadhyay, and Sahoo 2013). Further, the organization of the apparel sector in global value chains links producers in the region to international markets, facilitating knowledge spillovers and skill acquisition for workers.

There is a huge window of opportunity now for South Asia, given that China, the dominant producer for the last ten years, has started to cede some ground because of higher wages. But the region faces strong competition from East Asia—with Cambodia, Indonesia, and Vietnam already pulling ahead. Plus, the sector suffers from production inefficiencies and policy bottlenecks that have prevented it from achieving its potential.

Against this backdrop, this report hopes to inform the debate by measuring the employment gains that the four most populous countries in South Asia—Bangladesh, India, Pakistan, and Sri Lanka (hereafter "SAR countries")—can expect in this new environment of increased competition and scrutiny. Its main message is that it is important for South Asian economies to remove existing impediments and facilitate growth in apparel to capture more production and create more employment as wages rise in China. The successful manufacturers will be those who can supply a wide range of quality products to buyers rapidly and reliably—not just those who offer low costs.

Transformational Jobs in Apparel

The World Bank (2013) describes jobs as the cornerstone of both economic and social development. Jobs provide individuals with pathways out of poverty and toward better livelihoods. They allow workers to acquire new skills, firms to increase their productivity, and economies to flourish as a result. They can also have significant social spillovers, bringing together people from different ethnic and social backgrounds to increase social cohesion and create a sense of fairness. Thus, the value of a job to society can be far greater than its value for the jobholder.

Jobs in apparel can be transformational for both individuals and society. Apparel production requires relatively low capital investment, and a large part of production—which includes cutting, sewing, and finishing activities—remains labor intensive. In addition, the skills required by new production workers in the industry are relatively basic and can be acquired over short periods of time. For example, a sewing machine operator requires four to six weeks of training, with a primary level education sufficing for training purposes (Baruah et al. forthcoming). These relatively low barriers to entry attract thousands of low-income workers. Empirical evidence confirms that apparel was one of the largest employees in low- and middle-income countries between 1963 and 2007, employing up to 0.5 percent of the population (figure 1.1). This rate was well above that of other, more sophisticated industries (like machinery, automobiles, chemicals, and fabricated metals) that become important employers as countries move to high-income status.

The ability of apparel production to generate jobs for the poor offers developing countries a path to reduce poverty.[1] A World Bank study contends that in Madagascar the sustained export-driven growth in the textile and apparel sectors led to a substantial increase in the income of poor households with a consequent decrease in poverty (Nicita and Razzaz 2003). In a scenario simulating five years of expansion of the apparel and textile sectors, the authors estimated that more than 1 million individuals would directly or indirectly receive some benefit. In Cambodia, a study finds that the expanding export-oriented apparel industry created job opportunities for the poor, with entry-level workers earning a monthly salary three times the food poverty line for Phnom Penh (Yamagata 2006).

Another striking feature of the apparel industry is that it employs large numbers of female workers. In fact, the sector is regarded as a "gateway" into formal manufacturing jobs for women whose alternative is agriculture or the informal labor market (including domestic service, construction, and childcare) (Lopez-Acevedo and Robertson 2012). This is especially important in South Asia, where women's engagement in the world of work is extremely limited. Women account for most unpaid work in the region, along with being overrepresented in the informal sector and among the poor (Elborgh-Woytek et al. 2013). Moreover, the female labor force participation rate in the region has remained stubbornly low at 30 percent (Nayar et al. 2012), which hinders South Asia's ability to reach its economic potential.

Stitches to Riches? • http://dx.doi.org/10.1596/978-1-4648-0813-5

Figure 1.1 The Apparel Sector Is One of the Most Important Employers in Developing Countries

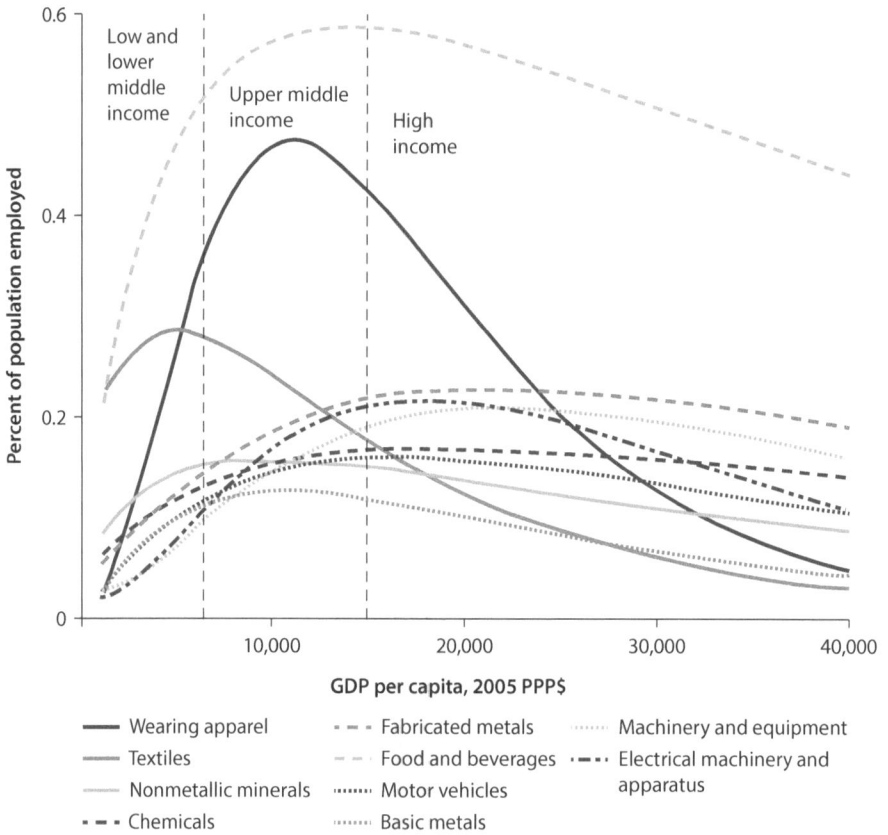

Source: UNIDO 2013.
Note: GDP = gross domestic product; PPP = purchasing power parity.

We know that a higher female participation rate could bring the region significant macroeconomic gains, in terms of increased total factor productivity (Loko and Diouf 2009) and higher GDP growth rates (Lawson 2008). We also know that it would generate significant positive social spillovers. Working women are more likely to assume a bigger role in economic decision making in their households (Anderson and Eswaran 2009) and in marriage and fertility decisions (Sivasankaran 2014). Moreover, the benefits are not limited to the working women but extend to their families, especially their children. In India, children of working mothers were found to have a much higher school attendance rate (Afridi, Mukhopadhyay, and Sahoo 2013). This matters greatly because human capital accumulation is thought to be a key driver of economic growth (Mankiw, Romer, and Weil 1992; Jones 2011).

In addition to the gains for apparel workers and their families, a competitive apparel sector can also offer significant gains for the economy.

Knowledge spillovers occur through international trade and participation in global value chains. Workers employed with foreign-owned companies or with firms integrated in international value chains acquire new technical and managerial skills. Firms that engage in export markets tend to become more productive and, in doing so, push other, less productive firms out of business. Knowledge spillovers from foreign direct investment (FDI) increase aggregate productivity, thus allowing economies to develop (World Bank 2013).

Economists contend that the apparel sector (along with footwear and textiles) was instrumental in the initial development of countries like Germany, Japan, Malaysia, the Republic of Korea, Singapore, the United Kingdom, the United States, and more recently China, Indonesia, Sri Lanka, Thailand, and Vietnam (Brenton and Hoppe 2007). Historically, developing countries have used success in apparel production as a first step toward industrialization. The experience gained in this sector allows them to progress from light manufacturing (apparel, footwear, and toys) to producing more sophisticated products (plastics, electric machinery, and electric parts). This process of structural transformation is documented in Kaname Akamatsu's "flying geese model" (1962), illustrated in figure 1.2. Countries like Japan, the ASEAN 4 (Indonesia, Malaysia, the Philippines, and Thailand of the Association of Southeast Asian Nations), and now South Asian economies, start off manufacturing nondurable consumer goods like apparel and then progress to durable consumer goods, and then capital goods of higher value.

The good news is that evidence suggests that greater competitiveness in the global apparel market will allow South Asia to create more jobs and benefit from several developmental spillovers along the way. However, the apparel industry has undergone major changes in the past 10 years that may limit its role in the region's development. Until 2005, global apparel trade was governed by a system of quotas under the Multifibre Arrangement (MFA), which restricted imports from developing countries to developed countries—although it also created opportunities for countries that might not otherwise have developed their apparel sector. The MFA preferences of the European Union (EU) for Bangladesh created the incentive to develop the apparel industry there, thus laying the foundation for future increases in apparel production. Other countries like China were motivated by the limits to establish production in developing countries that were not filling their quotas (Robertson 2012).

With the phaseout of the MFA in 2005, global apparel production is being allocated according to market incentives rather than regulation (Robertson 2012). The effects of the phaseout, combined with the 2007–08 global economic crisis, have resulted in buyers narrowing down their sources to a relatively small number of apparel exporters. In 2000, the top five apparel-exporting countries accounted for 55 percent of exports, but by 2012 their share had jumped to 71 percent. China has come to dominate the sector, and developing countries that enter the fray face increasing competition for foreign investments and contracts with leading apparel brands. Also likely to impact South Asia's

Figure 1.2 "Flying Geese" Model Depicts the Process of Industrialization for Developing Countries

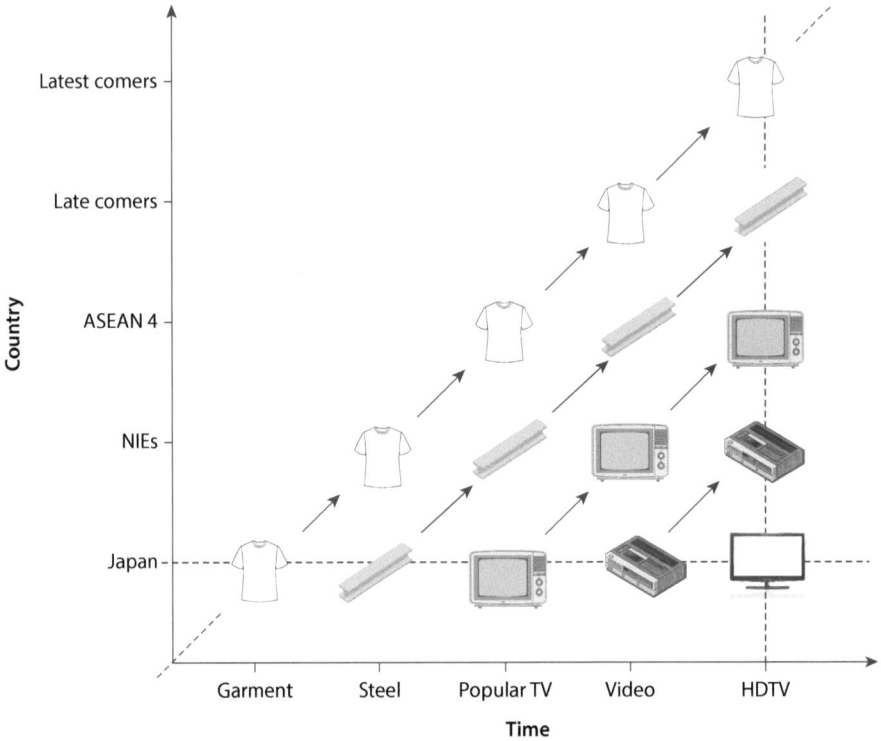

Source: GRIPS Development Forum; images from iStock.
Note: ASEAN 4 = Indonesia, Malaysia, the Philippines, and Thailand of the Association of Southeast Asian Nations; NIEs = newly industrialized economies.

competitiveness is the increasing international attention to labor standards in the region in response to pressure from corporate social responsibility (CSR) campaigns by nongovernmental organizations and compliance-conscious consumers and, more recently, because of the higher number of disasters in apparel factories. Notable among these are Bangladesh's Rana Plaza factory collapse in April 2013 (which killed more than 1,000 workers) and the fire at Tazreen Fashions in November 2012 (which killed 112 workers) (see box 2.2 and chapter 2).

Opportunities in the Global Apparel Market

The global apparel industry was valued at $355 billion in 2012—with the largest retail markets located in the United States and EU-15,[2] which together accounted for 63 percent of imports (UNSD 2014a). Most global apparel brands are also headquartered in the United States and the EU, yet the vast majority of apparel production actually takes place elsewhere. In fact, the production of apparel for the international market is organized in "global value chains"—which cover the full range of activities that are required to bring a product from its conception to its end use and are typically divided among multiple firms and spread out across wide swaths of geographic space.

We can visualize the various activities involved in apparel production by looking at figure 1.3. Each activity is associated with different levels of value addition, with values increasing from left to right, as we move from tangible to intangible activities. Lead firms perform the higher–value added activities (such as design, branding, and retail) but outsource most or all of the manufacturing to a global network of producers. Given the labor-intensive nature of apparel production, producer firms are usually located in developing countries that can offer vast supplies of low-wage labor. Apparel produced in these countries is in turn exported to the large retail markets for distribution and sale.

These organizational dynamics have made the global apparel manufacturing industry one of the largest export sectors in the world. In 2012, exports represented 68 percent of the industry, and 14 of the top 15 apparel exporters were developing countries.[3]

Moreover, each of the four SAR countries studied in this report has an established export-oriented apparel sector and is increasingly assuming a higher profile in the world apparel trade. Between 2000 and 2012, the growth rate of exports of these SAR countries combined was equivalent to the growth of China's apparel exports during this period, and greater than China's growth post–MFA.

Figure 1.3 Structure of the Global Value Chain for Apparel

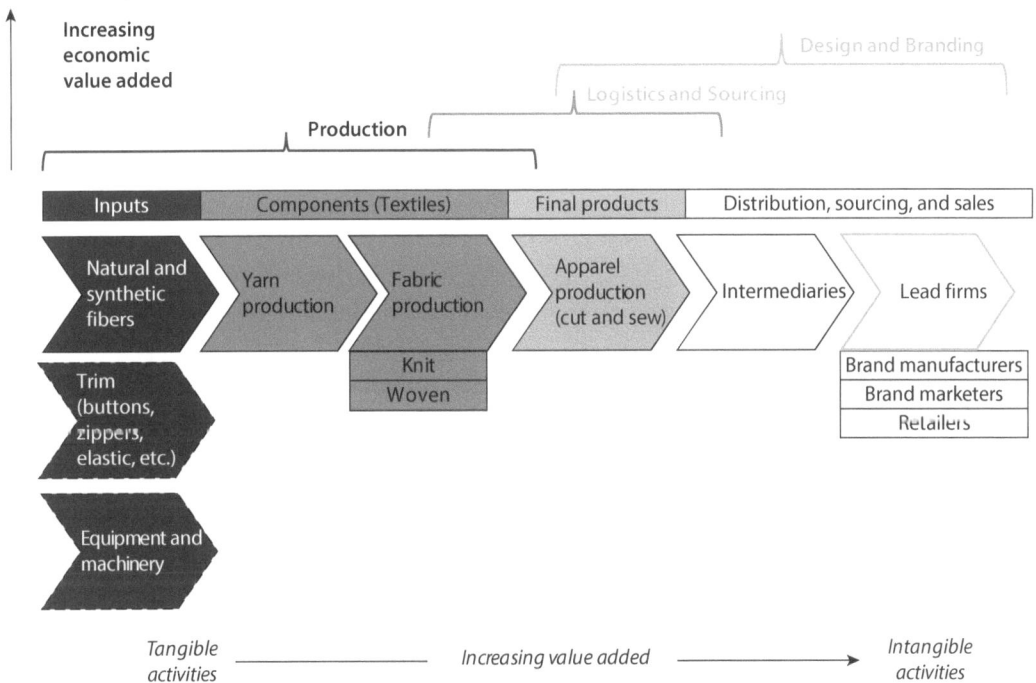

Green indicates highest value added activities + control/power over the chain

Source: World Bank (see chapter 2 of this report).

Indeed, since 2005, exports from SAR countries have increased by 83 percent, well above the world average of 31 percent and China's average of 59 percent.

The structure and characteristics of apparel industries in each of the SAR countries vary considerably (see box 1.1). The sectors in Bangladesh and

---

Box 1.1 South Asia's Apparel Profiles Vary Greatly among Countries

Bangladesh has the largest apparel export industry of the four SAR countries in terms of value ($22.8 billion) and global market share, accounting for 6.4 percent of global apparel exports in 2012 (UNSD 2014a). The apparel industry is also extremely important to the economy, account-ing for 83 percent of total exports (UNSD 2014c). The industry is dominated (over 90 percent) by locally owned firms (BEPZA 2013; Yunus and Yamagata 2014), but foreign direct investment (FDI) played a central role in initiating the industry by providing links to foreign buyers, tech-nology, and knowledge transfer. Bangladesh is a primary destination for basic commodity items produced in long runs, predominately made from cotton, including trousers, knit and woven shirts, and sweaters/sweatshirts (Tewari 2008; Birnbaum 2014; UNSD 2014b).

India ranks second in terms of value ($12.5 billion) and global market share (3.5 percent in 2012); although, unlike in Bangladesh and Sri Lanka, apparel's share of total exports is quite low at 5 percent (UNSD 2014c). Overall it has a more diversified export structure than the other SAR countries (UNSD 2014a)—India and Pakistan have a well-developed fiber (cotton), textile, and apparel-manufacturing base, with the textile industry larger than the apparel industry in terms of export value. FDI has played a limited role (less than 1 percent) as a share of overall investment in the textile and apparel industry, and as a share of the country's overall FDI inflows (UNCTADSTAT 1970–2012; NCAER 2009; Saheed 2012; National Stakeholders 2014). India is primarily an exporter of cotton products, including knit and woven tops, skirts, men's bottoms, and embellished and embroidered apparel (Tewari 2008; UNSD 2014b).

Sri Lanka ranks third in terms of value ($4.4 billion) and global market share (1.2 percent in 2012), although apparel makes up a relatively high share of total exports at 45 percent (UNSD 2014a, 2014c; Sri Lanka DCS 2014). Similar to Bangladesh, FDI played a central role in initiating the industry in Sri Lanka; but today the industry is dominated by joint ventures and domestically owned firms. Sri Lanka's export profile differs from that of other SAR countries because the country is a source of intimate apparel, trousers, and swimwear; and exports are equally divided between cotton and manmade fiber (MMF) products. Sri Lanka's exports are more niche and fashion-oriented items rather than volume products (Tewari 2008; UNSD 2014b).

Pakistan comes in fourth in terms of value ($4.2 billion) with the same global market share (1.2 percent) as Sri Lanka, although apparel's share of total exports is lower at 19 percent (UNSD 2014a, 2014c). FDI has not played an important role; in the apparel sector, the share of foreign-owned firms is estimated to be less than 2 percent, with only a slightly higher share in the textile sector (Hamdani 2009; National Stakeholders 2014). Pakistan specializes in basic cotton, woven, denim, and chino trousers, low-priced knitwear such as polo shirts and T-shirts, and fleece sweatshirts.

Source: World Bank (see chapter 2 of this report).

Sri Lanka are dominated by large, formal firms that are geared toward the global market. On the other hand, India and Pakistan have a sizeable informal apparel sector where firms employ fewer than 10 workers. Despite these disparities, much of the competitiveness of these countries is driven by favorable demographics and low wages. The region's steady supply of young workers entering the labor market provides apparel-making capacity at a sufficient scale to meet demand from large markets like the United States and the EU. As table 1.1 illustrates, labor costs in these countries are also much lower than in China—ranging from a low of $0.51 per hour in Bangladesh to a high of $1.06 per hour in India. In addition, the SAR countries enjoy a distinct advantage in backward linkages with the textile sector. Keep in mind that textiles are the major input in apparel production and can make up almost 70 percent of production costs. India and Pakistan are top cotton producers, with significant production also taking place in Bangladesh.

Yet, despite being endowed with an abundant supply of some of the most critical inputs in apparel production, SAR countries have not come close to realizing their full potential. Although they have increased their combined market share from 7.5 percent to 12.3 percent between 2000 and 2012 (table 1.1), they were far outperformed by China, which accounts for 41 percent of the market. Even with its higher labor costs, China is able to attract buyers by offering a wide range of apparel, produced at high levels of productivity with short lead times. No SAR country has succeeded in offering the same range of goods and services.

Even so, the tide may be turning as China's rising wages and appreciating currency prompt buyers to look to other production destinations to stay competitive. A 2013 survey of leading global buyers in the United States and EU found that 72 percent of respondents planned to decrease their share of sourcing from China during the next five years (2012–2016) (McKinsey & Company 2011, 2013). Rising prices in China are also encouraging Chinese investors to invest in apparel firms in countries like Cambodia and Vietnam, which affects the domestic investment available to Chinese firms. In addition, there is evidence that China itself is looking to shift

Table 1.1 SAR Countries' Labor Costs Are Much Lower than China's
(The Competitiveness of SAR Countries in the Apparel Sector, 2012)

Country	Rank in top 15 apparel exporters	Apparel exports as a share of world apparel exports (percent)	Apparel exports as a share of country exports (percent)	Average apparel monthly earnings (US$/per hour)
Bangladesh	2	6.4	82.8	0.51
India	7	3.5	5.2	1.06
Pakistan	13	1.2	19.0	0.58
Sri Lanka	14	1.2	44.8	0.55
China	1	41	7.1	2.60

Source: World Bank calculations using COMTRADE data.

production to higher value-added industries like electronics. Although it remains the world's largest apparel exporter, apparel as a share of China's total exports in 2012 accounted for only 7.1 percent—about half of the 15.6 percent in 1990.

For buyers looking for new export destinations to match the scale of China's production, the SAR countries would seem an obvious choice. But South Asia is also well positioned to capture new apparel markets, not just the existing ones. The demand for apparel is highly income elastic and will continue to grow as populations become more well off. For example, demand for apparel from the top five importers (the United States, the United Kingdom, Japan, Germany, and France) has been stable relative to per capita incomes between 2004 and 2013 (figure 1.4). While we can expect similar trends in the demand for apparel from high-income countries in the future, we are also likely to see an expansion in global demand as incomes increase in countries like Brazil, China, the Russian Federation, and South Africa. In fact, the fastest growing retail markets since 2005 are the Asia Pacific and Latin American regions (both had a compound annual growth rate of 10 percent), followed by Eastern Europe (7 percent), the Middle East and Africa (6 percent), and Australasia (5 percent).

Of course, as incomes rise in developing countries that are apparel producers, domestic markets will also acquire increasing importance. For SAR, the domestic market has significant potential in India, Pakistan, and Bangladesh

Figure 1.4 Apparel Imports Have Been Steady in High-Income Countries
(Demand for Apparel Imports Relative to GDP in High-Income Countries)

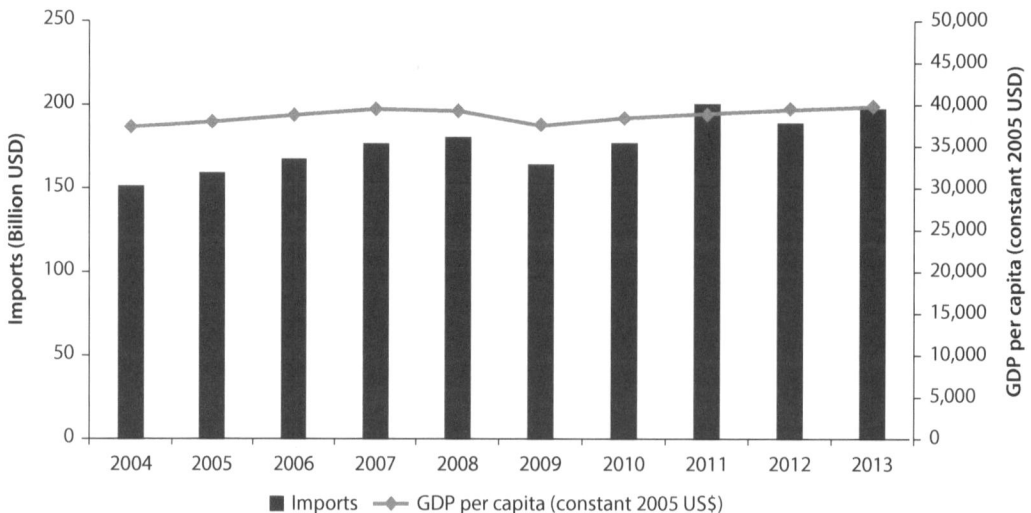

Sources: World Bank calculation based on COMTRADE and WDI data.
Note: High-income countries include France, Germany, Japan, the United Kingdom, and the United States. GDP = gross domestic product.

(with populations of about 1.25 billion, 182 million, and 157 million, respectively), but is more limited in Sri Lanka (with a population of 20 million).[4]

If SAR countries were to take advantage of the increasing opportunities to boost their share of the growing global apparel market, more jobs would also likely follow. But the extent to which they can do so will hinge on how competitive they are, which will be determined by lead firms (like H&M, Gap, and Walmart) that drive the global apparel value chain. And for firms making sourcing decisions, SAR countries are by no means the only possible candidates. East Asian countries like Cambodia, Indonesia, and Vietnam have established apparel sectors and are strong contenders.

Analytical Framework

Although the vital contribution of apparel to the development of countries during previous episodes of industrialization has been well documented, much less is known about how the changes of the past ten years have affected the sector's ability to deliver on its development promise today. A shift in global apparel production away from China would present a huge opportunity for SAR countries, but how much production can they capture in an increasingly competitive market, and will this lead to more jobs for their citizens?

This report seeks to understand how changes in the global market (such as rising apparel prices in China) would affect demand for apparel from SAR countries and, consequently, local wages and employment. To this end, our analytical framework—illustrated in figure 1.5—models both the dynamics of the global apparel sector and the decisions of firms and workers in SAR countries. We build our framework around a firm-level production function. The simple form of the production function that we use in our study assumes that the firm combines capital (K), labor (L), and technology (A) to produce output (y):

$$y = f(K, L, A). \tag{1.1}$$

This approach is particularly useful because it illustrates the connections between production and employment that we study. We focus on both the left- and right-hand sides of equation (1.1).

We begin with the left-hand side. Production, y, is sold in international markets. The demand for the product in international markets is assumed to be exogenous to local firms. Instead, demand is driven by buyers who have the choice of buying (often called "sourcing") from many different countries. To a large extent, buyers' sourcing decisions are motivated by the price of the product. Therefore, the left-hand side of equation (1.1) can be modeled using a familiar demand system that depends on the product's home price and its price in other markets. Indicating the home country with the subscript i, other countries with the subscript j, and output prices with p, the demand for the firm's output is equation (1.2):

$$y_i = D(p_i, p_j). \tag{1.2}$$

Stitches to Riches? • http://dx.doi.org/10.1596/978-1-4648-0813-5

Buyers make their sourcing decisions such that they meet their demand for apparel at the lowest possible cost.

To derive the demand curves, we model the buyer's cost-minimization decision as equation (1.3):

$$\min_{x_i} \; C(x_i, p_i) \;\; \text{s.t.} \;\; Y = f(x_i). \tag{1.3}$$

Given exogenous product prices p, buyers pick the imports from each country that minimize their total costs of meeting domestic demand for product Y given a production technology described by $f(.)$. As is well known, the derivative of the cost function in equation (1.3) is the factor demand equation for each country i that can be estimated as a system of equations with the imports on the left-hand side and the prices of each country and total imports on the right-hand side. An example of such a system that we estimate is equation (1.4),

$$x_i = \alpha_0 + \alpha_1 p_i + \alpha_2 p_j + \alpha_3 y + \delta_i \tag{1.4}$$

$$x_j = \beta_0 + \beta_1 p_i + \beta_2 p_j + \beta_3 y + \delta_j$$

in which country i represents one of our South Asian countries, country j represents China, and δ represents the usual error term. Symmetry requires constraining $\alpha_2 = \beta_1$. The system can be expanded to include additional countries. The estimated coefficients are then used to calculate the elasticity of substitution between countries. This elasticity of substitution tells us how much production of country i would increase for any given increase in prices in China.

While price is an important factor driving sourcing decisions, buyers are also concerned with other criteria like the quality and reliability of apparel producers. This makes countries *imperfect substitutes*—which means that buyers will not completely shift their orders (and therefore, in effect, production) between countries when the prices in China change. The non-cost factors that buyers consider when making sourcing decisions are critical to understanding a country's competitiveness, and also the elasticities derived from equation (1.4). These factors are also harder to quantify.

To understand the non-cost factors that are driving our substitution elasticities, we survey buyers to determine what criteria they consider when making sourcing decisions. In addition to cost competitiveness, the key factors that emerge are (i) productivity, (ii) quality, (iii) lead time and reliability, and (iv) social compliance and sustainability. We then use buyer perceptions to benchmark the performance of SAR countries and their main competitors (such as China, Vietnam, Cambodia, and Indonesia) on these parameters.

Since firms take international demand as given, once we have the estimates of demand for apparel from SAR countries we can turn to the right-hand side of equation (1.1). Apparel production is labor intensive and requires relatively low investments in capital (K), so our focus is on labor (L) and technology (A). As in any market, L (and wages paid to labor) is determined by the interplay of demand and supply. We analyze demand by following Hamermesh (1993), recognizing that labor demand is a derived demand. When deciding how many workers to hire, firms take the production as given and try to minimize costs. To model this, we return to the firm production function in equation (1.5), where y is firm output and z is a non-negative vector of inputs that includes capital (K), labor (L), and technology (A):

$$y = f(z). \tag{1.5}$$

Defining $w \gg 0$ as the vector of input prices that includes wages for labor (w) and the cost of capital (r), the firm's cost-minimization problem takes the form in equation (1.6):

$$\min_{z \geq 0} \; w \cdot z \quad s.t. \quad f(z) \geq y. \tag{1.6}$$

The demand for labor is a derivative of the cost function with respect to wages. Using the cost minimization function in equation (1.6), we derive the firm's labor demand in equation (1.7):

$$z(w,y) = \nabla_w c(w,y). \tag{1.7}$$

We assume that men and women represent two types of labor inputs, and firms can choose between the two. After taking logs, the system of equations in equation (1.8) gives us the labor demand elasticities for firm i,

$$\log\left(l_i^m\right) = \alpha_0^m + \alpha_1^m \log\left(w_i^m\right) + \alpha_2^m \log\left(w_i^f\right) + \alpha_3^m \log\left(y_i\right) + \alpha_4^m size_i + \alpha_5^m year + \varepsilon_i^m \tag{1.8}$$

$$\log\left(l_i^f\right) = \alpha_0^f + \alpha_1^f \log\left(w_i^m\right) + \alpha_2^f \log\left(w_i^f\right) + \alpha_3^f \log\left(y_i\right) + \alpha_4^f size_i + \alpha_5^f year + \varepsilon_i^f$$

where l_i^m is firm demand for male workers, l_i^f is demand for female workers, w is wages, y_i is firm production, and *size* and *year* allow us to control for the size of the firm, the price of capital (r) in a particular year, and other global changes over time. The labor demand elasticity estimates in equation (1.8) tell us how much more male or female labor a firm will demand for a given increase in production.

Having estimated how increases in firm production affect labor demand, we now turn to the responses of the workers who supply the labor. Drawing on household and labor force data, we estimate labor force participation decisions, specified in equation (1.9)

$$LFP_i = I\left(H_i \geq 0\right) \tag{1.9}$$

$$H_i = \beta_0 + \beta_1 \ln W_i + \beta_2 N_i + \beta_3 X_i + \varepsilon_i$$

in which $LFP_i = 1$ if a person participates in the labor force, H_i represents hours worked, W_i is an hourly wage rate, N_i is nonlabor income (asset income and other unearned income), X_i is a vector of an individual i's attributes (including marital status, education, household size, number of children, and a rural/urban dummy), and ε_i is an error term. The wage rate (W_i), an important determining factor of labor force participation, is likely to increase in the short term as firms demand more labor. The estimates from equation (1.9) allow us to assess how a change in the expected reservation wage would effect labor force participation decisions.

Because labor force participation rates are greatly affected by wages offered in apparel compared to other sectors, we conclude our analysis of labor supply by estimating the wage premiums in apparel using Mincer-type equations. The estimates of wage premiums suggest that higher wages in apparel can potentially pull nonparticipants into the labor force.

The combination of labor demand and labor supply helps illustrate how changes in output demand in global markets would ultimately affect employment, wages, and thus worker welfare.

Finally, we turn to the technology parameter A, which has a long history in economic analysis and has predominantly been estimated as a residual—that is, it captures those factors that affect production that are not captured by K and L. In the case of apparel, these might include the ease of accessing raw materials, the availability of land and investment, the cost and reliability of energy, infrastructure that allows for the transport of finished goods, and so on. Since A is hard to quantify, we undertake a qualitative analysis of the policies that affect all these factors and, consequently, the firm's apparel production. Our preceding analysis provides tentative estimates for the job creation potential of the apparel sector in the current scenario. Our analysis of A looks to the future, highlighting areas where policy intervention could greatly improve firm productivity and create even more good jobs for development.

Our Roadmap

The structure of this report closely follows the framework that is illustrated in figure 1.5. We begin at the left of figure 1.5 with an analysis of the global demand for apparel products. Chapter 2 first describes the global apparel market and then discusses findings from a buyers' survey that identified the key factors that shape buyers' preferences for a particular apparel producer in a particular country. It then undertakes a benchmarking exercise that compares the performance of SAR countries on these key factors to China (the sector leader) and their Southeast Asian competitors—Cambodia, Indonesia, and Vietnam (hereafter known as the Southeast Asian Benchmark [SEAB] countries). This exercise creates a picture of the competitiveness of the SAR countries in the current apparel market.

For its data, chapter 2 combines qualitative and quantitative information on the global apparel value chain from established sources (including COMTRADE, labor force and household surveys, World Bank Enterprise Surveys and Establishment Data, established literature on the apparel sector, and other sources) and interviews with major players in the apparel global value chain (including

Figure 1.5 Overarching Framework for *Stitches to Riches*

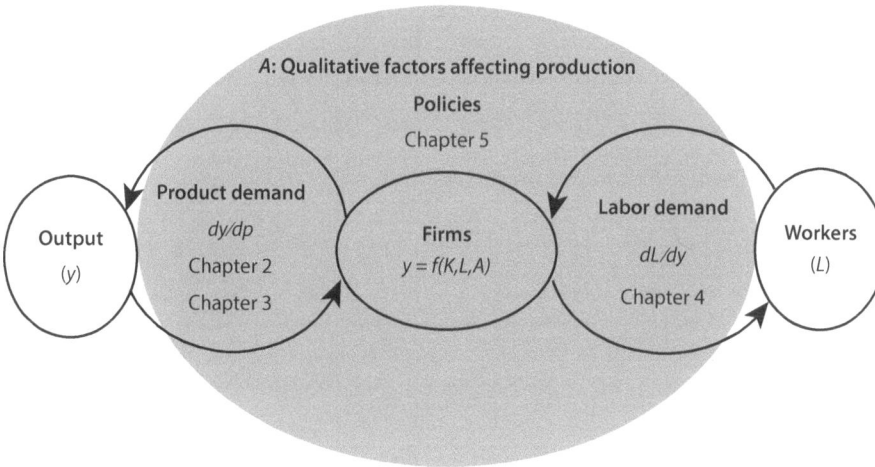

Note: *A* = technology; *K* = capital; *L* = labor; *y* = output.

global buyers; in-country stakeholders, such as relevant ministries, industry associations, unions/workers' groups, and sector experts; and international organizations such as the International Labour Organization).

The results of the benchmark analysis indicate that, overall, the SEAB countries and China are outperforming the SAR countries in terms of aggregate export performance, product diversity, and non-cost-related factors important to global buyers. SAR countries—with the exception of Sri Lanka—generally appear to be cost competitive for selected product categories, but are inhibited by product concentration and inferior performance compared to competitors in non-cost-related factors (including quality, lead times, reliability, and compliance).

So by how much could exports from our focus countries increase given rising apparel prices in China? Chapter 3 tackles this question by examining the output relationships represented on the left of the production function. To do this, it takes specific product-level import data over time and applies them to a system of demand equations in which each country's exports are treated as a unique product whose demand is a function of its own price, the price of competitor countries, and the total amount imported of that product.

For data, the chapter uses the following sources: World Integrated Trade Solutions (WITS), COMTRADE, Office of Textiles and Apparel (OTEXA), United Nations Conference on Trade and Development (UNCTAD), Trade Analysis and Information System (TRAINS), World Development Indicators (WDI), and International Finance Statistics (IFS).

Our results suggest that a 10 percent increase in Chinese apparel wages will result in a 13–25 percent (depending on country) rise in SAR countries' apparel exports to the United States, compared to a 37-51 percent increase for SEAB countries. Thus, unless South Asia successfully identifies and removes barriers to apparel exports—such as barriers to importing MMF and improving exporting logistics—other countries, such as Cambodia and Vietnam, stand to gain even more.

The next step is calculating how the changes in output affect labor demand on the right-hand side of our production function. Firms and workers take market conditions—such as labor costs and the global demand for a country's apparel exports—as exogenous and beyond their control. For that reason, an increase in demand for a country's exports that results from declining Chinese apparel exports will cause firms to alter the mix and level of employment. Chapter 4 explicitly and empirically models both firm-level labor demand and labor supply to estimate how local employment would be affected by an increased demand for SAR apparel exports (we also estimate elasticities of employment for key competitors). Further, it explores how workers respond when an increased demand for their labor results in a higher market wage.

For data, chapter 4 uses firm data that contain information about firm performance (such as sales, productivity, employment, and wages). Household and labor force surveys provide information on individual labor market outcomes (such as labor force participation, employment and earnings, education and training, and other individual and household-level variables).

Our main results show that on the demand side, using output as a proxy for exports, a 1 percent increase in apparel output is associated with a 0.3–0.4 percent increase in employment (both for men and women) in Bangladesh, Pakistan, and Sri Lanka. India's values are lower, with a 0.14 percent increase in demand for male workers and a 0.08 percent increase in demand for female workers. These SAR country results are consistent with labor demand elasticities found in the literature.

On the supply side, we find that a 1 percent increase in the expected wage increases the likelihood of women joining the labor force by between 16 percent in Pakistan and 89 percent in Sri Lanka. We also find that a wage premium exists in the apparel sector compared to agriculture that ranges from 8 to 27 percent, depending on the country—a premium that is even higher when only women are considered. However, this premium has stopped rising with the end of the MFA in 2005, raising questions about whether the region can hold on to its competitive edge.

We conclude this report with a look at the policy implications for South Asia (top of figure 1.5). Chapter 5 begins by using the estimates in chapters 3 and 4 to calculate potential employment gains for the SAR countries from increases in demand for apparel exports, assuming that current policies and conditions remain constant. However, the development of the apparel sector is a stated priority of governments across the SAR countries, and it is reasonable to expect that policy makers will attempt to put policies in place that will increase the competitiveness of their countries in the global apparel market. We explore how policies are linked to the stages of production in apparel, which policies matter most for this industry, how South Asia performs in these areas, and the key hurdles that need to be tackled to give the region a greater competitive edge.

Our key finding is that, with respect to jobs, South Asia exhibits significant employment generation potential as represented by elasticities of employment to prices. If its policies remain unchanged and Chinese wages rise 10 percent, our results show that employment could rise by 9 percent—with Pakistan and Bangladesh the top winners in the U.S. market, and Sri Lanka faring the best in the EU market. But, for this potential to be realized, South Asian economies need urgently to enact supporting policies. We find that, although reform priorities vary by country, most countries would benefit from increasing market access, easing barriers to the import of inputs such as MMFs, and facilitating foreign investment.

Notes

1. A literature review of studies mapping the link between jobs and transitions out of poverty concludes that, regardless of the methodology employed, more and better-paid work has been critical in lifting people out of poverty (Inchauste 2012). In Bangladesh, for instance, a recent World Bank study finds that higher incomes for adults explains over 50 percent of the reduction in the poverty headcount using the national moderate and extreme poverty lines, and over 60 percent using the $1.25 poverty line (Inchauste et al. 2012).

2. The EU-15 includes Austria, Belgium, Denmark, Finland, France, Germany, Greece, Ireland, Italy, Luxembourg, the Netherlands, Portugal, Spain, Sweden, and the United Kingdom.

3. Data are from COMTRADE (database), United Nations (accessed November 4, 2014), http://comtrade.un.org/data/.

4. Data are from the World Development Indicators (database), World Bank, Washington, DC (accessed October 16, 2015), http://databank.worldbank.org/data/reports .aspx?source=world-development-indicators.

Bibliography

AEPC (Apparel Export Promotion Council). 2013. "Disha: The Journey So Far." *Apparel India* 1 (5).

Afridi, Farzana, Abhiroop Mukhopadhyay, and Soham Sahoo. 2013. "Female Labour-Force Participation and Child Education in India: The Effect of the National Rural Employment Guarantee Scheme." Working Paper 95, Young Lives, London.

Ahmed, Faisal Z., Anne Greenleaf, and Audrey Sacks. 2014. "The Paradox of Export Growth in Areas of Weak Governance: The Case of the Ready Made Garment Sector in Bangladesh." *World Development* 56: 258–71.

Akamatsu, Kaname. 1962. "A Historical Pattern of Economic Growth in Developing Countries." *The Developing Economies* 1: 3–25.

Anderson, Siwan, and Mukesh Eswaran. 2009. "What Determines Female Autonomy? Evidence from Bangladesh." *Journal of Development Economics* 90 (2): 179–91.

Baruah, Raginee, Rana Hasan, Nidhi Kapoor, and Aashish Mehta. Forthcoming. *What Constrains the Growth of Good Jobs? The Case of Apparel Manufacturing.* Manila, the Philippines: Asian Development Bank.

BEPZA (Bangladesh Export Processing Zones Authority). 2013. *Annual Report 2010–2011*. Dhaka, Bangladesh: BEPZA. http://www.epzbangladesh.org.bd/web_admin/web_tender_files/BEPZA_2010-2011.pdf.

Bernard, Andrew B., and J. Bradford Jensen. 1995. "Exporters, Jobs, and Wages in U.S. Manufacturing: 1976–1987." *Brookings Papers on Economic Activity. Microeconomics* 1995: 67–119.

BGMEA (Bangladesh Garment Manufacturers and Exporters Association). 2014. "Trade Information." Retrieved April 22, 2014, from http://bgmea.com.bd/home/pages/TradeInformation.

Bhaskaran, Resmi, Dev Nathan, Nicolaa Phillips, and C. Upendranadh. 2010. "Home-Based Child Labour in Delhi's Garment Production: Contemporary Forms of Unfree Labour in Global Production." *Indian Journal of Labour Economics* 53 (4): 607–24.

Birnbaum, David. 2014. "Comment: Bangladesh's Garment Trend Lines Look Pretty Poor." just-style.com, June 8.

Brenton, Paul, and Mombert Hoppe. 2007. "Clothing and Export Diversification: Still a Route to Growth for Low-Income Countries?" Policy Research Working Paper 4343, World Bank, Washington, DC.

Elborgh-Woytek, Katrin, Monique Newiak, Kalpana Kochhar, Stefania Fabrizio, Kangni Kpodar, Phillipe Wingender, Benedict Clements, and Gerd Schwartz. 2013. *Women, Work, and the Economy: Macroeconomic Gains from Gender Equity*. IMF Staff Discussion Note. Washington, DC: International Monetary Fund.

Galor, Oded, and David N. Weil. 2000. "Population, Technology, and Growth: From Malthusian Stagnation to the Demographic Transition and Beyond." *American Economic Review* 90: 806–28.

Gereffi, Gary. 1999. "International Trade and Industrial Upgrading in the Apparel Commodity Chain." *Journal of International Economics* 48: 37–70.

Gifford, James, and Sean Ansett. 2014. "10 Things That Have Changed since the Bangladesh Factory Collapse." *The Guardian*, April 2. Accessed June 24, 2015. http://www.theguardian.com/sustainable-business/bangladesh-factory-collapse-10-things-changed.

Global Apparel Buyers. 2014. *Interviews with Global Apparel Buyers*. Interviewer: S. Frederick.

GRIPS Development Forum. n.d. "Flying Geese Model." *GRIPS Development Forum*. Accessed May 5, 2015. http://www.grips.ac.jp/forum/module/prsp/FGeese.htm.

Hamdani, Khalil. 2009. *Foreign Direct Investment Prospects for Pakistan*. Islamabad: Pakistan Institute of Development Economics.

Hamermesh, D. 1993. *Labor Demand*. Princeton, NJ: Princeton University Press.

Hirway, Indira. 2008. "Trade and Gender Inequalities in Labour Market: Case of Textile and Garment Industry in India." Paper presented at the International Seminar on Moving towards Gender Sensitization of Trade Policy, organized by UNCTAD, New Delhi, India. http://s3.amazonaws.com/zanran_storage/www.unctadindia.org/ContentPages/452292790.pdf.

ILO (International Labour Organization). 2010. "ILO Better Work Vietnam Fact Sheet." ILO.

———. 2013a. *Bangladesh Country Report: Trade and Employment*. Dhaka: ILO Country Office for Bangladesh.

———. 2013b. "Joint Action Plan to Promote Workplace Safety and Health Launched in Karachi." Press Release, October 4.

Inchauste, Gabriela. 2012. "Jobs and Transitions Out of Poverty: A Literature Review." Background Paper for the *World Development Report 2013*, World Bank, Washington, DC.

Inchauste, Gabriela, Sergio Olivieri, Jaime Saavedra, and Hernan Winkler. 2012. "What Is Behind the Decline in Poverty since 2000? Evidence from Bangladesh, Peru and Thailand." Policy Research Working Paper 6199, World Bank, Washington, DC.

India MOSPI-CSO (Ministry of Statistics and Programme Implementation, Central Statistics Office). 2013a. *Annual Survey of Industries 2010–2011.* Volume I. New Delhi: MOSPI-CSO.

India MOSPI-NSSO (Ministry of Statistics and Programme Implementation, National Sample Survey Office). 2013b. *Economic Characteristics of Unincorporated Non-agricultural Enterprises (Excluding Construction) in India.* New Delhi: MOSPI-NSSO.

Jones, Benjamin. 2011. "The Human Capital Shock: A Generalized Approach." NBER Working Paper Series 17487, National Bureau of Economic Research, Cambridge, MA.

Kelegama, S. 2009. "Ready-Made Garment Exports from Sri Lanka." *Journal of Contemporary Asia* 39 (4): 579–96.

Lawson, Sandra. 2008. "Women Hold Up Half the Sky." Global Economics Paper 164, Goldman Sachs, New York.

Lin, Justin Yifu. 2011. *From Flying Geese to Leading Dragons: New Opportunities and Strategies for Structural Transformation in Developing Countries.* Washington, DC: World Bank.

Loko, Boileau, and Mame Astou Diouf. 2009. "Revisiting the Determinants of Productivity Growth: What's New?" IMF Working Paper, International Monetary Fund, Washington, DC.

Lopez-Acevedo, Gladys, and Raymond Robertson, eds. 2012. *Sewing Success? Employment, Wages, and Poverty Following the End of the Multi-fibre Arrangement.* Washington, DC: World Bank.

Lucas, Robert E., Jr. 1988. "On the Mechanics of Economic Development." *Journal of Monetary Economics* 22: 3–42.

Mankiw, Gregory N, David Romer, and David N Weil. 1992. "A Contribution to the Empirics of Economic Growth." *Quarterly Journal of Economics* 107 (2) 407–37.

McKinsey & Company. 2011. *Bangladesh's Ready-Made Garments Landscape: The Challenge of Growth.* McKinsey & Company Apparel, Fashion & Luxury Practice.

———. 2013. *The Global Sourcing Map—Balancing Cost, Compliance, and Capacity: McKinsey's Apparel CPO Survey 2013.* McKinsey & Company Apparel, Fashion & Luxury Practice.

National Stakeholders. 2014. *Interviews with National Industry Stakeholders.* Interviewer: C. Staritz.

Nayar, Reema, Pablo Gottret, Pradeep Mitra, Gordon Betcherman, Yue Man Lee, Indhira Santos, Mahesh Dahal, and Maheshwor Shrestha. 2012. *More and Better Jobs in South Asia.* Washington, DC: World Bank.

NCAER (National Council of Applied Economic Research). 2009. *Assessing the Prospects for India's Textile and Clothing Sector.* New Delhi: NCAER.

Nicita, Alessandro, and Susan Razzaz. 2003. "Who Benefits and How Much? How Gender Affects Welfare Impacts of a Booming Industry." Policy Research Working Paper 3029, World Bank, Washington, DC.

Robertson, Raymond. 2012. "Introduction." In *Sewing Success? Employment, Wages, and Poverty Following the End of the Multi-fibre Arrangement*, edited by Gladys Lopez-Acevedo and Raymond Robertson, 7–17. Washington, DC: World Bank.

Saheed, Hassen. 2012. "Prospects for the Textile and Clothing Industry in India." *Textile Outlook International* (156): 86–127.

Sandhu, Kamran Yousef. 2011. "Challenges to Pakistan's Value Added Industry." Paper presented at the Third International Conference on Textile and Clothing, Institute of Textile and Industrial Science, Lahore. http://umt.edu.pk/ictc2011/Presentation .html.

Sivasankaran, Anitha. 2014. "Work and Women's Marriage, Fertility and Empowerment: Evidence from Textile Mill Employment in India." Job Market Paper, Harvard University, Cambridge, MA.

Sri Lanka DCS (Department of Census and Statistics). 2014. *Annual Survey of Industries 2012*. Colombo: Sri Lanka DCS.

Tewari, Meenu. 2008. "Deepening Intra-regional Trade and Investment in South Asia: The Case of the Textile and Clothing Industry." India Council for Research on International Economic Relations (ICRIER).

UNCTADSTAT. 1970–2012. *Inward and Outward Foreign Direct Investment Flows, Annual, 1970–2012*. http://unctadstat.unctad.org/TableViewer/tableView.aspx.

UNIDO (United Nations Industrial Development Organization). 2013. *The Industrial Competitiveness of Nations: Looking Back, Forging Ahead*. Competitive Industrial Performance Report 2012/2013. Vienna: UNIDO.

UNSD (United Nations Statistics Division). 2014a. *World Apparel (HS1992 61+62) Imports (1990–2012)*. Retrieved March 3–6, from UNSD.

———. 2014b. *World Apparel Imports (1992–2012) by Product Categories*. Retrieved May 13–15, 2014, from UNSD.

———. 2014c. *World Textile Product Imports (1995–2012) by Product Categories*. Retrieved May 13, 2014, from UNSD.

World Bank. 2013. *World Development Report 2013: Jobs*. Washington, DC: World Bank.

Yamagata, Tatsufumi. 2006. "The Garment Industry in Cambodia: Its Role in Poverty Reduction through Export-Oriented Development." IDE Discussion Paper 62, Institute of Developing Economies, JETRO, Chiba.

Yunus, Mohammad, and Tatsufumi Yamagata. 2014. "Bangladesh: Market Force Supersedes Control." In *The Garment Industry in Low-Income Countries: An Entry Point of Industrialization*, edited by Takahiro Fukunishi and Tatsufumi Yamagata, 77–104. Basingstoke, UK: Palgrave Macmillan.

## PART 1

What Is South Asia's Apparel Export Potential?

## CHAPTER 2

Benchmarking South Asia in the Global Apparel Industry

Key Messages

- There is a tendency toward consolidation in the industry, meaning that global buyers are looking to outsource production to fewer rather than more units.
- Our results show that South Asia performs relatively well on cost—but not on product diversification or on factors like quality, lead time and reliability, and social compliance, all of which are increasingly important to global buyers.
- India and Pakistan face the most hurdles—notably not enough product diversity; Sri Lanka needs to expand end markets or develop capabilities in other higher-value, lower-volume product categories; and Bangladesh, now reaping the benefits of low costs, needs to tackle social compliance and product diversity to remain competitive.

A Vital Industry for South Asia

As the global apparel industry continues to evolve—spurred by the phaseout of the Multifibre Arrangement (MFA) in 2005 and the 2008–09 global financial crisis—policy makers across South Asia are trying to weigh the costs and benefits of making policy changes that would facilitate apparel exports. Already, apparel (combined with textiles) is the region's largest manufacturing sector, major employer, and leading export sector. In 2012, the region exported $43.8 billion in apparel, representing 12 percent of global apparel exports (UNSD 2014a), with the formal apparel industry directly employing about 4.7 million people and the informal textile and apparel industries another 20.3 million.[1] But, in today's fiercely competitive environment, South Asia will need to move up the global value chain in apparel just to hang on to what it has, let alone make deeper inroads.

The author of this chapter, Stacey Frederick, is grateful for comments provided by the core team and for substantive contributions from Cornelia Staritz and Leonard Plank.

Exporters enter the industry producing basic products, which make up the bulk of global apparel trade. These products—like cotton knit shirts, socks, underwear, basic pants, and woven shirts—are produced in medium to high volumes and sold at lower average unit values. They are readily available from multiple countries and firms, although buying from a large pool of factories is costly and time consuming. In fact, an important trend emerging in the industry is consolidation—that is, buyers prefer to source from larger, more capable vendors who offer a variety of products at competitive prices paired with consistent quality, reliable delivery, sufficient lead times, and broader nonmanufacturing capabilities. In other words, merely exporting at a low cost is no longer a sufficient advantage for exporting apparel. Top exporters in basic product categories can produce large outputs, use automated equipment where it exists, and often employ thousands of workers in one factory.

A next step up for apparel producers is expanding into multiple high-end product categories and enlarging the size of their end markets, although this move does not necessarily translate into opportunities to significantly increase employment or global market share. More complicated products in terms of design or materials—like suits, skirts, coats, or high-end materials such as wool, linen, or silk—are typically produced in lower volumes, have higher unit values, and are exported by a limited set of countries and firms (Birnbaum 2014a).

This chapter begins with a look at how South Asian countries have recently (2005–2012) performed compared to one another and to other top apparel exporters in terms of overall apparel export values and market share, along with product category, fiber type, and end markets. For South Asia, four countries are used: Bangladesh, India, Pakistan, and Sri Lanka (hereafter, "the SAR countries" or "SAR"). For the main competitors, China and three Southeast Asian benchmark countries are used: Vietnam, Indonesia, and Cambodia (hereafter, "the SEAB countries" or "SEAB"). The chapter then tries to provide possible explanations for the variations seen in export patterns by identifying key attributes associated with export performance from the point of view of global buyers. Countries are then ranked along these parameters using qualitative data compiled from two recent sets of interviews with global apparel buyers. The goal is to benchmark South Asia's capabilities for high-volume product categories that could enable these countries to expand global market share and increase manufacturing employment opportunities.

The results of the benchmark analysis indicate that, overall, the SEAB countries and China are outperforming the SAR countries in terms of aggregate export performance, product diversity, and non-cost-related factors important to global buyers. SAR countries—with the exception of Sri Lanka—generally appear to be cost competitive for the selected product categories but are inhibited by product concentration and inferior performance compared to competitors in non-cost-related factors (including quality, lead times, reliability, and compliance).

Introduction to Benchmarking

Why is it important to do a benchmark analysis of the SAR apparel exporters? It enables us to put SAR countries' recent export performance in perspective of global trends and those of key competing countries. It also enables us to evaluate SAR countries' performance in key areas that matter to global buyers who want to increase apparel purchases. For this purpose, countries were chosen that have been among the top 10 *global* (rather than regionally focused) apparel exporters over the past decade. Furthermore, two recent surveys asked buyers to name hot spots for increased sourcing beyond China; in both surveys buyers' responses included Vietnam, Indonesia, and Cambodia (Lu 2014; McKinsey & Company 2011, 2013).

The benchmark analysis begins by comparing the SAR and SEAB countries in terms of aggregate export performance and by product category, fiber type, and end markets (assessing the size and importance in terms of exports and employment and structural characteristics like firm ownership [box 2.1]) (see also table 2B.1 in annex 2B).[2] It relies on trade data from United Nations Statistics Division's database (COMTRADE) and uses the time frame between 2005 and 2012 because it coincides with important institutional and regulatory changes in the industry. Until 2005, apparel trade was governed by a system of quotas under the MFA—a trade pact that restricted textile and apparel exports from developing to developed countries, although it also ended up spreading production to even more developing countries. Then, the 2008–09 global economic crisis led to a temporary reduction in global demand, evidenced by a 6 percent decline in world apparel exports between 2007 and 2009 (Gereffi and Frederick 2010; UNSD 2014a).

The next step in the benchmark analysis tries to (i) identify the key factors that affect export performance to provide possible explanations for the variations seen in export patterns and (ii) evaluate the SAR and SEAB countries in these key areas. To do this, a review of recent studies on global apparel buyers' sourcing strategies was conducted (Birnbaum 2013; Daher and Chmielewski 2013; KSA-AM 2007–2013; Nathan Associates 2005). See table 2A.1 in annex 2A for an overview of these surveys. This information was supplemented with primary data from interviews with global apparel buyers (2014). These firms are responsible for choosing suppliers; and, as such, their sourcing strategies and preferences have a profound effect on production, trade, and employment in apparel-exporting countries.

Next, the countries are ranked along these dimensions using data from two sources. The first is a recent survey of global apparel buyers, in which respondents were asked to rate seven key apparel-supplying countries on a number of factors, which included the main areas deemed to be important in this study (Birnbaum 2013). Results from that survey were supplemented with primary data collected during the interviews with global apparel buyers (2014) in which participants were asked about their perceptions of South Asian suppliers relative to competitors.

The global apparel industry is a characteristic buyer-driven value chain[3] in which global apparel brand owners or apparel buyers with headquarters in the United States and the European Union (EU) control the highest value-adding activities related to retailing, marketing, branding, and design and outsource production to a network of suppliers, largely based in Asia (Gereffi 1994, 1999; Gereffi and Frederick 2010; Gereffi and Memedovic 2003). Beyond apparel buyers, the main segments of the supply chain include apparel manufacturing, textile components (yarn and fabric) and trim, and fiber production.

Ranking Performance Based on Exports

Starting with how each country currently stands overall in terms of increasing apparel exports and gaining global market share, results show that, of the top 15 apparel exporter countries in the world, only emerging Asian apparel exporter countries have increased export values *and* global market shares in the context of the MFA phaseout and the global economic crisis (that is, during the 2005–2012 period). In contrast, more developed Asian apparel exporter countries and regional suppliers to the United States and the EU-15[4] have collectively lost export share (Gereffi and Frederick 2010; Staritz 2011). It is also important to note that globally there has been an overall consolidation of the supply base—in 2005 the top five apparel-exporting countries accounted for 63 percent of exports, and by 2012 this increased to 71 percent (UNSD 2014a). The export performance of the main apparel-exporting countries, as illustrated in figure 2.1, can be categorized as follows:

- *Growth suppliers:* This group—which includes China, all three SEAB countries, Bangladesh, and Pakistan—has increased export value and global market share since the early 1990s as well as in the post-MFA and postcrisis period. Despite modest growth in global market share, at 41 percent in 2012, China still holds an exceptional share of the global market.
- *Stable suppliers:* These countries—like Sri Lanka and India—have increased export value; but their global market shares are stable or declining, and growth rates are lower than the world average.
- *Declining suppliers:* These economies—like SAR and the Republic of Korea— have experienced declines in value and global market share during the phase-out and post-MFA period, and in some cases since the early 1990s.

In terms of value and global market share, as figure 2.2 shows, this time period has collectively been good for the SAR countries. Indeed, they boosted their share of global apparel trade at a compound annual growth rate (CAGR) of 9 percent, which was above the world average (4 percent) and greater than China (7 percent), yet slower than that of the SEAB countries (13 percent) (UNSD 2014a). At the country level, however, some have done a lot better than others—with export growth rising in Bangladesh (the top performer), and to a lesser extent in Pakistan, while slowing in India and Sri Lanka. There is also a big

Figure 2.1 Emerging Asian Countries Fared Well Post-MFA and Despite the Global Economic Crisis

(Top Apparel Exporting Countries, CAGR, 2005–12)

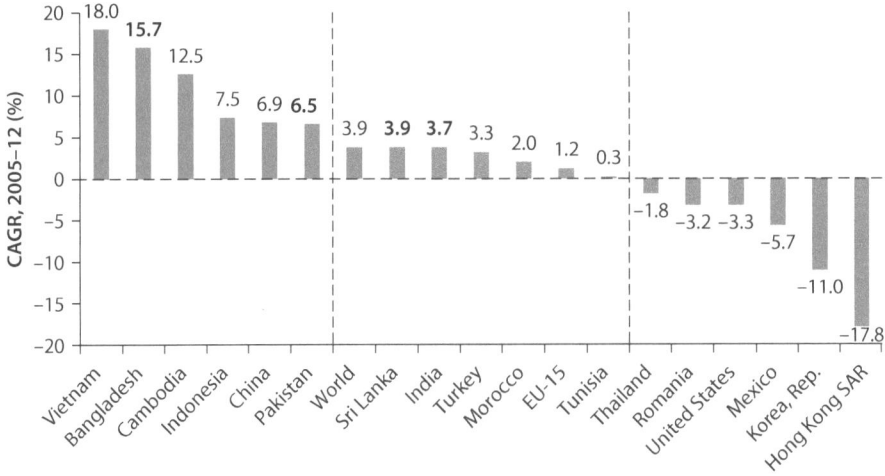

Source: UNSD 2014a.

Note: Includes countries/regions that were top 15 apparel exporters between 2000 and 2012; exports based on world (aggregate) apparel imports (HS92 61+62). SAR countries' values are in bold. CAGR = compound annual growth rate; EU-15 = Austria, Belgium, Denmark, Finland, France, Germany, Greece, Ireland, Italy, Luxembourg, Netherlands, Portugal, Spain, Sweden, and the United Kingdom.

Figure 2.2 South Asia Is Gaining Market Share but Not as Quickly as Southeast Asia

(SAR, SEAB, and China Apparel Exports, 2012, and Growth Rates, 2005–12)

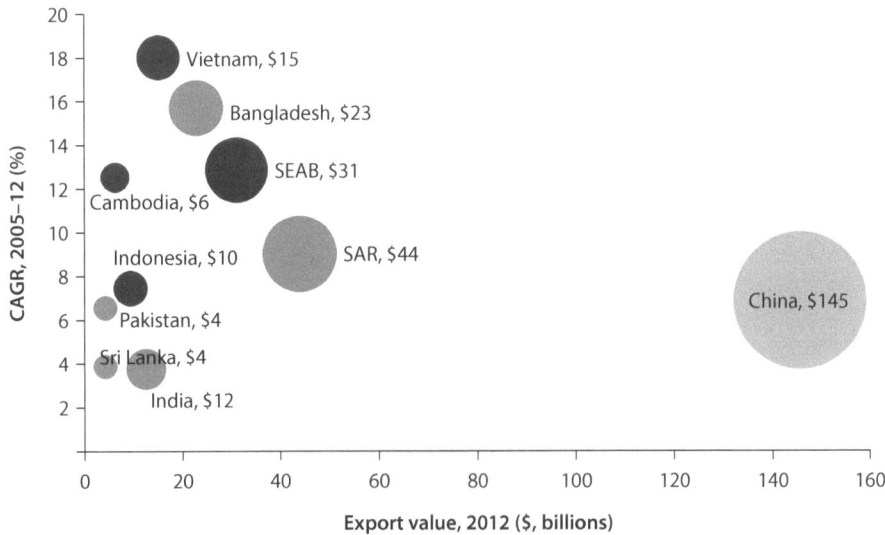

Source: UNSD 2014a.

Note: Exports based on world (aggregate) apparel imports (HS92 61+62). Number next to country name represents 2012 apparel export value ($, billions); Orange: SAR (South Asia sample) country; Blue: SEAB (Southeast Asian benchmark) country; Green: China. Size of bubble based on share of global apparel exports in 2012. In 2012, the value of global apparel trade was approximately $355 billion (UNSD 2014a). CAGR = compound annual growth rate.

Box 2.1 A Snapshot of South Asia's Major Apparel Exporters

A respectable global market presence: Bangladesh leads the pack with 6.4 percent of the global market, followed by India (3.5 percent), and Sri Lanka and Pakistan (1.2 percent). The same pattern holds for global value: Bangladesh ($22.8 billion), followed by India ($12.5 billion), then Sri Lanka ($4.4 billion), and Pakistan ($4.2 billion).

Mostly lower-end, cotton products: The profile is much the same for the SAR countries, except Sri Lanka. Bangladesh is a key destination for basic commodity items produced in long runs, mostly made from cotton (trousers, knit and woven shirts, and sweaters/sweatshirts) (Birnbaum 2014b; Tewari 2008; UNSD 2014b). India is primarily an exporter of cotton products (woven and knit tops, skirts, men's bottoms, and embellished and embroidered apparel) (Tewari 2008; UNSD 2014b). Pakistan also specializes in basic cotton apparel (woven denim and chino trousers, low-priced knitwear such as polo shirts and T-shirts, and fleece sweat-shirts). However, Sri Lanka's exports are equally divided between cotton and manmade fiber (MMF) products, and it is a niche and fashion-oriented producer (intimate apparel, trousers, and swimwear) (Tewari 2008; UNSD 2014b).

Mainly domestic ownership: In Bangladesh, the industry is dominated (over 90 percent) by locally owned firms (BEPZA 2013; Yunus and Yamagata 2014), but foreign direct investment (FDI) played a central role in initiating the industry by providing links to foreign buyers, technol-ogy, and knowledge transfer. In Sri Lanka, the FDI history is similar, although today ownership is both joint ventures and domestically owned firms. However, in India, which is dominated by locally owned firms, FDI has played a limited role (less than 1 percent) as a share of overall investment in the textile and apparel industry and as a share of the country's overall FDI inflows (National Stakeholders 2014; NCAER 2009; Saheed 2012a; UNCTADSTAT 1970–2012). The story is similar for Pakistan, with the share of foreign-owned firms estimated to be less than 2 percent for apparel and only slightly higher for textiles (Hamdani 2009; National Stakeholders 2014).

variation among the countries in terms of their share of the global apparel market as of 2012 (ranging from 1.2 percent for Sri Lanka and Pakistan to 6.4 percent for Bangladesh) (see box 2.1). And apparel's share of country exports ranges from 5 percent for India to 83 percent for Bangladesh, with Pakistan (19 percent) and Sri Lanka (45 percent) in the middle.

In terms of apparel export value—estimated at about $355 billion globally in 2012 (UNSD 2014a)—Bangladesh is the largest exporter, followed by India with roughly half the value of Bangladesh, and finally Sri Lanka and Pakistan with similar values. However, in contrast, all of the SEAB countries and China managed to increase both export value and global market share.

Drivers of Export Performance: Products and End Markets

As South Asia looks for ways to maximize export growth and increase global market share, key inputs will be current demand and future or emerging demand.

Current Demand

At this point, the SAR countries and SEAB countries alike are adequately producing and selling items that match global trends in current demand in top product categories, material, and end markets.

Product Categories and Fiber Types

Product diversity is important because most global buyers sell a mix of apparel from multiple product categories and fiber types and therefore prefer to source from vendors and countries with broader product availability to reduce complexity and costs associated with vendor management. The top three globally traded apparel product categories by export value have remained the same since at least 2000 and include trousers, knit shirts, and sweaters/sweatshirts, accounting for 46 percent of traded apparel in 2012 (UNSD 2014b) (figure 2.3). The bulk of production in these categories is made up of high-volume and midrange unit value products. SAR countries' exports in these three categories represented 57 percent of exports in 2012, compared to 50 percent for the SEAB countries and 41 percent for China (UNSD 2014c) (figure 2.6). Bangladesh and Pakistan's exports are concentrated in these three categories, and they are also the only two SAR countries with increasing global market share. India and Sri Lanka follow a strategy of higher-value exports in relatively smaller runs, focusing on value addition and more complex and differentiated items—like India's embellished and embroidered apparel and Sri Lanka's intimate apparel and swimwear.

As for fiber types, the two main materials are cotton and manmade fibers (MMFs), representing about 46 and 32 percent, respectively, of world apparel exports in 2012 (UNSD 2014c). At this point, SAR is heavily focused on

Figure 2.3 Trousers, Knit Shirts, and Sweaters/Sweatshirts Are Today's Largest Product Categories
(Global Apparel Product Categories: Export Value and CAGR, 2005–12)

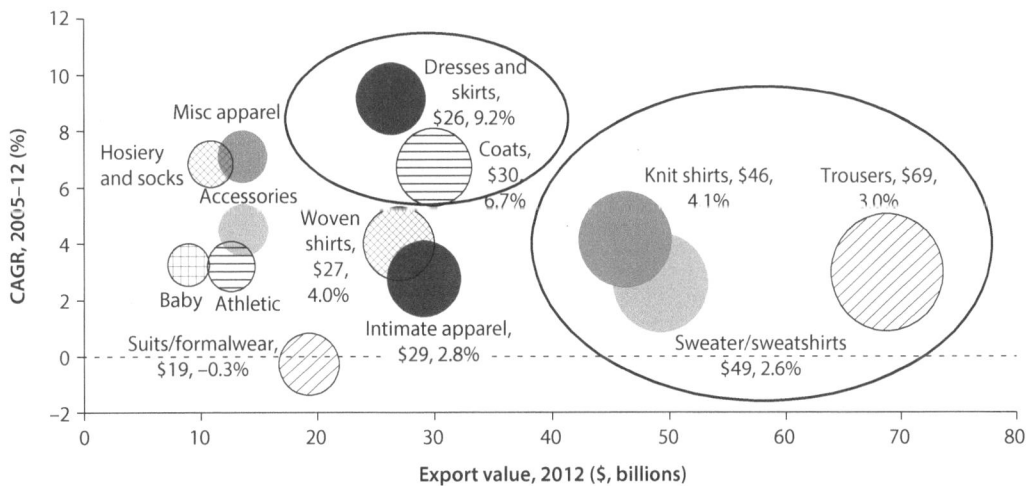

Source: UNSD 2014b.
Note: Classifications created by author. The size of the bubble represents the 2012 global export value. CAGR = compound annual growth rate.

cotton-based apparel products (nearly 75 percent of apparel exports), unlike its competitors (SEAB, at 47 percent, and China, at 39 percent) and the world at large (an average of 46 percent) (figure 2.4) (UNSD 2014c). This focus is desirable for meeting current demand but will be detrimental for satisfying future demand and product diversity. That said, Sri Lanka differs from the rest of SAR in that it is already using 50 percent MMF in its production.

End Markets

Diversifying end markets not only increases growth prospects—given that the mature and currently top two markets (the United States and the EU-15) are experiencing a slowdown in demand—but also reduces risks and dependency on certain markets and buyers. Between 2005 and 2012, the SAR countries became less dependent on these markets, with their share of exports to the United States and the EU-15 decreasing from 88 percent to 77 percent. However, this level is still above that of the SEAB countries (58 percent) and China (49 percent) (UNSD 2014a) (figure 2.5).

Sri Lanka diversified the most, which is good given its greater focus on niche products, followed by Bangladesh.[5] Pakistan's diversification has generally been on par with the SAR region. However, India has had minimal diversification over

Figure 2.4 SAR, Unlike Its Competitors, Focuses Heavily on Cotton
(Composition of Apparel Exports by Region and Fiber Type, 2012)

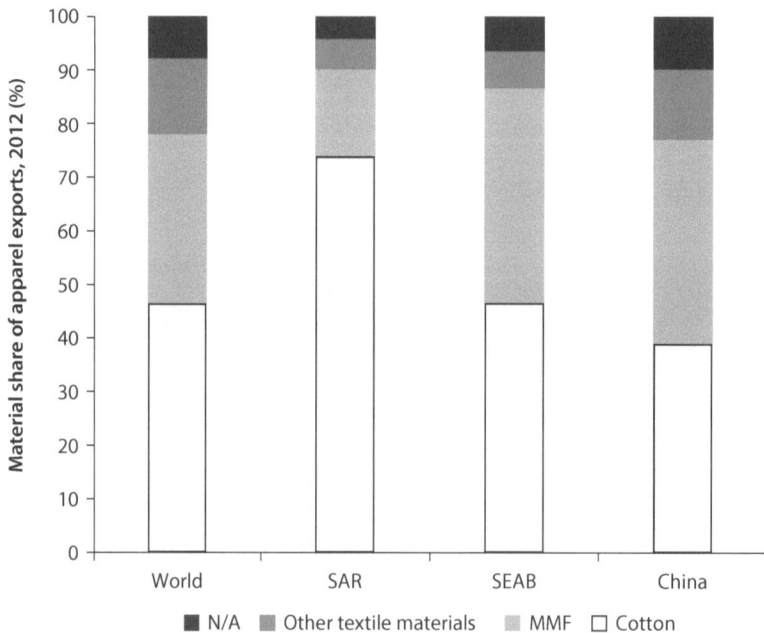

Source: UNSD 2014c.
Note: Exports represented by world imports; classifications created by author. MMF = manmade fiber; SAR = South Asian sample countries (Bangladesh, India, Pakistan, and Sri Lanka); SEAB = Southeast Asian benchmark countries (Cambodia, Indonesia, and Vietnam). N/A indicates the material is not available in trade data classification definition.

Stitches to Riches? • http://dx.doi.org/10.1596/978-1-4648-0813-5

Figure 2.5 China Has the Most Diversified End Market Export Profile
(Share of Exports to the EU-15 and United States by Value and Region, 2012)

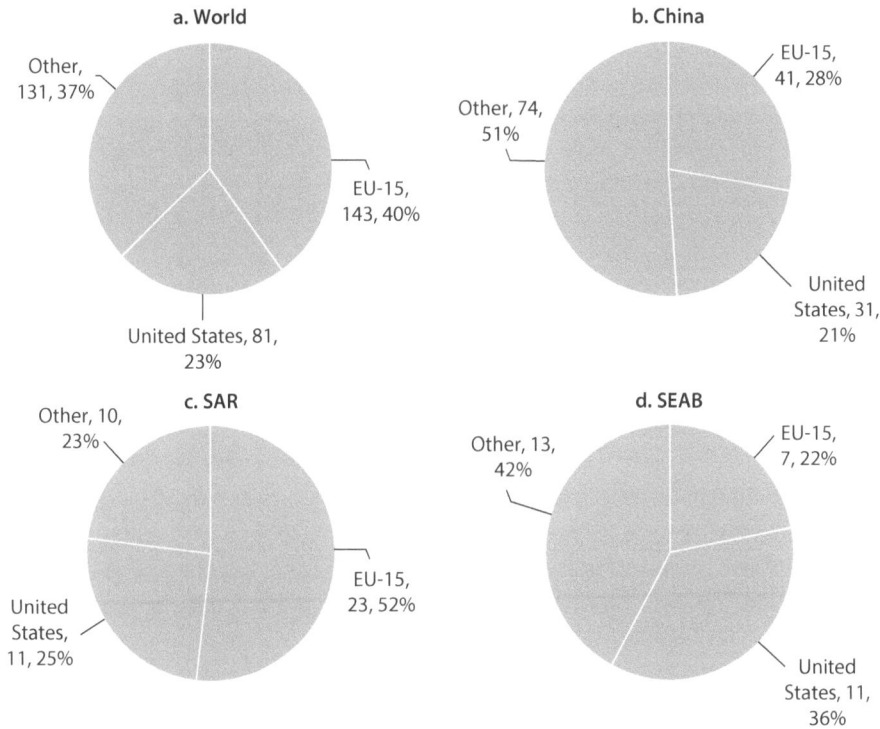

a. World
Other, 131, 37%
EU-15, 143, 40%
United States, 81, 23%

b. China
EU-15, 41, 28%
Other, 74, 51%
United States, 31, 21%

c. SAR
Other, 10, 23%
EU-15, 23, 52%
United States, 11, 25%

d. SEAB
Other, 13, 42%
EU-15, 7, 22%
United States, 11, 36%

Source: UNSD 2014a.
Note: Numbers in figure above reflect export values in billions for 2012 followed by share. EU-15 = Austria, Belgium, Denmark, Finland, France, Germany, Greece, Ireland, Italy, Luxembourg, Netherlands, Portugal, Spain, Sweden, and the United Kingdom; SAR = South Asian sample countries (Bangladesh, India, Pakistan, and Sri Lanka); SEAB = Southeast Asian benchmark countries (Cambodia, Indonesia, and Vietnam).

the last seven years, although it was already a more diversified exporter than the other SAR countries.

The two top import markets for apparel are the EU-15 and the United States, with 63 percent of global imports in 2012 (UNSD 2014a). For SAR, the EU-15 is the most significant export destination in terms of value ($22.9 billion) and share of exports (52 percent), followed by the United States at 25 percent. Moreover, exports to the EU-15 are growing at a much faster rate than those to the United States—largely thanks to EU preferential market access (see chapter 5 for details).[6] As for SAR's competitors, exports from the SEAB countries are also focused on the EU-15 and the United States, but they are more concentrated on the United States—which accounted for nearly half of its exports, followed by the EU-15 (22 percent) and Japan (9 percent).

Future Demand

To capture exports from China, SAR must diversify its product categories and produce more apparel that is based on MMF. This will require better backward linkages to MMF textile capabilities, which are mostly produced in Korea, Taiwan, and, to a lesser extent, China and Vietnam. Domestic or foreign investment will need to be targeted, or relationships with MMF suppliers established in nearby countries to minimize lead times.

Product Categories and Fiber Types

The strongest growth in global demand by fiber type is for apparel made from MMF, which rose by 6.7 percent over the 2005–2012 period and increased in share of global apparel trade from 26 percent to 32 percent. On the other hand, cotton's share of the global market decreased by a similar margin over the same time period (UNSD 2014c). Yet, unlike the SEAB countries and China, which mirrored these trends, SAR countries saw an increase in the share of apparel made from cotton between 2005 and 2012 and a decrease in the share of MMF.

Synthetics are important for coats, athletic apparel, and dresses/skirts—so there is a correlation between product categories and fiber type. The ability to produce a wider variety of apparel products requires access to textile inputs (either through domestic production or imports) and adequate production capacity. SAR's dependence on cotton products is reflective of the significant domestic cotton industry in India and Pakistan and the comparatively small size of MMF fiber production. In 2011–12 India produced 6.1 million tons of raw cotton fiber, well above the 1.2 million tons of MMF staple fibers (Saheed 2012a).[7] Heavier MMF and wool fabrics needed for the fall/winter season need to be imported (Jordan, Kamphuis, and Setia 2014), and India is not a significant exporter in product categories (like coats) requiring these fabrics.

The fastest growing, sizeable export product categories globally are dresses/skirts and coats (figure 2.6).[8] However, SAR countries' share of exports in these two categories has *decreased* in terms of the overall share of exports (from 12 to 10 percent between 2005 and 2012), whereas it has increased for the SEAB countries (from 15 to 18 percent) and China (from 16 to 19 percent).

End Markets

The SAR countries need to accelerate the diversification process in light of the fact that China has more diversified export markets than both the SAR or the SEAB countries. To evaluate emerging end market demand, both retail and trade data are considered because apparel for the local retail industry is often produced domestically—which can be significant (box 2.2)—before shifting to imports.

Globally, the fastest growing sizeable retail markets include Argentina, Australia, Brazil, China, India, the Russian Federation, Saudi Arabia, and the United Arab Emirates (Euromonitor/Passport 2014).[9] The largest and the fastest-growing import markets include Australia, Canada, China, Japan, Korea, and Russia (UNSD 2014a).[10] In the case of SAR, export destinations that accounted for more than 1 percent of its apparel exports in 2012 and had growth rates above the region's average include many of these countries: Australia, Canada, Japan, Russia, Saudi Arabia, and the United Arab Emirates. But the SAR countries may be missing key export opportunities in China, India, Korea, and Latin America.

Figure 2.6 Emerging Demand Includes Dresses/Skirts and Coats, Not SAR's Strength

(Share of Apparel Exports by Region, Country, and Product Categories, 2012)

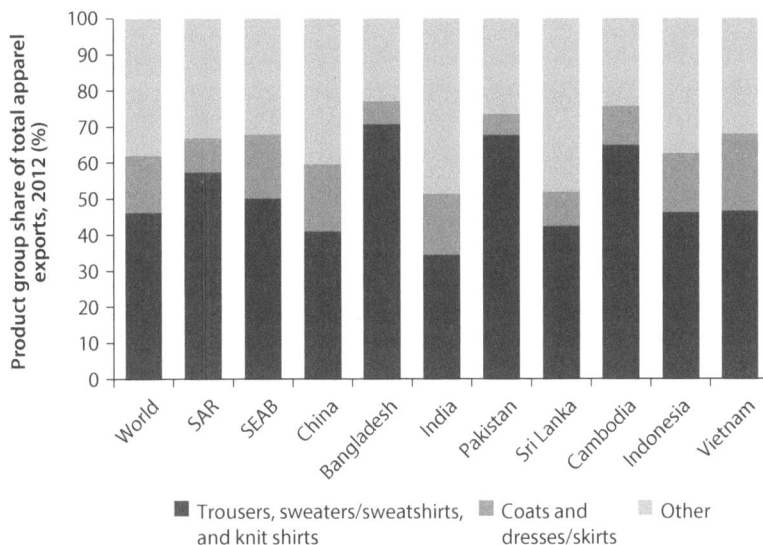

Trousers, sweaters/sweatshirts, and knit shirts ■   Coats and dresses/skirts ■   Other ▓

Source: UNSD 2014b.
Note: SAR = South Asian sample countries (Bangladesh, India, Pakistan, and Sri Lanka); SEAB = Southeast Asian benchmark countries (Cambodia, Indonesia, and Vietnam).

Box 2.2 Don't Forget Domestic Apparel Markets

The domestic markets in countries with large populations and expanding disposable incomes also present growth opportunities. Apparel produced domestically for the domestic market (so-called nontraded apparel) is often omitted in benchmarking studies because of a lack of a reliable, uniform dataset to measure production and consumption that does not cross borders. However, production for domestic consumption is sizeable and growing, particularly for large Asian economies such as China and India. For example, in 2012, the Asia-Pacific region accounted for about 32 percent of the global retail market, but only 24 percent of apparel imports, compared to nearly equal shares for North America and a much higher import than retail share for Western Europe (40 percent of imports and 25 percent of retail sales)(Euromonitor/Passport 2014; UNSD 2014a).

With populations in 2013 over 100 million, the domestic market represents a significant opportunity for India, and eventually Pakistan and Bangladesh, which have yet to fully develop organized formal retail sectors (World Bank 2014a). Sri Lanka's domestic market is not appealing to large exporting firms because it has limited high-end demand, although these firms have begun developing brands for the Indian market (National Stakeholders 2014).

The case for India is particularly strong because its average export performance may be partially attributed to an increasing focus on the domestic market, which is omitted in trade

box continues next page

Box 2.2 Don't Forget Domestic Apparel Markets *(continued)*

analysis. To put this in perspective, Bangladesh and Vietnam are the strongest performers in terms of export growth, yet neither has a sizeable formal retail apparel industry. The retail market in these two countries combined is less than $3 billion, whereas India's market is valued at $40 billion, which is almost entirely produced within the country. If production for the domestic and export markets are combined, India's value jumps to $53 billion, compared to $24 and $20 billion in Bangladesh and Vietnam, respectively. Of course, on top of boosting manufacturing, a bigger domestic retail market also can create jobs and increase revenue attributable to services related to marketing and retail. Several large apparel exporters in India have developed brands for the domestic market and, in some instances, their own retail chains (Tewari 2009).

End market diversification is influenced by tariff rates faced in importing countries (and thus market access preferences) and access to end market buyers. Historical relationships and established well-known capabilities within a country or region are key factors that can pose challenges to countries wishing to sell to new buyers or offer new products. The dominance of local firms and a long tradition in local entrepreneurship are important advantages of South Asian apparel exporter countries because this makes industries more embedded, leads to higher learning potential, and reduces the likelihood of relocation (National Stakeholders 2014; Staritz 2011). However, the lack of FDI is also a threat because foreign investors provide the potential for technology transfer, access to buyers, spillovers, and, hence, learning and upgrading opportunities. From a foreign investment standpoint, the SAR countries are less aligned with East Asia and China than the SEAB countries. Given this scenario, SEAB (particularly Vietnam) is poised to receive more of China's spillover because of the ability of East Asian multinational corporations to shift orders to branch plants located in SEAB countries (see chapter 5).

Key Factors for Global Buyers

The next step in this analysis is to identify the key factors shaping export performance to help explain variations in export patterns. Apparel buyers account for an array of factors when making sourcing decisions that are specific to the supplier country and firm; and, although variations exist, a number of common trends emerge. Based on multiple surveys of global apparel buyers conducted over the last decade (Birnbaum 2013; Daher & Chmielewski 2013; KSA-AM 2007–13; Nathan Associates 2005) and interviews during this project (Global Apparel Buyers 2014), the key factors apparel buyers consider when selecting a supplier relate to firm capabilities—notably, cost; quality, lead time, and reliability, including access to inputs; full package services; and social and, to a lesser extent, environmental compliance.

We will now analyze the SAR and SEAB countries along these parameters using data from two recent studies. The first is a benchmark analysis that was commissioned by India's Apparel Export Promotion Council (AEPC) to determine the causes of India's declining market share of U.S./EU apparel industries (Birnbaum 2013). As part of the project, 30 senior sourcing executives at EU and U.S. brand importers and retailers were interviewed and asked to rate seven garment-exporting countries on factors important to sourcing decisions (Birnbaum 2013). Interviewees rated the target countries in each area as high (4 points), medium (2 points), or low (−2 points). The questions covered cost (free on board [FOB] price), quality, lead time, reliability, and compliance. The results were used to rank the countries with available data (Bangladesh, Cambodia, China, India, Indonesia, and Vietnam).[11] Factory owners were also interviewed. The results of this survey were compared with those of interviews with seven U.S.- and EU-based global buyers in fall 2014 in which they were asked to rank countries' performance along the same dimensions. Because Sri Lanka and Pakistan were not included in the first study, these interviews, along with information from other sources, were used for those countries (see annex 2C for survey).

Costs and Competitiveness

Production costs and quality have always been important and have become even more so given the stepped-up competition after the MFA and the global economic crisis. These two firm-specific criteria ranked the highest in importance in all buyer surveys reviewed.

To evaluate cost competitiveness, the analysis began by comparing the countries' actual performance on price using 2013 global export unit value data for seven product categories (table 2B.2 in annex 2B). The results showed that Bangladesh, Cambodia, and Pakistan offer the lowest unit values; Indonesia and India fall in the middle; and China, Vietnam, and Sri Lanka post the highest unit values (table 2.1). Next the countries were compared

Table 2.1 Cost Is Important, but Offering the Lowest Unit Values Is Not Necessary
(Cost Competitiveness: Unit Value and Export Rank Analysis by Country)

Country	Unit value rank	Export rank	Cost competitiveness
China	◆	◉	▲
Bangladesh	◉	◉	◉
India	▲	▲	▲
Pakistan	◉	◆	◉
Sri Lanka	◆	◆	◆
Vietnam	◆	◉	▲
Cambodia	◉	◆	◉
Indonesia	▲	▲	▲

Source: Based on analysis of unit value data provided in table 2B.2 and global apparel export ranks in 2012.
Note: Green circle: top three countries based on data analysis (factor is not a problem); Orange triangle: middle two countries (factor may become an issue); Blue diamond: bottom three countries (factor is likely an issue).

Stitches to Riches? • http://dx.doi.org/10.1596/978-1-4648-0813-5

based on their global export rank in the same product categories, and the results were compared with the unit value results to place the countries into the following groups:

- *China and Vietnam:* They have relatively high unit export values compared to competitors yet are top exporters in every category—perhaps helped by being the lead exporters in emerging product categories in which there are fewer competitors.[12]
- *Bangladesh, Indonesia, Sri Lanka, and, to a lesser extent, India:* These countries' unit values and export ranks are similar. Bangladesh offers low unit values and ranks as a top exporter across multiple product categories. Indonesia offers midrange unit values and generally ranks as the fourth- or fifth-largest exporter of the eight countries analyzed. Sri Lanka had among the highest unit values in nearly every category and was also not a top exporter—and was the one country flagged on cost competitiveness. India's results were the least consistent—it offers midrange unit values in trousers and sweaters/sweatshirts yet is not a top exporter.
- *Cambodia and Pakistan*[13]: Both countries offer lower unit values, but neither is a top exporter—yet the reason does not appear to be cost competitiveness.

Perhaps equally important as actual unit values are buyers' perspectives on the cost competitiveness of a country. Indeed, the results of the Birnbaum buyer survey (table 2.2) are similar to the actual unit value results (table 2.1)—except that buyers appear to perceive India as less cost competitive than it actually is and Vietnam as being more competitive than it actually is. Overall, Bangladesh is perceived to be the most cost competitive, followed by Vietnam, Cambodia, China, Indonesia, and India (Birnbaum 2013). Based on these results, cost appears to be a primary issue for Sri Lanka, and may currently be or become an important factor for China, India, Indonesia, and Vietnam.

Table 2.2 Productivity Is a Major Factor in Determining Competitiveness
(Competitiveness on Cost-Related Factors: Wages and Buyers' Perceptions on Productivity and Price)

Country	Buyers' perceptions of:				Minimum wages		Cost-related issues
	Price (FOB)		Productivity				
China	▲	4	●	1	◆	8	Wages, price perception
Bangladesh	●	1	◆	5	●	1	Productivity perception
India	◆	6	◆	6	▲	4	Productivity and price perception, wages
Vietnam	●	2	▲	3	▲	5	Productivity perception, wages
Cambodia	▲	3	▲	4	●	3	Productivity and price perception
Indonesia	◆	5	●	2	◆	7	Price perception

Source: Buyers' perceptions on price (FOB) and productivity based on data from Birnbaum 2013; minimum wages based on data in table 2B.3 (not shown: Sri Lanka ranked two and Pakistan six); cost-related issues based on World Bank analysis.
Note: Green indicates top two countries (factor is not an issue); orange is for the middle two countries and indicates caution; blue is used for the bottom two ranking countries (factor is an issue). FOB = free on board.

Raw Materials, Labor, and Productivity

For apparel manufacturers the largest cost components are raw materials/inputs (two-thirds), followed by labor (one-fifth), and rent and utilities (less than one-fifth). As such, two critical elements in reducing cost are raw material inputs and labor, although the ability of the apparel supplier to alter the price of raw materials is limited. In apparel production, fabrics are the most expensive input, and the quality of textiles is directly related to the final product's quality. However, unlike apparel, textile production is more capital, skill, and scale intensive, which can pose a challenge to establishing domestic backward linkages (Staritz and Frederick 2014). Furthermore, buyers often nominate textile mills to ensure consistency and negotiate pricing. This situation leaves countries with only a few options: ensure import tariffs are low from the primary supplying countries, encourage foreign investment from nominated mills within country, or ask buyers to add domestic textile firms to their list of approved textile suppliers.

Because apparel production is labor intensive, the availability of labor and labor costs plays an important role in the sector's competitiveness. In many Asian countries, wages have risen substantially in recent years because of workers' protests and competition from other more attractive sectors, with the latter being particularly important in Sri Lanka, some regions in India, as well as in China, Indonesia, and Vietnam (Birnbaum 2014c). These developments and the problematic social implications of low wages show that competitiveness based only on low wages is not an effective or desirable long-term strategy. Wage increases often have to be compensated with increased productivity because buyers are generally not prepared to accept proportional increases in prices despite corporate social responsibility (CSR) efforts (National Stakeholders 2014).

In all four SAR countries, labor costs remain quite low despite wage increases. Minimum wages per month are the lowest in Bangladesh ($68), followed by Sri Lanka ($71), India ($101), and Pakistan ($120) (table 2B.3 in annex 2B). In contrast, minimum wages in the SEAB countries and China tend to be higher, ranging from $100 in Cambodia to $211 in China (table 2B.3).

China provides evidence that higher wages do not have to translate into higher apparel prices if productivity-increasing measures take place at the firm and country levels. After a decade of near-continuous wage rises, the average price of Chinese apparel exported to the United States in fall 2013 was lower than in both 2012 and 2008 (Flanagan 2014). A determinant of success for apparel manufacturers is the ability to introduce new processes, work organization, and technology, all of which improve operational performance and productivity. Productivity levels are also affected by worker and manager skills as well as by the broader business environment, access to credit, and infrastructure.

How do the SAR countries and their competitors fare in the eyes of buyers in terms of productivity? China ranked significantly higher than the other countries; Cambodia, Indonesia, and Vietnam fared similarly; and Bangladesh and India were the bottom two performers (table 2.2). Two elements that can affect productivity are worker quality and turnover. When factory owners were asked to rate countries based on worker quality, China and India were viewed as having the highest quality workers; Cambodia, Indonesia, and Vietnam were generally considered average; and Bangladesh was rated the lowest (Birnbaum 2013). Owners also provided data on monthly worker attrition. India had the highest turnover, with an average of 11 percent. This was significantly higher than China, where monthly attrition was 3 percent (Birnbaum 2013).

In Sri Lanka, large export-oriented firms have high productivity levels and sophisticated production processes (National Stakeholders 2014; Wijayasiri and Dissanayake 2008). The labor force is also better skilled than in most other Asian countries (although with skill gaps in the northern and eastern regions) (National Stakeholders 2014). This can be attributed to a good general education system, as well as specific education and training facilities for the apparel sector at different levels, including university degrees in technical areas and design. One problem that stands out in Sri Lanka is the limited availability of workers in the apparel sector—the perception of poor working conditions prompts workers to seek employment in other sectors.

As for the competitors, in Indonesia, Vietnam, and particularly Cambodia, there is a lack of skilled workers with experience in technology, marketing, and design as well as in middle management (Frederick and Staritz 2012). In Cambodia, the vast majority of top and middle managers, technical workers, and supervisors are foreigners (Natsuda, Goto, and Thoburn 2009).

Non-cost Factors

Whereas price is important, buyers do not necessarily buy from the supplier that offers the *lowest* price. They also look for consistent quality, reliable delivery, acceptable lead times, and broader nonmanufacturing services. Results thus far have indicated that Bangladesh, India, and Pakistan are generally cost competitive in the selected product categories but are not always top exporters. A major reason appears to be that, with the exception of full package services (box 2.3), global buyers perceive these countries as less competitive than the SEAB countries when it comes to quality, lead time, and compliance (table 2.3).

Quality: Besides being cost competitive, suppliers must also be able to consistently offer quality products. Quality is influenced by the raw materials used, the skill level of the sewing machine operator, and the thoroughness of the quality control team. Based on combined results from the buyer surveys and interviews, the countries fall into the following three groups, ranging from strongest to weakest: (1) China, Vietnam, and Sri Lanka; (2) Indonesia, Cambodia, and Bangladesh; and (3) India and Pakistan.

Lead time and reliability: These reflect the productivity and efficiency of processes at the firm level as well as how the supply chain is organized, including availability of textile and trim inputs locally or via efficient, cost-competitive import networks. Factors impacting lead time and reliability at the country level are not apparel specific and include the efficiency and availability of transportation networks and customs procedures. Standard apparel-specific lead time data are difficult to obtain at the country level because the definition often differs and standard times vary considerably by product, source of material, size of the

Box 2.3 Offering the Full Package

When deciding where to source apparel, global apparel buyers prefer to work with suppliers that provide the "full package"—that is, manufacturing and supply chain management-related services in addition to assembly activities (such as textile [fabric or yarn] and trim sourcing and financing and apparel product development services). The majority of firms in all SAR and SEAB countries are capable of providing full package services, a key reason why these countries have been able to maintain their position among the top 15 apparel-exporting countries in the face of consolidation.

As basic apparel producers try to move up the value chain into lower-volume, higher-value product categories, it is vital for them to have apparel product development and design capabilities. India, and to a lesser extent Sri Lanka, are somewhat involved in product development–and sample development–related services (National Stakeholders 2014). Indeed, apparel product development services (including material sourcing, original apparel design, and sampling) are India's strongest areas compared to competitors (Birnbaum 2013). Sri Lanka has also moved into design and even brand development for the regional market, driven primarily by large manufacturers that have established plants within the SAR region in India and Bangladesh. Its goal is to become a regional hub that invests and coordinates production networks, with a focus on high-tech and high-end apparel, lingerie, and fabric development (National Stakeholders 2014). Such a move would lead to fewer domestic apparel manufacturing jobs and exports, but would create new (although fewer) service-related jobs in logistics, design, and research and development.

Table 2.3 South Asia Less Competitive than Southeast Asia in Non-cost Areas
(Country Comparison: Non-Cost-Related Factors Impacting Performance)

	Buyers' perceptions of:					
Country	Quality		Lead time and reliability		Social compliance and sustainability	
China	●	1	●	1	▲	3
Bangladesh	◆	5	◆	5	◆	6
India	◆	6	◆	6	◆	5
Vietnam	●	2	●	2	●	2
Cambodia	▲	4	▲	4	▲	4
Indonesia	▲	3	▲	3	●	1

Source: Based on data from Birnbaum (2013) and from buyers and stakeholders surveys conducted for this study.
Note: Countries were ranked from 1 to 6 on each factor, with 1 being the best and 6 being the worst. Ranks for quality and lead time/reliability are the same, so only one line is visible. Green indicates top two countries (factor is not an issue); orange is for the middle two countries and indicates caution; blue is used for the bottom two ranking countries (factor is an issue).

shipment, and distance to market. Lead time is generally measured as the time between when the order is placed and when the shipment is received by the buyer, but it can also reflect the time between the receipt of raw materials and shipment of the final product. Given these issues, the following analysis is based on buyers' perspectives of country's competiveness regarding lead time and reliability.

Based on survey and interview results related to lead time[14] and reliability (Birnbaum 2013; Global Apparel Buyers 2014), the countries can be placed in the following groups, ranging from strongest to weakest: (1) China, Vietnam, and Indonesia; (2) Sri Lanka and Cambodia; and (3) Bangladesh, India, and Pakistan. China has consistently been regarded as having the shortest lead times throughout the last decade (Muzzini and Aparicio 2013; World Bank 2005, 2013b). Factories in China are cited as having the best productivity levels, technology, speed, and production capacity, which are all enabled by well-established industrial clusters and infrastructure systems (Frederick and Gereffi 2011).[15]

One way to minimize lead time, while also increasing domestic value added and potentially reducing cost, is to produce textiles domestically. SAR countries are performing better than the SEAB countries but are behind China.[16] The same pattern is evidenced when comparing the value of output from textile establishments across countries as well as the changes over time[17] and by comparing textile machinery shipment and installed capacity statistics. At the country level, Bangladesh is capable of producing about two-thirds of its fabric needs, which are predominately cotton. India and Pakistan have full capabilities for cotton products (fiber, yarn, and fabric). But a downside for India is that it is the only major garment-exporting country that has not attracted global trim suppliers. A large share of trim must be imported through Hong Kong SAR, which adds to both costs and delivery time (Birnbaum 2013). The textile industry is the least developed in Sri Lanka—in the early 2000s, an estimated 80–90 percent of fabrics were imported.

Another way to shorten lead times is to buy textiles regionally, which is increasingly occurring in South Asia, with SAR countries accounting for 18 percent of the region's fabric imports in 2012 (UNSD 2014d). The primary fabric exporters are India and Pakistan, and the main recipients are Bangladesh and Sri Lanka. However, SAR countries are still far behind China, which accounted for 63 percent of SAR's fabric imports in 2012. A major constraint to increasing regional trade within SAR is the lack of an MMF textile supply base in all countries.

In India, reliability, lead time, quality (particularly consistency), and productivity are intertwined and to some extent stem from inefficiencies in the domestic textile supply base. Local textile mills largely provide only greige goods, so apparel factories must purchase these unfinished fabrics and send them to converters to be dyed and finished. But, after processing, it is not uncommon for factories to discover the fabrics are damaged, meaning that the factory must replace the fabric, take the loss on the initial purchase, and ship the product late, or use the damaged fabric and hope the buyer doesn't notice. In either case, the apparel supplier will be viewed as unreliable (Birnbaum 2013). This situation is further exacerbated by the fact that an estimated 65 percent or more of fabric production in India is on power looms, which are relatively inefficient systems that lead to inconsistencies and lower-quality products (AEPC 2013). To improve productivity and reliability, these could be replaced by modern shuttleless weaving equipment.

Social compliance and sustainability: These have become central criteria in buyers' sourcing decisions in response to pressure from CSR campaigns by nongovernmental organizations (NGOs), compliance-conscious consumers, and, more recently, the higher number of disasters in apparel factories. Noncompliant countries face an acute risk of damaging their country brand. In Cambodia, the government's brutal reaction that led to the death of four workers induced major buyers to cut back orders or threaten to leave (Barrie 2014). In Bangladesh, concerns over factory safety and adverse publicity associated with these concerns have deterred some buyers (Birnbaum 2014a).

Although environmental concerns and sustainability are more of a concern for the textile industry, these also apply to apparel, particularly in the areas of dyeing and finishing. To evaluate compliance, questions from Birnbaum (2013) on social compliance and sustainability were combined and an average rank was created and compared with data from the global buyer interviews (2014). Both provided similar findings. The countries can be placed into the following categories, ranging from strongest to weakest: (1) Sri Lanka, Indonesia, Vietnam, and China; (2) Cambodia; and (3) India, Bangladesh, and Pakistan.

Overall, buyers and factory owners perceived all countries to be performing better in social than environmental compliance (based on total points awarded) (Birnbaum 2013). The most salient labor-related issues in all four SAR countries include the lack of freedom of association and collective bargaining, and thus unionization, which contributes to other problems—such as low wages, long work hours, a large share of contract and informal employment (particularly in Bangladesh and Pakistan), and poor building and occupational health and safety (OHS) standards (National Stakeholders 2014). There are also enforcement issues related to the limited capacity of labor inspectorates (see chapter 1 for more details on compliance).

Better, but Still Lagging behind Competitors

So how do all of these results add up? As the apparel competition intensifies, the SEAB countries and China are outperforming the SAR countries in terms of export growth, product diversification, and non-cost-related factors. SAR countries are cost competitive but suffer from a lack of product diversity and below-average performance in quality, lead times, reliability, and social compliance. If they hope to hang on to their current market shares and further expand, top areas for improvement include product and end market diversity and, with the exception of Sri Lanka, reliability and compliance. At the country level, however, there are tremendous variations among countries within these regions in terms of strengths and weaknesses in the apparel and textile industry (see box 2.4). The following main conclusions can be drawn regarding the different benchmarking dimensions:

All SAR countries have gained global market share and boosted export values, but there are tremendous variations among them. Both Bangladesh and Pakistan have increased exports at a faster growth rate than the world average—with Bangladesh enjoying the largest increase in global market share whereas Pakistan's growth was more modest. Although apparel exports in

Box 2.4 How South Asia Countries Are Handling the Intense Apparel Competition

The South Asian Countries

Bangladesh is performing exceptionally well on cost in nearly every product category analyzed and in the eyes of global buyers (table 2B.2). Its low labor costs appear to make up for shortfalls in meeting buyers' desired criteria in other areas (table 2.2). It now needs to focus on compliance, quality, reliability (and lead times) (table 2.3), and product diversity into MMF-based products and emerging product categories. It is a top exporter in all product categories currently demanded, but it is not showing signs of entering areas that will matter in the future and is heavily dependent on cotton-based apparel. Plus, after major disasters in recent years, compliance has become a major risk. These challenges will have to be resolved convincingly if the industry's long-term prosperity is to be secured. The outcomes of the recently agreed initiatives and the reaction of buyers in the next year will be critical.

India still has a lot of room for improvement regarding productivity and perception (table 2.2). Like China, it has midrange unit values compared to competitors, despite buyers' perceptions of having comparatively higher free on board (FOB) prices. Where India and China differ, however is across all other criteria in which India ranks among the bottom in all categories (table 2.3). Quality, lead time, reliability, and compliance are all issues in India, in addition to product diversity. India benefits from having a vertically integrated cotton-textile-apparel supply chain, but it will need to expand into MMF to gain global market share. Its capabilities in product development and design place it in an ideal position for fashion apparel production, but this advantage is not critical for a large export-oriented apparel industry.

Pakistan is cost competitive in most product categories, but it is not a top performer in any of the export categories analyzed. One major problem is a lack of product diversity, with the country almost entirely dependent on cotton products and trouser exports. Other problems are reliability, compliance, and political stability and safety—especially regarding foreign direct investment (FDI). Pakistan also has a large labor pool, but productivity is hurt by the limited availability of good sector-specific training institutes and gaps in technical, design, and middle management skills (Yusuf 2013).

Sri Lanka is not a top exporter in any of the main product categories, and its unit values in these categories are higher than those of its competitors. Cost is the main issue, driven at least partly by relatively high and rising labor costs (minimum wages are low, but actual wages are much higher) and a labor shortage. The country also needs to improve on lead times and product range and availability. Its product portfolio is largely made up of higher-value, niche products (unlike the other SAR countries), and its workforce includes people with broader capabilities in product development, design, and marketing. These capabilities help as it continues to upgrade in apparel, but do not necessarily translate into higher global market share or more jobs. That said, it is viewed positively in other areas, notably compliance and stability (table 2.3).

The Competitors

China and Vietnam are performing better than expected when analyzing unit values alone. China's prices are in the middle for nearly every major product category, although it ranks in

box continues next page

Box 2.4 How South Asia Countries Are Handling the Intense Apparel Competition *(continued)*

the top two countries in all other criteria considered vital when choosing a partner. In fact, China remains very competitive even with production cost increases—no doubt explained by high productivity, an integrated supply chain, product variety, and service capabilities. Vietnam's rank by unit value varies across product categories, but it delivers in all other areas as the first- or second-ranked country. China and Vietnam's ability to deliver in all of the non-cost-related factors important to buyers is likely a key reason why they have been able to continue export growth despite higher unit values.

Cambodia offers low unit values, and its performance in other areas is generally average or acceptable. Cambodia is cost competitive, but lacks product diversity, is viewed as relatively unreliable, and provides only midrange quality.

Indonesia offers low to moderate unit values across all product categories and has a positive image with buyers across other indicators.

Sri Lanka and India have increased, their growth rates have remained below the world average, essentially remaining stable since 2005. Collectively, the export growth of the SAR countries is faster than the world and China yet slower than that of the SEAB countries.

There is a lack of product diversity and hence of alignment with global demand for MMF apparel. For all four SAR countries, product availability and diversity are key concerns. This primarily stems from a lack of MMF-based products in Bangladesh, India, and Pakistan, and from a general lack of diversity across product categories outside of intimate apparel and activewear in Sri Lanka. Hence, MMF products need to be expanded to capture exports from China. This problem also extends to domestic textile production capabilities. India and Pakistan are top cotton producers, but they have limited MMF availability and barriers to MMF textile imports remain.

SAR countries have substantially diversified their end markets away from the dominant EU-15 (and to a lesser extent the United States), but compared to China there is still a potential to diversify. Significant opportunities to expand apparel exports exist in nearby Asian countries, the Middle East, as well as Latin America. In particular, the SAR countries could add Argentina, Brazil, China, India, and Korea to their export portfolio.

SAR countries do well on most of the factors important to global buyers that affect export performance, although India in particular needs to tackle non-cost issues. These countries are generally cost competitive, with the exception of Sri Lanka. But compliance is a major issue in Bangladesh, stability is a major problem for Pakistan, and all other non-cost factors pose a problem for India. This presents issues for SAR because the SEAB countries are viewed as cost competitive and at or above average in all other areas.

Lack of foreign investment may be limiting visibility and links to the international market, including direct access to global buyers or indirectly through large multinational manufacturers. Expansion into a broader range of product categories and MMF apparel may be hindered by the fact that firms in the SAR countries are not part of production networks led by East Asian multinational corporations that have close, long-term relationships with global buyers, particularly in the United States. Domestic ownership does, however, put the SAR countries in a better position compared to the SEAB countries to develop exports to end markets outside the United States and EU-15, in which long-term buyer-supplier relationships do not yet exist.

Buyers will need a compelling reason to shift production out of China; and, at present, the SEAB countries—especially Vietnam—appear to be best positioned. Currently, Bangladesh is the best performer, whereas India and Pakistan face the most hurdles and share many of the same shortcomings and Sri Lanka faces labor and capacity constraints. Overall, SAR's aforementioned deficiencies in terms of meeting the requirements of global buyers coupled with the lack of product diversity and availability will need to be addressed for these countries to continue to increase apparel exports and expand global market share.

Annex 2A: Data Description

This chapter combines qualitative and quantitative information on the global apparel value chain from established sources—including COMTRADE and from interviews with major players in the apparel global value chain. Surveys were carried out with global apparel buyers from the United States and the EU to gain insight into the types of sourcing networks used and how sourcing decisions are made, to gather country-specific information on apparel sourcing, and to provide primary data on the perceptions of the strengths and weaknesses of the South Asian countries. To facilitate the benchmarking process, buyers were asked to identify the top five firm, country, and overall factors affecting the buyer's sourcing decision process and were then asked to rate the performance of their top two supplier countries and the four SAR countries for the factors they previously determined to be the most important.

Interviews with representatives of international organizations (such as the International Labour Organization [ILO] and Better Work) and in-country stakeholders (such as relevant ministries, industry associations, unions and workers' groups, and sector experts) were also conducted. These interviews provide clarity when there are minimal secondary data on issues such as working conditions, implementation of policies, informal sectors, productivity and skills, and functional capabilities. The interviews also facilitate country benchmarking by asking open questions on general perceptions about supplier countries, including perceived strengths and weaknesses of these countries; the specificities of and differences between the countries; and comparisons to other sourcing destinations.

Table 2A.1 Data Sources

Export performance: Aggregate and product and end market analysis	
End markets and products	UNCOMTRADE (HS 61+62)
All sections: National stakeholder interviews	
National stakeholder interviews	Phone interviews were conducted with 12 supporting organizations in the SAR countries, including research institutes, industry associations, unions, and organizations.
Buyer surveys (group/year)	
Global apparel buyer interviews (2014)[a]	Primary interviews were conducted with seven global apparel buyers as part of this study. Interviews with global apparel buyers cited as "Global Apparel Buyers 2014."
Birnbaum/Apparel Export Promotion Council (AEPC)(October 2012)[a]	AEPC asked Third Horizon (THL) to do a benchmark study to determine causes of India's declining market share of U.S./EU apparel industries and to provide a strategy outline to reverse the decline. As part of the project, THL interviewed (i) factory managers/owners in seven garment-exporting countries (Bangladesh, Cambodia, China, India, Indonesia, Turkey, and Vietnam) to compare their work with factories in India (146 interviews), (ii) senior sourcing executives at EU and U.S. brand importers and retailers, to ask about India and to rate the seven countries on factors important to sourcing (30 interviews), and (iii) management at India-based and transnational garment factories to examine government's role in the industry (22 interviews)(Birnbaum 2013).
Apparel Magazine/Kurt Salmon Associates (KSA)(2007–13)	*Apparel Magazine* and KSA conduct an annual sourcing survey. The first was in 2006 and had 35 questions with 120+ respondents; the most recent was published in 2013 (KSA-AM 2007–13).
Deloitte Private Label Sourcing Survey (2012)	Deloitte conducted an online survey through self-hosting and an independent research company throughout 2012. There were 266 respondents that provided input across three spend categories (apparel, general merchandise, and grocery) and 11 subcategories. Because respondents could submit responses for multiple subcategories, over 600 responses were collected. Approximately 75 percent of respondents were from companies with annual revenues greater than $100 million, and nearly 50 percent of the companies represented had more than 25,000 employees. Respondents were asked to rate a list of factors on a scale from 1 to 7 on their importance when selecting a vendor to source from (Daher and Chmielewski 2013).
Nathan Associates (2005)	In 2005, Nathan Associates conducted a survey of 20 U.S. buyers who source or have sourced apparel from Sub-Saharan Africa (SSA) over the period July–September 2005. The survey polled major sourcing decision makers on their intentions to import apparel from SSA in the near to midterm as well as their sourcing strategies and the factors driving their decisions, with specific emphasis on SSA and the major Asian producers of China and India. Participants came from four segments: brand specialty retailers (9), brand and private label manufacturers (8), department stores (2), and mass merchants (1). Their annual import volume (FOB) ranged from $20 million to $5 billion with the majority of respondents recording turnover of $100 million or more (11 reported turnover of more than $1 billion) (Nathan Associates 2005).

table continues next page

Stitches to Riches? • http://dx.doi.org/10.1596/978-1-4648-0813-5

Table 2A.1 Data Sources *(continued)*

Factors	
FOB price, productivity, quality, lead times	Based on buyer survey ranks from Birnbaum (2013).
Reliability	Based on buyer survey ranks from Birnbaum (2013); compared with perceptions provided from Global Apparel Buyers (2014) interviews.
Labor	Minimum wage data provided in appendix table.
Compliance	Birnbaum (2013): point totals from questions on compliance and sustainability for buyers and an average rank was created and compared with perceptions provided from the Global Apparel Buyers (2014) interviews.

Source: See citations within table.
a. The buyer survey was used in the benchmark analysis.

Annex 2B: Characteristics of Apparel Industries in the SAR and SEAB Countries

Table 2B.1 Size and Significance of Textile and Apparel Industries

Country	T&A formal employment	T&A informal employment	Apparel no. of establishments	Apparel foreign ownership share (%)	T&A FDI ($M) & timeframe	T&A share of country's FDI (%)	Apparel export value ($B), 2012	Apparel share of country's exports (%)
Bangladesh	2.76 mil (A, 2012) 0.81 mil (T, 2012)	180,000 (A, 2011) 680,500 (T, 2011) 860,500 (T&A, 2011)	6,984 (A, 2012)	5–9 (2002, 2011)	1,157 (2002–11)	16	22.8	83
Cambodia	350,000 (A, 2012)	—	315 (A, 2012)	93–95 (2008, 2012)	948 (2007–11)	24	6.2	67
China	4.5–10 mil (A, 2009, 2012)	—	100,000 (A, 2012)	40 (2007)	—	—	145.5	7
India	0.9 mil (A, 2011) 1.5 mil (T, 2011) 2.4 mil (T&A, 2011)	5.5 mil (A, 2010) 5.8 mil (T, 2010) 12.4 mil (T&A, 2010)	9,168 (A, 2011)	<1 (2014)	200 (2000–10)	<1	12.5	5
Indonesia	502,930 (A, 2011) 1.04 mil (T&A, 2011)	—	1,830 (A, 2011)	—	1,669 (2006–11)	3	9.6	5
Pakistan	734,805 (A, 2010) 613,792 (T, 2010) 1.3–3 mil (T&A, 2010–14)	7 mil (T&A, 2014)	3,500 (A, 2014)	< 2 (2009, 2014)	350 (2001–11)	1	4.2	19
Sri Lanka	280,872 (A, 2011) 333,300 (T&A, 2011)	—	1,553 (A, 2011)	15–20 (1999)	502 (2000–09)	14	4.4	45
Vietnam	1.01 mil (A, 2012)	—	4,950 (A, 2012)	19–50 (2009, 2012)	2,023 (2007–11)	5	15.2	12
SAR Total	4.7 million (A, 2010–12)	20.3 million (T&A, 2010–14) w/o SL	19,621	n.a.	2,209	2	43.8	14

Sources: Formal employment and establishments (est.): Bangladesh (BBS 2013b); Cambodia (Saheed 2013); China 2012 (Saheed 2014); China 2009 (UNIDO 2013; Zhu & Pickles 2014); India 2011 (India MOSPI-CSO 2014) est. with 10+ workers, formal and informal combined similar to 2013/14 estimates of 12 and 17 mil. (Birnbaum 2013; National Stakeholders 2014); Indonesia 2011 (Statistics Indonesia 2000–11), est. 20+ workers; Pakistan 2014 (National Stakeholders 2014); Pakistan 2010 (Sandhu 2011); Sri Lanka 2011 (Sri Lanka DCS 2014), est. with 5+ persons engaged; Vietnam (GSO Vietnam 2014). Informal Employment: Bangladesh (BBS 2013a) (mfg. units, < 10 workers); India (India MOSPI-CSO 2013). Pakistan (National Stakeholders 2014); there are also approximately 10,000 unregistered T&A establishments supplying the domestic market. Apparel Foreign Ownership: Bangladesh[1] (Haider 2007; Muzzini & Aparicio 2013); Cambodia (Natsuda, Goto, & Thoburn 2009; Saheed 2013); China (NBS 2007); India (National Stakeholders 2014); Pakistan (Hamdani 2009; National Stakeholders 2014); Sri Lanka (Kelegama and Wijayasiri 2004); Vietnam (ILO 2010; Saheed 2012c); Vietnam 2011–14 (Goto 2014), 19 percent based on number of firms, 50 percent based on production output. FDI: Total FDI (not shown) (UNCTADSTAT 1970–2012); Bangladesh (ITC, Various); Cambodia (Saheed 2013); India (Saheed 2012a); Indonesia (Saheed 2012b); Pakistan (Saheed 2009; Yusuf 2013); Sri Lanka (Saheed 2010); Vietnam (Saheed 2012c). Exports: (UNSD 2014a); Share of all **exports** (UNSD 2014e).

Note: A = apparel; FDI = foreign direct investment; SAR = South Asian sample countries (Bangladesh, India, Pakistan, and Sri Lanka); SEAB = Southeast Asian benchmark countries ((Cambodia, Indonesia, and Vietnam); T = textiles; T&A = textiles and apparel; — = not available; n.a. = not applicable.

Table 2B.2 World Unit Value Cost Comparison, 2013

Export rank/ indicator/ country	Rank and world unit values based on number of items, 2013						World export rank, by product category, by value, 2013					
	Trousers (1)	Sweaters/ sweatshirts (2)	Knit shirts (3)	Coats (4)	Woven shirts (6)	Dresses and skirts (7)	Trousers (1)	Sweaters/ sweatshirts (2)	Knit shirts (3)	Coats (4)	Woven shirts (6)	Dresses and skirts (7)
1 China	4/$6.5	8/$7.7	5/$4.1	7/$17.4	4/$7.2	7/$8.5	1	1	1	1	1	1
3 Bangladesh	3/$6.3	6/$6.2	2/$2.9	3/$13.3	2/$6.2	1/$5.0	3	3	3	4	4	9
6 India	5/$6.9	4/$5.2	3/$3.8	4/$16.0	7/$7.8	8/$8.6	11	8	5	13	3	3
11 Pakistan	8/$8.2	3/$4.8	1/$2.8	1/$7.8	3/$6.7	3/$6.1	9	11	14	14	29	33
10 Sri Lanka	7/$7.5	7/$6.3	7/$4.6	5/$16.7	8/$9.2	6/$8.4	13	17	15	24	10	12
5 Vietnam	6/$7.0	1/$4.6	8/$4.6	8/$20.5	5/$7.2	4/$6.8	5	4	6	3	7	5
8 Cambodia	2/$6.3	5/$5.5	4/$3.9	2/$10.9	1/$6.2	2/$5.3	7	6	9	8	11	10
7 Indonesia	1/$6.0	2/$4.6	6/$4.2	6/$16.9	6/$7.6	5/$6.9	6	7	8	5	6	6
World	$7.8	$7.0	$3.9	$19.8	$8.3	$9.7	n.a.	n.a.	n.a.	n.a.	n.a.	n.a.

Source: UNSD 2015.

Note: Unit values based on number of items; unit values include cotton and MMF products. Numbers in parentheses after product categories indicate the product categories rank in 2013 in global apparel exports. MMF = manmade fiber. n.a. = not applicable.

Table 2B.3 Average Apparel Monthly Earnings, Minimum Wages, and Productivity

Country	Apparel average monthly earnings		Current monthly minimum wages		Labor productivity in manufacturing		Labor productivity in apparel	
	Earnings (US$)	Year	Minimum wage (US$)	Min. wage effective	Value added per worker (US$)	Number of observations	Value added per worker (US$)	Number of observations
Bangladesh	64	2010	68	2013 (Dec)	—	—	—	—
Cambodia	—	—	100	2014 (Feb)	—	—	—	—
Sri Lanka	107	2010	71	2013 (Jan)	—	—	—	—
Pakistan	74	2009	120	2014 (July)	—	—	—	—
Vietnam	—	—	90–128 (109)	2014 (Jan)	—	—	—	—
India	81	2010	71–130 (101)	2013 (Oct)	5,855	4,774	5,657	179
Indonesia	—	—	68–200 (134)	2014 (Jan)	—	—	—	—
China	—	—	130–293 (211)	2014 (Feb)	19,724	1,349	15,258	98

Source: Apparel Avg. Monthly Earnings: Bangladesh (BBS); India (India MOSPI-NSSO), Sch.10; Pakistan (FBS) (represents textiles and apparel); Sri Lanka (Sri Lanka DCS), conversion based on national currency and US$ foreign exchange rates from oanda.com using July 1 midpoint bid/ask rate. Minimum wages: Bangladesh and India (Donaldson 2014); Bangladesh, India, and Indonesia (Emerging Textiles 2014); Cambodia ILO/Natlex; Pakistan (Wage Indicator; National Stakeholders), applies to unskilled workers; China (Wage Indicator), lowest and highest provinces, 2013/14; Sri Lanka Apparel-Specific: Wage Board Ordinance Gazette, 2012. Labor productivity numbers are from the World Bank Enterprise Surveys for India (2014) and China (2012).
Note: — = not available.

Annex 2C: World Bank Global Buyer Survey

Company Name:
Physical Headquarters (HQ) Location:
Apparel Sales (2013, $):
Apparel Purchases (2013, $, Value):
Type of Establishment: Retailer or Apparel Brand Owner (or share of both):
Interviewee Name, Title and E-mail:
Interview Date:

    1.1. Please indicate % of apparel purchases in 2013 (*should total 100%*)
        A. Knit tops: _____
        B. Woven tops: _____
        C. Intimate apparel, hosiery and socks: _____
        D. Athletic/active wear: _____
        E. Formalwear (suits, suit jackets, ensembles): _____
        F. Dresses and skirts: _____
        G. Pants/trousers/bottoms (specific share of denim vs. non-denim): _____
        H. Outerwear (coats, jackets): _____
        I. Accessories/other miscellaneous apparel: _____
        J. Baby: _____

    1.2. Please indicate the % of apparel purchased by gender
        A. Women:
        B. Men:
        C. Children:

1.3. Please indicate the % of apparel purchases by fiber
   A. Cotton:
   B. MMF:
   C. Other:

2. Global Sourcing Practices

2.1. Indicate the sourcing strategies your firm uses based on % of apparel purchase value (2013).

Sourcing strategy	Where/how activities take place	% of apparel purchase value
(1) Direct Ownership		
	(A) 100% company-owned factories	%
	(B) Joint-venture ownership (less than 100% ownership)	%
(2) Direct Sourcing (buyer has direct contact with manufacturers' headquarters or factory)		**%**
	(A) Global headquarters	%
	(B) Corporate overseas sourcing office (regional or country-specific)	%
(3) Indirect Sourcing (3rd party such as an agent identifies and has contact with apparel suppliers)		**%**
	(A) Global intermediaries (trading houses, agents)	%
	(B) Regional or country-specific agents (agents based in sourcing country/region)	%
	(C) Home country importer/wholesaler	%

Note: A, B, and C for each should sum to the % listed in 1–3; and 1–3 should sum to 100 %.

2.2. Please indicate the types of apparel firms you source from by % apparel purchase value (2013):
   A. Cut, Make and Trim (CMT) (your firm or an agent finances fabric/trim purchases): _____
   B. Full Package (FOB) Producer (finance fabric and input purchases): _____
   C. Full Package Producer (FOB + identify suppliers—see question below): _____
   D. Full Package Producer (FOB + apparel services)[18]: _____
   E. Full Package Producer (FOB + services + design): _____
   F. Full Package Development (above plus new product development): _____
   G. Full Package Development (above plus product branding & marketing): _____

2.3. Please indicate your degree of involvement in identifying textile (fabric and yarn) and trim suppliers by assigning % based on overall apparel purchases (2013):

Involvement/segment	Fabric suppliers	Yarn suppliers	Trim suppliers (e.g., buttons, zippers, thread)
My firm identifies and nominates suppliers	%	%	%
An agent identifies or nominates suppliers	%	%	%

Involvement/segment	Fabric suppliers	Yarn suppliers	Trim suppliers (e.g., buttons, zippers, thread)
Decision-making is shared between an agent and the apparel supplier	%	%	%
Decision-making is shared between my firm and the apparel supplier	%	%	%
The apparel supplier identifies suppliers but these must be approved by my firm	%	%	%
The apparel supplier is solely responsible for identifying suppliers	%	%	%
Total	**100%**	**100%**	**100%**

2.4. How many days lead time from order to your first shipment (including fabric purchase, but excluding design and sample time) do you expect your main suppliers to be capable of?
   A. Maximum number of days: _____
   B. Highest performing supplier number of days: _____

2.5. Which of the following three factors is the MOST IMPORTANT for your firm when making sourcing decisions? Label with an "X."
   A. Product-specific characteristics:
   B. Firm/factory-specific characteristics:
   C. Country-specific characteristics:

2.6. Does the country you source from vary depending on the final retail market for the product? (i.e., do you use different suppliers for sales in Europe versus the United States versus others?)

2.7. Please identify and rank the **top five *firm-level* factors (light gray section)**, the **top five *country-level*** factors **(dark gray section)** and **from those ten**, the **top five *overall factors*** from both sections based on importance in making sourcing decisions (1 most important, 2 second most important, etc.). NOTE: you will also use the information you provide here in the question below.

Factors/sourcing criteria	Firm- and country-specific ranks	Overall rank
Firm-specific		
Price (manufacturing cost; total production cost)		
Quality and consistency of supply		
Lead time		
Capacity (ability to meet a minimum order)		
Reliability of delivery		
Flexibility in production capacity (ability to produce small or large orders)		
Financial stability of firm		
Ability to procure and finance inputs (FOB/full package)		
Product offering and range (i.e., Section 1)		
Product development and innovation capabilities		
Design capabilities		
Labor relations and compliance with labor standards		
Compliance and/or certification to environmental standards		

Stitches to Riches? • http://dx.doi.org/10.1596/978-1-4648-0813-5

Factors/sourcing criteria	Firm- and country-specific ranks	Overall rank
Country-specific		
Energy/electricity and water prices		
Macroeconomic conditions (e.g., exchange rate movement, interest rates)		
Transportation and logistics infrastructure (roads, ports, flights)		
National policy support (i.e., incentives)		
Political stability		
Bureaucratic efficiency (no red tape, corruption, customs)		
Tariff rates and trade preferences (final product manufacturing country and shipping destination)		
Labor regulation policies and enforcement		
Labor pool and worker skill capabilities		
Industry cluster characteristics (e.g., other apparel mfg., suppliers, associations)		
International access to competitive inputs (e.g., duty-free imports)		
Local/regional availability of competitive inputs (i.e., fabric/yarn)		

3. Global Sourcing by Geography

    3.1. Please list the top five countries you sourced apparel-related products from in 2013 and estimate the share of apparel purchases (2013) from these countries and the four SAR countries. If possible, please also list any general observations on the types of products you purchase from each country and the main competitor country (if any).

Country*	Apparel purchase value (%, 2013)	Product characteristics	Country competitor
Country 1	%		
Country 2	%		
Country 3	%		
Country 4	%		
Country 5	%		
India	%		
Bangladesh	%		
Sri Lanka	%		
Pakistan	%		
Share of above	%		

(*): Replace Country 1, Country 2, etc. with actual country names.

    3.2. For the top five **overall** factors selected in Section 2, please rate the top two countries you sourced from in 2013 and the four SAR countries using the following scale. If you do not source from one of the SAR countries, please rank based on your perception of the country (results based on perception will be analyzed separately).

- 2 = "A": Performance exceeds expectations
- 1 = "B": Above average performance
- 0 = "C": Average/acceptable performance
- −1 = "D": Below average performance
- −2 = "F": Unacceptable

Factors/sourcing criteria	Country #1	Country #2	India	BNG	SL	PAK
Firm-specific						
Price (mfg., cost; total production cost)						
Quality and consistency of supply						
Lead time						
Capacity (ability to meet min. order)						
Reliability of delivery						
Flexibility in production capacity (ability to produce small or large orders)						
Financial stability of firm						
Ability to procure and finance inputs (FOB/full package)						
Product offering & range (i.e., Section 1)						
Product development & innovation capabilities						
Design capabilities						
Labor relations and standards compliance						
Compliance and/or certification to environmental standards						
Country-specific						
Energy/electricity and water prices						
Macro-economic conditions (e.g., exchange rate movement, interest rates)						
Transportation and logistics infrastructure (roads, ports, flights)						
National policy support (i.e., incentives)						
Political stability						
Bureaucratic efficiency (no red tape, corruption, customs)						
Tariff rates and trade preferences (final product manufacturing country and shipping destination)						
Labor regulation policies and enforcement						
Labor pool and worker skill capabilities						
Industry cluster characteristics (e.g., other apparel mfg., suppliers, associations)						
International access to competitive inputs (e.g., duty-free imports)						
Local/regional availability of competitive inputs (i.e., fabric/yarn)						

4. South Asia (open-ended)

    4.1. Considering your experience sourcing from South Asia (Pakistan, Bangladesh, Sri Lanka, and India), what are the most important weaknesses and strengths of the South Asia region generally and for the four individual countries?

Country	Strengths	Weaknesses
South Asia		
Bangladesh		
India		
Pakistan		
Sri Lanka		

    4.2. If you could make policy recommendations to the four South Asian countries to improve their competitiveness and to increase sourcing, what would be the two most important for each country?

Notes

1. The estimate for informal employment in the textile and apparel sector does not include Sri Lanka for which there are no data.

2. Table 2B.1 describes the importance of the industry in each country by showing the share of apparel exports in total merchandise exports, employment in the apparel (and textile) industry, number of establishments, and relative importance of FDI in the sector and of FDI in the country.

3. Global value chains can be differentiated into producer and buyer driven. In producer-driven chains (which are common in capital- and technology-intensive products such as automobiles, electronics, and machinery) large, integrated, and often multinational firms coordinate production networks. Control is generally embedded in the lead firm's control over production technology.

4. The EU-15 consists of Austria, Belgium, Denmark, Finland, France, Germany, Greece, Ireland, Italy, Luxembourg, the Netherlands, Portugal, Spain, Sweden, and the United Kingdom.

5. Industry associations in Bangladesh were very effective in supporting market diversification in the context of reduced demand from the United States and EU-15 during the global economic crisis (National Stakeholders 2014).

6. The average MFN applied tariff for the EU is 11.5 percent for apparel (WTO 2013). However Bangladesh and Pakistan (as of 2014) are eligible for 0 percent tariffs under the "Everything but Arms" (EBA) and GSP+ schemes, and Sri Lanka and India qualify for the preferential GSP rate (a 20 percent reduction from the MFN rate, averaging 9.2 percent).

7. In 2011–12 India produced 6.1 million tons of raw cotton fiber, well above the 1.2 million tons of MMF staple fibers (Saheed 2012a).

8. "Sizeable" categories considered were those representing over 5 percent of global trade, an export value over $25 billion in 2012, and CAGRs above the world average for 2005–2012. Accessories, miscellaneous apparel, and hosiery/socks also have CAGRs above the world average, but these are relatively small product markets.

9. This includes countries outside of the EU-15 with retail market values greater than $10 billion in 2013 and above world average CAGR for 2005–2012. Apparel includes womenswear, menswear, childrenswear, hosiery, and accessories at retail selling price (RSP). The trade value represents world apparel imports for similar categories represented by Harmonized System (HS) chapters 61 and 62.

10. This includes countries in the top 10 in 2012 that had growth rates above the world average between 2005 and 2012. Note that dresses/skirts and coats were the first- and fourth-fastest growing product categories in terms of value during this period.

11. Turkey was the seventh country in this study, but it is not included in this analysis, so the ranks were recalculated based on only the six countries included in this analysis.

12. Coats and dresses/skirts are both outliers in terms of unit costs. The top two exporters for coats (China and Vietnam) and dresses/skirts (China and India) also have the highest unit values. As two of the fastest growing product categories, this may reflect the fact that there are limited capabilities in these emerging product categories; and, as such, top exporters are able to charge premiums given the lack of competition.

13. Given that Pakistan is solely focused on cotton products, cost competitiveness may be somewhat skewed for product categories in which MMF make up larger shares.

14. Lead time represented the time between the arrival of fabric (ready to cut) to garments packed and ready to ship.

15. China's apparel industry also takes advantage of scale economies within firms (large, vertical factories with all supply chain sectors and value-adding activities in one place) and through product/cluster-specific supply-chain cities that specialize in the production of one product (Frederick & Gereffi 2011).

16. The share of fabric imports over total apparel exports in 2012 for the SAR countries was 20 percent, compared to 42 percent for SEAB and 6 percent for China (UNSD 2014b, 2014d). A caveat with using this data is that it includes all imported fabric used for domestic- and export-oriented apparel production. Therefore these values are best used as a proxy to compare regions rather than as absolute shares.

17. Based on ISIC 17 data from UNIDO 2013.

18. Apparel services include: pattern making, sample making, marker making, and/or translating CAD files.

Bibliography

AEPC (Apparel Export Promotion Council). 2013. "Interministerial Workshop on the Apparel Sector." Background Note, AEPC.

Barrie, Leonie. 2014. "Analysis: U.S. Apparel Imports Show Continuing China Competitiveness." just-style.com, August 14. http://www.just-style.com/analysis/us -apparel-imports-show-continuing-china-competitiveness_id122560.aspx.

BBS (Bangladesh Bureau of Statistics). 2013a. *Cottage Industry Survey 2011*. Dhaka: BBS.

———. 2013b. *Survey of Manufacturing Industries (SMI) 2012*. Retrieved from: http://www.bbs .gov.bd/WebTestApplication/userfiles/Image/LatestReports/SMI-%202012.pdf

———. Various. *Bangladesh Household Income and Expenditure Survey (HIES)*. Dhaka: BBS.

BEPZA (Bangladesh Export Processing Zones Authority). 2013. *Annual Report 2010– 2011*. Dhaka: BEPZA. http://www.epzbangladesh.org.bd/web_admin/web_tender _files/BEPZA_2010-2011.pdf.

BGMEA (Bangladesh Garment Manufacturers and Exporters Association). 2014. "Trade Information." March 13, 2014 Accessed April 22, 2014. http://bgmea.com.bd/home /pages/TradeInformation.

Birnbaum, David. 2013. "Competitiveness of India's Apparel Export." Report prepared for the Apparel Export Promotion Council (AEPC). New Delhi: APEC.

———. 2014a. "Bangladesh Industry Development Moving Backwards." just-style.com, April 16. http://www.just-style.com/comment/bangladesh-industry-development -moving-backwards_id121251.aspx.

———. 2014b. "Comment: Bangladesh's Garment Trend Lines Look Pretty Poor." just-style.com, June 8.

———. 2014c. DRAFT: Bihar Apparel Industry Development Project: Final Report I. Bangkok, Thailand: World Bank.

Clothesource. 2008. The Great Apparel Sourcing Issues of 2008—and How to Deal with Them Just-Style Management Briefing (March). Bromsgrove, UK: Aroq Limited.

Daher, Mike, and Joe Chmielewski. 2013. "Private Label Sourcing Strategies to Differentiate and Defend: Insights from the 2012–2013 Private Label Sourcing Survey." Report prepared for Deloitte Consulting LLP.

Donaldson, Tara. 2014. "2014: Global Sourcing to Be More Costly as Worldwide Minimum Wages Continue to Rise." Sourcing Journal. https://www.sourcingjournal online.com/minimum-wages-steadily-rising-low-cost-sourcing-countries-td.

Emerging Textiles. 2014. Labour Costs in Apparel Manufacturing Countries (Monthly Report). http://www.emergingtextiles.com/?q=art&s=140129-labour-costs.

Euromonitor/Passport. 2014. "World Apparel Market Statistics: 1999–2013." Euromonitor International (accessed March 24, 2014).

FBS (Federal Bureau of Statistics). Various. Pakistan Labor Force Survey (LFS). FBS. http://www.pbs.gov.pk/labour-force-publications.

Flanagan, Mike. 2014. "The Flanarant: Can You Choose Your Productivity Philosophy?" just-style.com, February 19.

Frederick, Stacey, and Gary Gereffi. 2011. "Upgrading and Restructuring in the Global Apparel Value Chain: Why China and Asia Are Outperforming Mexico and Central America." International Journal of Technological Learning, Innovation and Development 4 (1/2/3): 67–95.

Frederick, Stacey, and Cornelia Staritz. 2012. "Developments in the Global Apparel Industry after the MFA Phaseout." In Sewing Sucess? Employment, Wages and Poverty following the End of the Multi-fibre Arrangment, edited by G. Lopez-Acevedo and R. Robertson, 41–86. Washington, DC: World Bank.

Gereffi, Gary. 1994. "The Organization of Buyer-Driven Global Commodity Chains: How U.S. Retailers Shape Overseas Production Networks." In Commodity Chains and Global Capitalism, edited by G. Gereffi and M. Korzeniewicz, 95–122. Westport, CT: Praeger.

———. 1999. "International Trade and Industrial Upgrading in the Apparel Commodity Chain." Journal of International Economics 48: 37–70.

Gereffi, Gary, and Stacey Frederick. 2010. "The Global Apparel Value Chain, Trade and the Economic Crisis: Challenges and Opportunities for Developing Countries." Policy Research Working Paper 5281, World Bank, Washington, DC.

Gereffi, Gary, and Olga Memedovic. 2003. *The Global Apparel Value Chain: What Prospects for Upgrading by Developing Countries*. Vienna: United National Industrial Development Organization (UNIDO).

Global Apparel Buyers. 2014. *Interviews with Global Apparel Buyers*. Interviewer: S. Frederick.

Goto, Kenta. 2014. "Vietnam: Upgrading from the Export to the Domestic Market." In *The Garment Industry in Low-Income Countries: An Entry Point of Industrialization*, edited by Takahiro Fukunishi and Tatsufumi Yamagata, 105–32. Basingstoke, UK: Palgrave Macmillan.

GSO (General Statistics Office) Vietnam. 2014. *Statistical Yearbook of Vietnam 2013*. Hanoi: GSO Vietnam.

Haider, Mohammed. 2007. "Competitiveness of the Bangladesh Ready-Made Garment Industry in Major International Markets." *Asia-Pacific Trade and Investment Review* 3 (1): 3–27.

Hamdani, Khalil. 2009. *Foreign Direct Investment Prospects for Pakistan*. Islamabad: Pakistan Institute of Development Economics.

ILO (International Labour Organization). 2010. "ILO Better Work Vietnam Fact Sheet." ILO.

India MOSPI-CSO (Ministry of Statistics and Programme Implementation-Central Statistics Office). 2013. *Annual Survey of Industries 2010–2011*. Vol. I. New Delhi: MOSPI-CSO.

———. 2014. *Annual Survey of Industries 2011–2012*. Vol. I. New Delhi: MOSPI-CSO.

India MOSPI-NSSO (Ministry of Statistics and Programme Implementation, National Sample Survey Office). 2013. *Economic Characteristics of Unincorporated Non-agricultural Enterprises (Excluding Construction) in India National Sample Survey (NSS)*, 2584. New Delhi: MOSPI-NSSO.

———. Various. *National Sample Survey (NSS): Employment and Unemployment Situation in India*. New Delhi: MOSPI-NSSO. http://www.data.gov.in/dataset-group-name /national-sample-survey.

ITC (International Trade Centre). Various. "Investment Map." Geneva, Switzerland: ITC. http://www.investmentmap.org.

Jordan, Luke Simon, Bertine Kamphuis, and S.P. Setia. 2014. "A New Agenda: Improving the Competitiveness of the Textiles and Apparel Value Chain in India." Working Paper, World Bank, Washington, DC.

Kelegama, Saman. 2009. "Ready-Made Garment Exports from Sri Lanka." *Journal of Contemporary Asia* 39 (4): 579–96.

Kelegama, Saman, and Janaka Wijayasiri. 2004. "Overview of the Garment Industry in Sri Lanka." In *Ready-Made Garment Industry in Sri Lanka: Facing the Global Challenge*, edited by Saman Kelegama. Colombo: Institute of Policy Studies.

KSA-AM (Kurt Salmon Associates-Apparel Magazine). 2007–2013. *Excellence in Global Sourcing Survey*. Kurt Salmon Associates and Apparel Magazine.

Lu, Sheng. 2014. "2014 U.S. Fashion Industry Benchmarking Study." Department of Textiles, Fashion Merchandising and Design, University of Rhode Island.

McKinsey & Company. 2011. *Bangladesh's Ready-Made Garments Landscape: The Challenge of Growth*. McKinsey & Company Apparel, Fashion & Luxury Practice.

————. 2013. *The Global Sourcing Map—Balancing Cost, Compliance, and Capacity: McKinsey's Apparel CPO Survey 2013*. McKinsey & Company Apparel, Fashion & Luxury Practice.

Muzzini, Elisa, and Gabriela Aparicio. 2013. *Bangladesh: The Path to Middle-Income Status from an Urban Perspective*. Washington, DC: World Bank. http://elibrary.worldbank .org/doi/book/10.1596/978-0-8213-9859-3.

Nabi, Ijaz, and Naved Hamid. 2013. "Garments as a Driver of Economic Growth: Insights from Pakistan Case Studies." International Growth Centre.

Nathan Associates. 2005. *Survey of U.S. Apparel Buyers: Sourcing from Sub-Saharan Africa in the Post-quota Era*. Nathan Associates Inc.

National Stakeholders. 2014. *Interviews with National Industry Stakeholders*. Interviewer: C. Staritz.

Natsuda, Kaoru, Kenta Goto, and John Thoburn. 2009. "Challenges to the Cambodian Garment Industry in the Global Garment Value Chain." RCAPS Working Paper 09-3, Ritsumeikan Center for Asia Pacific Studies, Ritsumeikan Asia Pacific University.

NBS (National Bureau of Statistics). 2007. *China's Annual Survey of Industrial Firms (ASIF) (1998–2008)*. Beijing: NBS.

NCAER (National Council of Applied Economic Research). 2009. *Assessing the Prospects for India's Textile and Clothing Sector*. New Delhi: NCAER.

Palpacuer, Florence, Peter Gibbon, and Lotte Thomsen. 2005. "New Challenges for Developing Country Suppliers in Global Clothing Chains: A Comparative European Perspective." *World Development* 33 (3): 409–30.

Saheed, Hassen. 2009. "Prospects for the Textile and Garment Industry in Pakistan." *Textile Outlook International* 142: 55–102.

————. 2010. "Prospects for the Textile and Clothing Industry in Sri Lanka." *Textile Outlook International* 147: 79–119.

————. 2012a. "Prospects for the Textile and Clothing Industry in India." *Textile Outlook International* 156: 86–127.

————. 2012b. "Prospects for the Textile and Clothing Industry in Indonesia." *Textile Outlook International* 155: 70–109.

————. 2012c. "Prospects for the Textile and Clothing Industry in Vietnam." *Textile Outlook International* 159: 71–110.

————. 2013. "Prospects for the Textile and Clothing Industry in Cambodia." *Textile Outlook International* 161: 119–58.

————. 2014. "Prospects for the Textile and Clothing Industry in China." *Textile Outlook International* 168: 79–133.

Sandhu, Kamran Yousef. 2011. "Challenges to Pakistan's Value Added Industry." Paper presented at the Third International Conference on Textile and Clothing, Institute of Textile and Industrial Science, Lahore. http://umt.edu.pk/ictc2011/Presentation .html.

Sri Lanka DCS (Department of Census and Statistics). 2014. *Annual Survey of Industries 2012*. Colombo: Sri Lanka DCS.

————. Various. *Sri Lanka Labor Force Survey (LFS)*. DCS. http://www.statistics.gov.lk /page.asp?page=Labour%20Force.

Staritz, Cornelia. 2011. *Making the Cut? Low-Income Countries and the Global Clothing Value Chain in a Post-quota and Post-crisis World*. Washington, DC: World Bank.

Staritz, Cornelia, and Stacey Frederick. 2014. "Chapter 7: Sector Case Study—Apparel." In *Making Foreign Direct Investment Work for Sub-Saharan Africa: Local Spillovers and Competitiveness in Global Value Chains*, edited by T. Farole and D. Winkler, 209–44. Washington, DC: World Bank.

Statistics Indonesia. 2000–2011. "Annual Manufacturing Survey (establishments with 20+ workers)" Accessed September 29, 2014, Badan Pusat Statistik (BPS). http://www.bps.go.id/eng/menutab.php?kat=2&tabel=1&id_subyek=09.

Tewari, Meenu. 2008. *Deepening Intra-regional Trade and Investment in South Asia: The Case of the Textile and Clothing Industry*. India Council for Research on International Economic Relations (ICRIER).

———. 2009. "The Textiles and Clothing Industry." In *Study on Intraregional Trade and Investment in South Asia*, 40–69. Mandaluyong City, Philippines: Asian Development Bank (ADB).

UNCTADSTAT. 1970–2012. *Inward and Outward Foreign Direct Investment Flows, Annual, 1970–2012*. http://unctadstat.unctad.org/TableViewer/tableView.aspx.

UNIDO (United Nations Development Organization). 2013. "Industrial Statistics Database: INDSTAT4 (2013 edition)." Accessed May 6, 2014, from UNIDO. http://www.unido.org/en/resources/statistics/statistical-databases/indstat4-2013-edition.html.

UNSD (United Nations Statistics Division). 2014a. *World Apparel (HS1992 61+62) Imports (1990–2012)*. Retrieved March 3–6, 2014, from UNSD.

———. 2014b. *World Apparel Imports (1992–2012) by Product Categories*. Retrieved May 13–15, 2014, from UNSD.

———. 2014c. *World Apparel Imports (2000, 2005, 2009, 2012), HS (six-digits)*. Retrieved June 20, 2014, from UNSD.

———. 2014d. *World Fabric and Yarn/Thread Exports (1990–2012) by Product Categories*. Retrieved April 1, 2014, from UNSD.

———. 2014e. *World Total and Apparel (HS1992) Imports (All Years)*. Retrieved August 11, 2014, from UNSD.

———. 2015. *World Apparel Imports (2013)(HS92)*. Retrieved January, 14 2015, from UNSD.

Wijayasiri, Janaka, and Jagath Dissanayake. 2008. *Case Study 3: The Ending of the Multi-fiber Agreement and Innovation in Sri Lankan Textile and Clothing Industry*. Paris: Organisation for Economic Co-operation and Development.

World Bank. 2005. "End of MFA Quotas: Key Issues and Strategic Options for Bangladesh Readymade Garment Industry." Bangladesh Development Series Paper 2, World Bank, Dhaka.

———. 2012. *World Bank Enterprise Survey: China*. Washington, DC: World Bank.

———. 2013. "Volume 3: Sector Studies, Chapter 13: Value Chain Analysis for Polo Shirts." In *Bangladesh Diagnostic Trade Integration Study (DTIS)*, 107–59. Washington, DC: World Bank.

———. 2014a. *World Bank Enterprise Survey: India*. Washington, DC: World Bank.

———. 2014b. *World Development Indicators (WDI), Population (Total) in 2013*. Washington, DC: World Bank.

WTO (World Trade Organization). 2013. *Tariff Download Facility, Applied MFN Tariffs*. Retrieved March 25, 2014, from WTO. http://tariffdata.wto.org/Default.aspx.

Yunus, Mohammad, and Tatsufumi Yamagata. 2014. "Bangladesh: Market Force Supersedes Control." In *The Garment Industry in Low-Income Countries: An Entry Point of Industrialization*, edited by Takahiro Fukunishi and Tatsufumi Yamagata, 77–104. Basingstoke, UK: Palgrave Macmillan.

Yusuf, Shahid. 2013. "Can Chinese FDI Accelerate Pakistan's Growth?" IGC Working Paper, International Growth Centre (IGC), London.

Zhu, Shengjun, and John Pickles. 2014. "Bring In, Go Up, Go West, Go Out: Upgrading, Regionalisation and Delocalisation in China's Apparel Production Networks." *Journal of Contemporary Asia* 44: 36–63.

## CHAPTER 3

South Asia's Potential Share of China's Apparel Trade

Key Messages

- Our estimates suggest that apparel production is actually fairly mobile and responsive to price changes, helping to shed light on an issue that has lacked much quantification.
- If Chinese prices increase 10 percent, U.S. imports from South Asia would increase by 13–25 percent (depending on the country).
- But, if Chinese prices increase 10 percent, U.S. imports from Southeast Asia would increase by 37–51 percent (depending on the country).

An Intense Competition

Developing countries seeking to gain a foothold in the apparel industry, seen as one of the most internationally mobile industries, often lament the intense competitive pressure between countries. The competition is driven by the constant threat of shifting production across countries. In the early 2000s, many developing countries feared that the end of the Multifibre Arrangement (MFA)—a trade pact that restricted their textile and apparel exports to developed countries—would allow China to capture a significant share of global apparel production. Their fears were not unwarranted: China's share of U.S. apparel imports increased dramatically from about 13 percent in 2000 to 38 percent in 2013.

Since then, however, rising wages in China have contributed to a shift in production away from China toward lower-wage countries, and the rate of U.S. apparel imports from China has been slowing down, although as of 2014 it has yet to start to fall.[1] Not surprisingly, given the thousands of jobs that have been

The authors, Raymond Robertson and Benjamin Goldman, are grateful for comments provided by the core team.

created in China in apparel production over the past decade, other developing countries—especially in South Asia—are increasingly considering ways to boost their own apparel exports.

How much of the global apparel production can they hope to capture? That is the question that this chapter tries to answer—specifically how much South Asian apparel exports would increase for a given increase in Chinese apparel prices and how this sum would compare to the estimated sum for South Asia's most likely competitors. Although estimates of how much production might shift in response to rising Chinese prices are important for policy makers, few accurate estimates of the magnitude of production shifts across countries are available because the paradigm of production shifting in value chains is relatively new.

Our approach is based on a model in which the developed countries are characterized as "buyers" who can choose how much to source from each developing country. It is grounded in the foundations of a traditional gravity model (examines trade volumes), directly calculating elasticities (measures how much import and export quantities will change if relative prices change), and Feenstra (1994) (measures gains from trade in differentiated products). In our model, buyers use several criteria to make their decisions, such as logistics, quality, and prices. And, because prices are not the only variable that buyers care about, the countries are *imperfect substitutes*—which in economics jargon means that buyers do not completely shift their orders (and therefore, in effect, production) between countries when the prices in one country change.

The degree to which buyers shift their orders in response to price changes (holding all other variables constant) is called the *elasticity of substitution*. It is this figure that we focus on for four South Asian countries: Bangladesh, India, Pakistan, and Sri Lanka. We then compare it with the elasticity of substitution for three potential competitors: Vietnam and Cambodia in Southeast Asia, and Mexico in Latin America. The target markets are the two largest apparel buyers: the United States and the European Union (EU). Vietnam and Cambodia have become increasingly important in the global apparel market because Chinese investors have been attracted by lower wages and the proximity to China. Since 2000, Mexico's share of the U.S. apparel market has fallen as China's has risen, although some recent anecdotal evidence suggests that some production may be returning to Mexico (Agren 2013).

Our results suggest that a 10 percent increase in Chinese apparel prices will result in a 13–25 percent (depending on country) rise in South Asian countries' apparel exports to the United States, and a 37–51 percent increase in Southeast Asian countries. Thus, unless South Asia successfully identifies and removes barriers to apparel exports—such as barriers to importing manmade fibers (MMF) and poor exporting logistics—other countries, such as Cambodia and Vietnam, stand to gain even more.

A Snapshot of U.S. and EU Imports

To estimate the degree of competition across countries, it is important to start with the importer countries because they compare source countries when making purchasing decisions.

U.S. Apparel Imports

For the United States, the latest data from the U.S. Department of Commerce's Office of Textiles and Apparel (OTEXA)—which posts monthly U.S. import values and the volume of apparel products dating back to 1989—shows that China's share has increased dramatically over time (figure 3.1). In addition, although China and Mexico had approximately equal shares of the U.S. market in 2000, their shares have sharply diverged. Indeed, several of the larger producers in 2000 (like Mexico) were no longer significant producers in 2009, and our focus countries that are not present in 2000 (like Vietnam) emerge as significant exporters in 2009.

At the individual product level, we find that, over the past 25 years, the United States imported 2,774 different apparel products, averaging 15,828.3 million square meters of apparel imports per year. The total value of these imports has shot up from $27.76 billion in the early 1990s to $67.10 billion in 2014, as the

Figure 3.1 China Dominates U.S. Apparel Imports

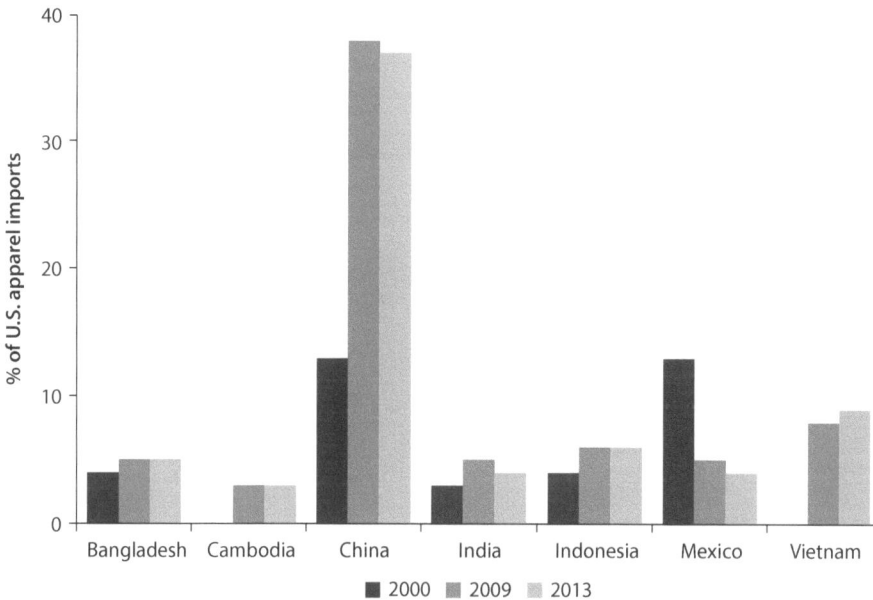

Source: U.S. Department of Commerce's Office of Textiles and Apparel (OTEXA).
Note: We define apparel as HS 61 and 62. HS stands for Harmonized System. Code 61 includes articles of apparel and clothing accessories that are knitted or crocheted, and Code 62 includes articles of apparel and clothing accessories that are not knitted or crocheted.

mean weighted price has steadily dropped from $3.86 per square meter to $3.22 per square meter—with the U.S. and Chinese apparel prices closely tracking each other (figure 3.2).

That said, the U.S. import apparel story has varied greatly for our focus countries between 1990 and 2014 (table 3.1). The first period (1990–94) was dominated by China, India, and Mexico, which all exported in excess of $800 million to the United States per year. Of our competitor countries, Cambodia and Vietnam exported the least, reflecting the fact that their apparel industries were not yet export oriented as they transitioned away from communist regimes. China was the top exporter with an average value of $4.30 billion per year, offered the greatest variety with 1,397 different apparel products, and posted the highest mean price per square meter of apparel at $3.93. At the other extreme, Vietnam exported only 34 products at a mean-weighted price of $1.24 per square meter.

In the second period (1995–99), Cambodia and Vietnam markedly increased not only the value of their apparel exports and product variety but also their prices. China also saw a large increase in value but a drop in product variety and a rise in price. It is worth noting that India and Mexico made large gains as well, with Mexico seeing the largest value increase—putting it on par with China, a phenomenon that would persist until the mid-2000s. The cheapest apparel in this period came from Vietnam, and the most expensive came from China.

Period three (2000–04) saw Vietnam top the $1 billion mark—a dramatic increase from $0.5 billion in the first period—coupled with a price per square

Figure 3.2 U.S. and Chinese Apparel Prices Move Together

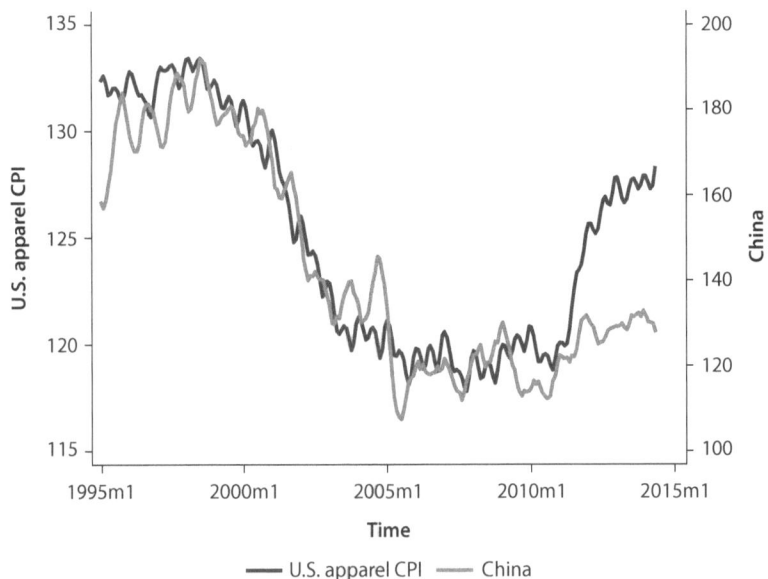

Source: U.S. Department of Commerce's Office of Textiles and Apparel (OTEXA) and the U.S. Bureau of Labor Statistics.
Note: Data shown are the seven-month rolling average of monthly price indexes (for the U.S. apparel CPI) and import unit values. CPI = consumer price index; m1 = January (the first month of the monthly data).

Table 3.1 Value of U.S. Apparel Imports Shot Up as Prices Fell
(Summary Statistics of U.S. Imports from Specified Countries)

Country	Variable	1990–94	1995–99	2000–04	2005–09	2010–14
Bangladesh	Value/year	620.038	1,274.412	1,851.623	2,955.109	3,820.038
	Total products	643	744	832	946	906
	Mean weighted price	2.035	2.240	2.167	2.478	2.784
Cambodia	Value/year	0.107	208.649	1,079.089	2,098.834	2,152.991
	Total products	17	424	582	784	709
	Mean weighted price	2.115	2.726	2.450	2.844	2.418
China	Value/year	4,304.011	5,423.497	7,827.469	21,801.411	25,451.369
	Total products	1,397	1,309	1,440	1,680	1,568
	Mean weighted price	3.933	5.087	3.995	3.058	2.994
India	Value/year	833.162	1,389.502	1,984.621	3,106.117	2,833.883
	Total products	885	1,049	1,221	1,371	1,319
	Mean weighted price	3.871	4.062	3.868	3.829	3.565
Mexico	Value/year	1,133.626	5,240.671	7,646.690	4,783.722	3,298.287
	Total products	859	1,250	1,237	1,324	1,141
	Mean weighted price	3.093	3.185	3.457	4.091	3.971
Pakistan	Value/year	310.740	633.903	983.465	1,408.265	1,326.674
	Total products	613	733	908	1,080	1,033
	Mean weighted price	2.203	2.850	2.217	2.122	2.367
Sri Lanka	Value/year	630.086	1,135.156	1,467.042	1,527.037	1,301.422
	Total products	710	785	825	920	730
	Mean weighted price	2.982	3.653	3.591	3.930	4.130
Vietnam	Value/year	0.506	26.176	1,163.193	4,054.980	6,056.289
	Total products	34	407	994	1,253	1,185
	Mean weighted price	1.243	2.003	3.055	3.570	3.292
World	Value/year	27,760.61	44,169.86	61,212.72	71,431.65	67,108.07
	Total products	1,912	1,660	1,666	1,790	1,619
	Mean weighted price	3.86	3.83	3.51	3.45	3.22

Source: World Bank calculations based on data from U.S. Department of Commerce's Office of Textiles and Apparel (OTEXA).
Note: This analysis uses OTEXA data (rather than COMTRADE), which provide detailed information on unit quantities and prices; certain categories with missing quantities were dropped. Value/year is given in millions of dollars per year, and price data are in 1990 dollars. The mean weighted price is weighted by exported product shares per period. Products are identified by a 10-digit Harmonized Tariff System (HTS) code, and the quantities are measured in different units (such as pounds, dozens, or pieces). To harmonize the quantity measurements, we apply OTEXA-provided conversion factors to convert the various units into square meter equivalents.

meter just above $3.00. China continued its steady growth and maintained a pace of nearly $8 billion per year. The mean world price per square meter was $3.51, with China, India, and Sri Lanka producing above-average-price apparel while Bangladesh, Cambodia, Mexico, Pakistan, and Vietnam were all below average. The cheapest apparel came from Bangladesh, at a mean weighted price of $2.17 per square meter.

In period four (2005–09), China began producing $21.8 billion of apparel per year. No other country's exports came within $15 billion of China's volume, although apparel exports grew for all countries except Mexico, which saw a significant drop—a reflection of a large increase in its prices while China's dropped sharply. China was also producing 1,680 different products by the 2000s,

Stitches to Riches? • http://dx.doi.org/10.1596/978-1-4648-0813-5

just 110 products short of what the United States imported in period four. Pakistani prices fell in period four, making it the cheapest source of apparel. The fact that buyers care about issues besides price is cast into sharp relief in the Pakistani case because, although Pakistan's prices were the lowest, it did not capture the majority of apparel production.

Period five (2010–14) saw a continuation of robust Chinese export growth with value reaching $25.45 billion per year—and nearly every apparel product imported by the United States produced by China (1,568 of 1,619 different products). India, Mexico, Pakistan, and Sri Lanka all saw a reduction in apparel exports. Pakistan was the cheapest source of apparel whereas Mexico and Sri Lanka were the two most expensive exporters.

Over these five periods, the key driving variable was the change in average apparel prices, which could reflect two different types of forces at work. One type of change is referred to as *between* products. It occurs when countries change the mix of products they export (for example, moving from low-price to high-price products); even if the prices of those products remain constant, the average prices would appear to rise. The other type of change is referred to as *within* products. It occurs when countries produce the same product but experience a change in the price of those products.

So which type of price change dominated? To answer this question, we broke down the price changes into changes *within* products and *between* products for two periods: 2000–04 and 2010–14. The main message of table 3.2 is that the price of apparel generally rose, and there was an overall shift into lower-priced products. The net result was a drop in overall apparel prices. Comparing the last two columns supports this finding in that the average individual prices of new products are generally lower than the overall average prices. Starting with price drops, China and India were the only two countries where this occurred (table 3.2). China's price drop of $1.22 between the two periods can be

Table 3.2 A Tendency for Higher Apparel Prices and Lower-Priced Products
(Decomposition of Price Changes between 2000–04 and 2010–14)

Country	Within	Between	Total	New price	Overall price
Bangladesh	0.2032	0.0823	0.2855	2.0302	2.7845
Cambodia	−0.1208	0.2421	0.1213	1.9172	2.4176
China	−0.1498	−1.0669	−1.2167	2.6997	2.9935
India	0.4689	−0.9507	−0.4818	2.9505	3.5653
Pakistan	−0.0340	0.3040	0.2700	2.1344	2.3672
Sri Lanka	0.6141	−0.4368	0.1774	3.4179	4.1304
Vietnam	0.7101	−0.6629	0.0472	2.7886	3.2919
World	0.1888	−0.3468	−0.1581	2.8212	3.2212

Source: World Bank calculations based on data from U.S. Department of Commerce's Office of Textiles and Apparel (OTEXA).
Note: Total is a sum of *within* and *between*. *Within* is equal to the change in prices from the two periods analyzed multiplied by the mean share, by product. *Between* is equal to the change in the share from the two periods analyzed multiplied by the mean price, by product. The new price is the weighted price of the products that were exported only in period 2. The overall price is the weighted price of all products in period 2. Period 1 represents 2000–04, and period 2 represents 2010–14.

explained by both a movement toward producing cheaper products (responsible for $0.95 of the drop) and a drop in price within the products the two countries produced ($0.15 of the drop). India's price drop of $0.48 during the two periods, however, reflected a rise of $0.47 within products and a $0.95 decrease between products.

Mexico saw the largest rise in prices between the two periods. Its products got more expensive by $0.69, but it saw only a small drop ($0.16) that resulted from manufacturing cheaper products. Vietnam experienced the largest growth of prices within products, as prices grew by $0.71 within products despite dropping by $0.66 between products. The largest decline within products was from Cambodia ($0.12). Of the countries that saw price growth, Vietnam had the largest decline in price growth between products while Pakistan had the largest increase, with an increase in price of $0.30.

European Union Apparel Imports

In Europe's apparel market, we can see several trends that vary from what occurred in the United States over comparable periods. For example, between 2010 and 2014, EU imports contracted while prices rose—unlike in the U.S. market, where prices fell along with imports. These variations may be explained by different historical patterns. While some countries have traditionally exported more to Europe, others (like Cambodia) have only recently begun to sharply step up their EU exports thanks to changes in EU preferences. A meaningful comparison between the two markets is complicated because European import data follow a different industry classification scheme than the available U.S. data. Even so, the latest data from EUROSTAT show that China dominates both U.S. and European apparel imports (table 3.3). Between 2010 and 2014, China averaged $8.76 billion worth of apparel exports to European nations—more than three times the amount exported by Bangladesh, its closest competitor. And, as in the U.S. market, China continued to consume a larger market share since 2000.

However, the two markets differ in their import relationships with countries other than China. Mexico exported very little apparel to Europe (less than $20 million a year), although it exported more than $1 billion a year to the United States by the end of the 2000s. Cambodia and Vietnam, at least until recently, exported more to the U.S. market than to Europe.

Also, average import prices are quite different for the two biggest apparel markets, with those for the United States falling and those for the EU rising. The tables suggest that one possible reason is that the United States expanded product variety and specifically shifted into cheaper products. The EU, on the other hand, imported fewer, higher-priced goods between 2010 and 2014.

The changes in prices and varieties varied across exporting countries. While Vietnam and Cambodia saw large increases in variety at the turn of the century (at the end of communist regimes) with the U.S. market, their variety held fairly constant with Europe. Much of this can be attributed to European data beginning in 2000, though. Similarly, we see more overlap in product exports in the European data than in the U.S. data. At first glance, it appears countries behave

Table 3.3 Values of EU Apparel Imports Grow Even as Prices Rise
(Summary Statistics of European Imports from Specified Countries)

Country	Variable	2000–04	2005–09	2010–14
Bangladesh	Value/year	525.367	2,808.341	2,742.978
	Total products	208	229	214
	Mean weighted price	1.310	2.698	3.624
Cambodia	Value/year	61.514	359.305	442.119
	Total products	127	205	208
	Mean weighted price	4.338	4.334	5.413
China	Value/year	1,650.979	14,043.128	8,767.733
	Total products	233	233	215
	Mean weighted price	3.861	3.878	5.131
India	Value/year	427.914	2,385.252	1,292.628
	Total products	232	233	215
	Mean weighted price	3.187	3.162	4.101
Mexico	Value/year	5.552	31.924	18.686
	Total products	162	219	207
	Mean weighted price	5.678	7.754	10.844
Pakistan	Value/year	124.984	533.535	416.241
	Total products	216	230	215
	Mean weighted price	3.360	3.782	5.562
Sri Lanka	Value/year	209.904	757.576	440.895
	Total products	211	225	205
	Mean weighted price	0.773	3.354	3.097
Vietnam	Value/year	160.964	641.799	587.169
	Total products	222	232	214
	Mean weighted price	5.919	5.064	7.869
World	Value/year	14,916.120	53,465.190	30,895.656
	Total products	233	233	215
	Mean weighted price	2.300	4.857	6.088

Source: World Bank elaboration based on data collected and provided by EUROSTAT.
Note: This analysis uses EUROSTAT data (rather than COMTRADE), which provide detailed information on unit quantities and prices; certain categories with missing quantities were dropped. Value/year is given in millions of dollars per year. The mean weighted price is weighted by quantities by period. The mean weighted price is 1990 real price per kg. The values in the table are given in real 1990 dollars. The total product measure is given by a six-digit Harmonized System (HS) code, a slightly broader version than the 10-digit Harmonized Tariff System (HTS) code given in the U.S. import summary statistics. European import data range from 2000 to 2014 (U.S. data begin in 1990).

more competitively in the European market whereas they tend to specialize in the United States.

Model and Estimation Approach

Now that we have detailed data on U.S. and EU apparel imports over time, we can estimate the relationship between Chinese prices and U.S. and EU apparel imports from countries other than China. Our approach and model are described fully in Annex 3A. Candidate estimation approaches include a standard gravity model, direct estimation of elasticities, and Feenstra's model.

The gravity model is a standard empirical tool used to examine trade volumes. It assumes that trade volumes can be modeled as a function of the size of the trading economies (often measured as gross domestic product [GDP] per capita), the distance between the two countries, and a varied list of other factors that might affect trade (such as sharing a common border and a common language, resource differences, and trade agreements). However, because of several shortcomings, we cannot apply the gravity model directly (see annex 3B).

In our robustness section, we compare our elasticity estimates with those produced using the gravity approach as well as estimates produced following Feenstra's (1994) method. The main difference between our results and Feenstra's (1994) approach is that our main results rely on data that vary across time and country (because we use panel data) whereas Feenstra's (1994) approach uses data across countries in a single time period (cross-sectional data). We therefore apply Feenstra's (1994) approach to a cross section of U.S. import data from 2013. However, when applying this cross-sectional approach, we encounter the same estimation issues documented by Feenstra (1994) and later Broda and Weinstein (2006), and we find that these issues preclude getting reasonable estimates. As a result, we focus on our main (panel data) results.

We begin by pooling the data into a panel data set, which enables us to produce "average" elasticity estimates while also controlling for differences across products that may stem from demand or consumer preferences. For weighting, we use country-specific total import values to deal with the potential issue of undue influence from small-volume categories.

As in any typical demand equation, we are assuming that how much apparel (the dependent variable) buyers want to purchase from each country will depend on the price that country offers, the prices other countries offer, and the total income of the buyer. We expect that, if, say, India increases its prices, buyers will buy less from India. We also expect that, if other countries raise their prices, buyers will want to buy less from them and more from India. And if buyers' incomes increase, they will want to buy more from India.

To focus on each country's relationship with China, we estimate a separate three-equation system for each of the following focus countries: Bangladesh, Cambodia, India, Pakistan, Sri Lanka, and Vietnam. The three equations represent imports from our focus country, U.S. imports from China (as the fundamental comparison country), and U.S. imports from Latin America (as a common comparison group). Using i to denote our focus countries (Bangladesh, Cambodia, India, Pakistan, Sri Lanka, and Vietnam), the equations we estimate[2] are shown below in equation (3.1).

$$A_{it} = \varphi_0 + \beta_1 P_{it} + \delta_1 P_{China,t} + \delta_2 P_{LatinAmerica,t} + \varphi_1 Y_t + e_{it}$$

$$A_{China,t} = \gamma_0 + \delta_1 P_{it} + \beta_2 P_{China,t} + \delta_3 P_{LatinAmerica,t} + \gamma_1 Y_t + e_{it}$$

$$A_{LatinAmerica,t} = \lambda_0 + \delta_2 P_{it} + \delta_3 P_{China,t} + \beta_3 P_{LatinAmerica,t} + \lambda_1 Y_t + e_{it} \qquad (3.1)$$

The first equation, indexed by i, represents the price of our focus country, and the next two equations are for the prices in China and Latin America. U.S. or EU imports of apparel are represented by A, and prices are represented by the P variables. The Y terms near the end of each equation represent the income of the importing country. The β terms are estimated and capture the "own price" effect on imports. For example, the β_1 in the first equation is an estimate of how much imports from, say, India, would fall if Indian apparel prices increased.

The δ terms are estimates that capture the "cross-price" effects. For example, δ_1 captures the change in imports from India if Chinese prices increase. The δ terms from these equations are used to calculate the elasticity of substitution for each country, which are the main estimates we are interested in for this chapter. The dependent variable is the share of imports in each 10-digit Harmonized Tariff System (HTS) good from the country specified in each of the three equations in each system.

Our results highlight several key findings (table 3.4):

If a country's apparel price rises, the U.S. and EU markets will import less from that country. This can be seen in row 1, which shows negative signs for the inverse relationship between price and quantity, in line with what we expected. The magnitudes are generally similar across countries and equations, but larger absolute values suggest more elastic demand curves. Cambodia, which produces lower-value goods, such as T-shirts, has a more elastic demand than Sri Lanka, which produces higher-value goods, such as women's undergarments. Pakistan also seems to have a relatively high elasticity, which indicates that a rise in prices in Pakistan would result in a larger fall in U.S. imports than for other countries.

China is the most vulnerable in terms of quantity drops if its prices rise. When comparing China's own-price elasticities to those of other countries, it is clear that a rise in Chinese prices would result in a larger fall in Chinese production than a rise in prices in other countries. This result is important because it suggests that rising Chinese prices will result in production leaving China in relatively large amounts, although it is not clear where the production would go.

Currently, an increase in global apparel demand favors China. This can be seen in the rows marked "Q World," which show how the United States would respond toward each country given a general increase in apparel demand. The coefficients for the South Asian and Southeast Asian countries (shown in the row marked "1: Q World") are negative (except Vietnam) whereas the coefficients for China (shown in the row marked "2: Q World") are all positive. This reveals a preference for China while prices are held constant—that is, unless they rise.

Rising world prices could shift demand to our focus countries. The uniformly positive and relative large values for the "Rest of World P" suggest that rising prices in the rest of the world will cause the United States to import more from our focus countries, including China and Latin America. These values are smallest (in absolute value) for Vietnam, whose apparel production increased later than that in the other countries.

Table 3.4 Higher Chinese Prices Will Benefit China's Competitors
(SUR Weighted Fixed Effects Using Shares)

Variables	(1) Bangladesh	(2) Cambodia	(3) India	(4) Pakistan	(5) Sri Lanka	(6) Vietnam
1: X own price	−0.046***	−0.057***	−0.046***	−0.053***	−0.046***	−0.049***
	(0.001)	(0.001)	(0.001)	(0.001)	(0.001)	(0.001)
1: Q world	−0.007***	−0.005***	−0.010***	−0.012***	−0.011***	0.001
	(0.001)	(0.001)	(0.001)	(0.001)	(0.001)	(0.001)
2: China own price	−0.058***	−0.068***	−0.053***	−0.059***	−0.052***	−0.063***
	(0.001)	(0.001)	(0.001)	(0.001)	(0.001)	(0.001)
2: Q world	0.041***	0.036***	0.042***	0.041***	0.045***	0.032***
	(0.001)	(0.001)	(0.001)	(0.001)	(0.001)	(0.001)
3: LAM own price	−0.037***	−0.034***	−0.035***	−0.040***	−0.046***	−0.017***
	(0.001)	(0.001)	(0.001)	(0.001)	(0.001)	(0.001)
A: China-X	0.003***	0.015***	0.005***	0.006***	−0.005***	0.025***
	0.000	0.000	0.000	0.000	0.000	0.000
B: LAM-X	−0.018***	−0.018***	−0.013***	−0.012***	−0.012***	−0.020***
	0.000	0.000	0.000	0.000	0.000	0.000
C: China—LAM	−0.006***	−0.007***	−0.005***	−0.006***	−0.006***	−0.007***
	0.000	0.000	0.000	0.000	0.000	0.000
Rest of world P	0.061***	0.060***	0.054***	0.059***	0.063***	0.044***
	(0.001)	(0.001)	(0.001)	(0.001)	(0.001)	(0.001)
3: Q world	−0.025***	−0.025***	−0.029***	−0.030***	−0.029***	−0.022***
	(0.001)	(0.001)	(0.001)	(0.001)	(0.001)	(0.001)
Constant	0.393***	0	0	0.555***	0	0
	(0.018)	0.000	0.000	(0.017)	0.000	0.000
Observations	264,293	244,909	284,071	257,613	260,567	264,175

Note: Standard errors in parentheses. Table 3.4 shows the regression results. Each column represents the results from a three-equation system with homogeneity and symmetry constraints imposed. The first equation (with the "1" prefix) is for the country "X" listed at the top of each column. The second equation (with the "2" prefix) represents China. The third equation (with the "3" prefix) represents Latin America. P represents prices. Q represents quantities. LAM represents Latin America. The dependent variable is the share of imports in each 10-digit HTS (Harmonized Tariff System) good from the country specified in each of the three equations in each system. The "A" prefix represents variables that appear in, and are constrained across, equations 1 and 2. The "B" prefix represents variables that appear in, and are constrained across, equations 1 and 3. The "C" prefix represents variables that appear in, and are constrained across, equations 2 and 3 (China and Latin America). The "Rest of World P" variable appears in all three equations and is constrained to have the same coefficient in all three equations. This variable is a proxy for all other possible input factors available to the buyers when making purchasing decisions. SUR = seemingly unrelated regression.
***$p<.01$, **$p<.05$, *$p<.1$.

A technical note here is that it is useful to double-check the panel estimates (which combine all of the products into an average) by estimating the system one product at a time (that is, estimating a separate elasticity for each product). The results are best viewed in a frequency chart, given that hundreds of products generate hundreds of elasticity estimates. As figure 3.3 shows, the summary statistics (such as the mean) are similar to, and support, the panel data approach. However, we also learn that the range is large, extending from about −10 to 1, meaning that there are some products that are outliers, with much greater or much less elasticity than the bulk of the products.

Figure 3.3 Individual Product Estimates Center around the Pooled Ones

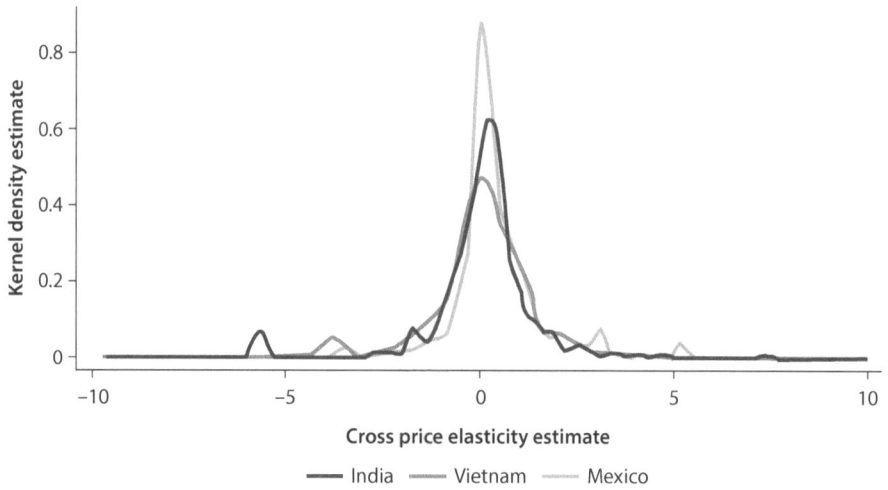

Source: World Bank calculations using data from the U.S. Department of Commerce's Office of Textiles and Apparel (OTEXA).
Note: The curve represents the probability density of country *x*'s price elasticity with China for all apparel exports.

Elasticity of Substitution Estimates

Now that we have a sense of the relationship between Chinese prices and U.S. and EU apparel imports from countries other than China, we can use this information to produce estimates of the elasticity of substitution across countries. The final critical step is to adjust the demand coefficients shown in row 1 of table 3.4 to account for the share that these products represent of the total. In other words, in the case of Bangladesh, if its own price rises 1 percent, the 4.6 percent drop in quantity demanded from the United States is a relatively large response. This estimate shows that apparel demand is very elastic—much more so than for other goods.

To generate the elasticity of substitution estimates, we combine the estimates from table 3.4 with the import shares of each country as follows in equation (3.2).

$$\sigma_{jk} = \frac{1}{\alpha_j \alpha_k} \gamma_{jk} + 1 \qquad\qquad (3.2)$$

This formula generates both the elasticity of substitution and the own-price elasticity of demand (see annex 3A for further details). Applying this formula to our estimation results generates several additional important results (table 3.5). *A 10 percent increase in China's prices would result in the United States reducing imports from China by about 7.9 percent, or almost $700 million.* This may seem small to those who know that U.S. demand has exhibited a very elastic response to the drop in global apparel prices. But keep in mind that this is a constant-income elasticity, which means that the income effect[3] is excluded. If the income effect were included, the increase in imports would be larger.

A 10 percent increase in Chinese export prices would result in the United States increasing imports from our South Asian focus countries. As table 3.5 shows, India and Bangladesh would experience an increase in exports of 14.62 percent (about $414 million) and 13.58 percent (about $518.76), respectively. Sri Lanka would experience an increase of less than 1 percent, whereas Pakistan would experience an increase of 25.31 percent (about $336 million). These are relatively large shifts (apparel production across countries is elastic for all but Sri Lanka).

South Asia's competitor countries would benefit even more from rising Chinese prices. Vietnam's exports would increase by 37.70 percent (about $2.2 billion), and Cambodia's exports would increase by 51.25 percent (about $1.1 billion).

Rising Chinese prices would have little, if any, effect on Bangladeshi and Pakistani exports to the EU. The EU estimates are larger for Sri Lanka and India than the U.S. estimates, but the estimates for Bangladesh and Pakistan are much smaller—in fact, negative and not statistically significant. Indian and Sri Lankan exports to the EU would increase by 18.95 percent and 22.49 percent, respectively. These results are consistent with the current production relationships between our focus countries and the EU.

How accurate are these findings? The elasticities in table 3.5 are probably more accurate than those estimated using a nonlinear estimation method or a standard gravity model (annex 3B). This is because they are not subject to the same set of estimation issues as described in annex 3B as the other two models (the gravity and Feenstra) that we used to double-check our results. In addition, our elasticity estimates are broadly consistent with what one might expect. Keep in mind that elasticities can be either: (i) below one, referred to as *inelastic*, suggesting very little response to a given shock; (ii) equal to one, referred to as *unitary elastic*, suggesting a response about equal to the shock (a 10 percent increase in a price would result in a 10 percent change in quantity); or (iii) greater than one, referred to as *elastic*, suggesting a big response.

The conventional wisdom about apparel-producing countries facing strong competition from other countries leads us to expect elasticity values greater than one, which is exactly what most of our results show. In Bangladesh,

Table 3.5 Southeast Asia Benefits More Than South Asia
(Elasticity of Substitution, U.S. and EU Imports)

	Bangladesh	Cambodia	India	Pakistan	Sri Lanka	Vietnam
U.S.	1.358[a]	5.125[a]	1.462[a]	2.531[a]	0.024	3.770[a]
	(0.039)	(0.093)	(0.027)	(0.086)	(0.058)	(0.029)
EU	−0.238	2.525	1.895[a]	−0.060	2.249[a]	1.644[a]
	(0.534)	(2.031)	(0.455)	(1.068)	(0.745)	(0.960)

Source: World Bank calculations using data from the U.S. Department of Commerce's Office of Textiles and Apparel (OTEXA).
Note: SUR with homogeneity and symmetry and fixed effects and weights. Estimates based on table 3.1 following equation (6) in annex 3A. SUR = seemingly unrelated regression. The numbers in this table are elasticities for a 1 percent increase in prices of Chinese apparel. The change in the exports of a given country heading the columns would be the elasticity times a given percent change in China. A negative value means a decline.
a = statistically significant at 1 percent.

Stitches to Riches? • http://dx.doi.org/10.1596/978-1-4648-0813-5

for example, a 10 percent increase in Chinese prices would induce an increase in apparel exports of nearly 14 percent.

That said, when interpreting elasticities, it is important to remember that elasticities measure the *percent* change in response to a given percent change in prices—and percent changes are sensitive to the size of the base. For example, an increase of one unit is much larger when the base is 2 (resulting in a 50 percent change) than when the base is 10 (resulting in a 10 percent change). Thus, the relatively large elasticities of Cambodia, Sri Lanka (for exports to Europe), and Pakistan (for exports to the United States) partially reflect the small base. As shown in table 3.3, these countries have smaller exports to these regions in absolute value.

Reaping the Most from Higher Imports

The main policy question that drives this analysis is whether or not it would benefit South Asian countries to invest in policies that would allow them to capture more of the apparel production that is shifting out of China as Chinese prices rise. The first result from this analysis, which is hardly surprising to developing country apparel producers, is that apparel producers face intense international competition in the sense that apparel production is very responsive to price changes. The other edge to this sword, however, is that policies to attract apparel production may be effective. The elasticity estimates suggest that the expected gains from following current policies are not trivial, but other countries that have pursued more aggressive apparel-friendly policies (such as Vietnam and Cambodia with the Better Work programs) stand to gain much more than the South Asian countries.

These results also suggest that current production relationships significantly affect the potential for capturing apparel production leaving China. Sri Lanka, for example, is much more closely tied to the EU market, and, therefore, it would be interesting to identify what kinds of products China is producing and exporting to the EU that are potential products for Sri Lankan production.

The estimated substitution elasticities are an important part of an analysis that predicts the employment effects of a rise in prices in China. If Chinese prices increase by 10 percent, we now have estimates of how much exports from the different South Asian countries would increase. The next step is to generate estimates of how much employment responds to changes in exports. Increasing exports would increase labor demand. How this increase in labor demand translates into rising employment requires estimating the employment-output elasticities, which is done in chapter 4. This report then combines the two sets of elasticity estimates in chapter 5 to generate the potential employment gains.

Annex 3A: Theoretic Foundation of the Estimation Approach

The elasticity of substitution is a standard parameter in both theoretical and empirical economics. To illustrate how the elasticity of substitution of production across countries is derived and estimated, we begin with the assumption that the international apparel chain has three principal components: consumers, buyers, and producers. Consumer demand for apparel products is determined by income and preferences. Global import data suggest that consumers of internationally traded apparel are located primarily in developed countries. We do not model consumer demand explicitly but instead assume that buyers make production decisions on the basis of (exogenous) consumer demand and exogenous input costs. Consistent with descriptions of global value chains (for example, Gereffi 1999), buyers contract with producers in (usually) developing countries to assemble apparel. The assembled apparel is then exported to developed countries, where it may be packaged and sold to consumers. Although these production decisions could be modeled using a production function approach, the dual cost-minimization approach offers a more straightforward representation of factor demands. In this model, buyers seek to minimize the cost C_{ikt} of meeting consumer demand for product i at time t:

$$\min C_{ikt} = \sum_k X_{ikt} P_{ikt} \; s.t. \; Y = f\left(X_{k \in K}\right) \tag{3A.1}$$

In this formulation, X_{ikt} represents the inputs from country k necessary to produce product i at time t. P_{ikt} represents the cost of production in each country k that is a member of the potential apparel-producing countries K.

The solution to the cost-minimization problem can be expressed with a minimum cost function:

$$C^* = g(Y, P_1, ..., P_K) \tag{3A.2}$$

As is well known, the minimum cost function is homogenous of degree one in prices. The main advantage of this cost function is that the derivative of the cost function with respect to any given input price yields the demand for that input (Shepard's lemma). For example,

$$\frac{\partial C^*}{\partial P_j} = X_j. \tag{3A.3}$$

Our main focus is to estimate the degree of substitutability between different apparel-producing countries from the point of view of the buyers. In other words, we are interested in the elasticity of substitution between countries, σ_{jk}, which is derived directly from the parameters of the minimum cost function,

$$\sigma_{jk} = \frac{\sum_{n=1}^{N} P_n X_n}{X_j X_k} \frac{\partial^2 C^*}{\partial P_j \partial P_k}. \tag{3A.4}$$

The cost function is commonly represented with the translog cost function, which, when expressed in natural log form and suppressing the time and product subscripts, can be expressed as

$$\ln C^* = v_0 + v_y \ln Y \sum_n v_n P_n + \frac{1}{2} \sum_n \sum_j \gamma_{nj} \ln P_n \ln P_j \sum_n \gamma_{ny} \ln Y. \tag{3A.5}$$

The derivative of the cost function yields the factor demand (expressed as the share of total costs):

$$\frac{\partial C^*}{\partial P_k} = \frac{X_k P_k}{\sum_k X_k P_k} = \alpha_k = v_k + \sum_j \gamma_{jk} \ln P_k + \gamma_{ky} \ln Y \qquad (3A.6)$$

This equation can be estimated directly as part of a system of equations for each factor k. The homogeneity condition described earlier is joined by the symmetry conditions $\gamma_{jk} = \gamma_{kj}$ that are implied by the symmetry of the bordered Hessian matrix of the derivatives of the cost function. Binswanger (1974) shows that the estimates of this function can be then combined to generate an estimate of the elasticity of substitution between the products of two countries.

$$\sigma_{jk} = \frac{1}{\alpha_j \alpha_k} \gamma_{jk} + 1 \qquad (3A.7)$$

Note that the α terms are defined in equation (3A.6) and represent the cost shares of factor k. In addition, the own-price elasticity of demand,

$$\sigma_{it} = \frac{\gamma_{it}}{\alpha_i} + \alpha_i - 1, \qquad (3A.8)$$

is also informative.

Following this theoretic framework, the goal of this chapter is to estimate the system of equations shown in (3A.6) and then calculate the elasticity of substitution coefficients between China, four South Asian countries (Bangladesh, India, Pakistan, and Sri Lanka), and three of the region's closest competitors (Vietnam, Cambodia, and Latin America). We use the parameters estimated from the system of demand equations to generate estimates of the cross-country and own-price elasticity of demand.

Annex 3B: Alternative Estimation Approaches

One reason why there are so few accurate estimates is that there is no consensus of the appropriate way to generate such estimates. The two leading alternative approaches use the gravity model and a nonlinear estimate approach. Greenaway, Mahabir, and Milner (2008) estimate the effect of China's production on exports of Asian countries using a gravity model. The gravity model is a standard model (perhaps even to the point of being the default model) in empirical international economics that estimates the effects of different variables, such as distance and GDP, on trade flows. The results from the gravity model of Greenaway, Mahabir, and Milner (2008) reveal small effects of China's production in the early 2000s on the exports of other Asian countries. Although these estimates are informative, they are potentially affected by three important estimation issues.

The first is that the gravity model does not control for total apparel demand. An increase in demand in the United States, for example, may increase imports from both China and South Asia regardless of the degree of substitutability between the two countries. To identify the elasticity of substitution between countries, it is important to control for total apparel imports, which reflect increased demand.

The second is that the gravity model approach compares the correlation between imports from one country (China) and other countries (for example, other Asian countries). Prices are not explicitly considered. This approach is therefore not especially appropriate for our question because we are specifically interested in the effects of rising prices in China. Harrigan and Barrows (2009) show that China's growth in the world apparel market significantly reduced U.S. import prices. Furthermore, quantities respond to prices, which means that any correlation between imports from two countries could be driven by a common third factor (prices), making the correlation between the two variables hard to interpret. Indeed, Harrigan and Barrows (2009) show that the drop in apparel prices corresponded to a significant increase in total U.S. apparel imports after the end of the MFA in December 2004. This result suggests that an increase in Chinese prices might induce U.S. apparel buyers to look for substitutions from other apparel-producing countries.

The third estimation issue is that the gravity model is not designed to produce estimates of the substitution elasticities. While the gravity model is a standard workhorse of international economics, gravity models do not directly estimate substitution elasticities and are not well suited for estimating the competitive effects that are the key to this study. Alternatively, it is possible to estimate directly the elasticity of substitution of apparel products across countries. If we estimate a system of global apparel demand equations, we can produce estimates of the effect of an increase in Chinese prices on the apparel exports of competing countries.

Estimating substitution elasticities directly overcomes the estimation issues that are present in the gravity model, but the direct approach raises its own challenges. The first issue is that the literature contains several different methods to estimate the substitution elasticities. Feenstra (1994) provides one notable alternative. Therefore, in our robustness section, we compare our elasticity estimates with those produced using the gravity approach as well as estimates produced following Feenstra's (1994) method. The main difference between our results and Feenstra's (1994) approach is that our main results rely on data that vary across time and country (because we use panel data), while Feenstra's (1994) approach uses data across countries in a single time period (cross-sectional data). We therefore apply Feenstra's (1994) approach to a cross section of U.S. import data from 2013. However, when applying this cross-sectional approach, we encounter the same estimation issues documented by Feenstra (1994) and later by Broda and Weinstein (2006), and we find that these issues preclude getting reasonable estimates.

A. Gravity Model

Greenaway, Mahabir, and Milner (2008) employ a gravity model of international trade to assess the effect that China's exports have on the exports of other Asian countries. Although a significant body of research debates the appropriate estimation approach for gravity models (for example, Anderson and van Wincoop 2003), gravity models tend to have common elements that take a form such as equation (3B.1),

$$x_{ijt} = \alpha + \beta_1 Y_{it} + \beta_2 Y_{jt} + \beta_3 D_{ij} + BZ_{ijt} + v_{ijt}, \qquad (3B.1)$$

in which x_{ijt} represents the trade (exports or imports) between countries i and j at time t. The Y variables represent national income, D represents distance, and Z represents a vector of other possible variables that affect trade (such as sharing a common border, speaking a common language, being landlocked or an island, and so on). Greenaway, Mahabir, and Milner (2008) include Chinese exports to country i at time t in the Z vector. A negative coefficient on Chinese exports is interpreted as evidence that an increase in Chinese exports is correlated with a decline in the exports of a given country j to country i.

To employ this approach, we use apparel trade data from COMTRADE for 271 countries (resulting in 26,234 country-pair observations) in the apparel trade covering the period 1992–2012. We add other variables to the trade data, including the GDP of each country, the pair-wise distance (in kilometers), the importer's ease of doing business rank, energy use by both the importer and the exporter, and the imports of materials (yarn and fabric).

Table 3B.1 summarizes the pair-wise interactions in the COMTRADE data. The data cover apparel trade between all countries dating back to 1992.

Table 3B.1 Summary Statistics of Gravity Pair-Wise Interactions

Year	Average country pair trade value, US$
1992	2,508,378
1993	2,997,225
1994	3,698,765
1995	4,247,369
1996	4,520,151
1997	4,788,523
1998	4,937,110
1999	5,070,939
2000	5,453,357
2001	5,504,827
2002	5,203,119
2003	6,377,380
2004	7,092,684
2005	7,570,669
2006	8,198,090
2007	8,984,211
2008	9,536,664
2009	8,471,154
2010	9,231,544
2011	10,594,164
2012	9,890,656

The average trade value between each country pair steadily increased over the course of the two decades. In 1992, the average apparel trade value per year was about $2.5 million US$. By 2012 countries were trading an average of $9.89 million US$ worth of apparel products with each other. There was not much deviation from the trend during the time period analyzed.

Table 3B.2 contains the gravity model estimation results. The resulting regression has 168,453 observations and has an R-squared value of 0.52. The results suggest that apparel imports from China are positively related to imports from our focus countries. This result suggests that increases in Chinese imports are positively related to imports from other countries, which is possibly explained by the fact that the gravity model does not account for common demand shocks. In other words, an increase in the demand for apparel in general could result in an increase in imports from China and other countries, which would mask the degree of competition between the two countries. Therefore, it is important to hold total imports constant to identify the substitution elasticities.

B. Feenstra (1994)

A traditional gravity estimation approach is not appropriate for aggregate apparel data because of the specific nature of different apparel products. A winter coat and

Table 3B.2 Gravity Model Results

Variable	General	Bangladesh	India	Pakistan	Sri Lanka
Country X dummy variable	n.a.	−9.64***	−1.16***	−1.31***	−8.53***
		(0.41)	(0.32)	(0.35)	(0.44)
ln (China's exports to importing country)	0.49***	0.48***	0.49***	0.49***	0.48***
	(0.00)	(0.00)	(0.00)	(0.00)	(0.00)
Country X interaction with China's exports	n.a.	0.49***	0.21***	0.14***	0.50***
		(0.02)	(0.02)	(0.02)	(0.02)
ln (importing country GDP PC)	0.44***	0.44***	0.44***	0.44***	0.44***
	(0.01)	(0.01)	(0.01)	(0.01)	(0.01)
ln (exporting country GDP PC)	−0.39***	−0.40***	−0.34***	−0.37***	−0.38***
	(0.01)	(0.01)	(0.01)	(0.01)	(0.01)
ln (distance km)	−1.36***	−1.36***	−1.36***	−1.36***	−1.37***
	(0.01)	(0.01)	(0.01)	(0.01)	(0.01)
Importer land locked	0.16***	−0.16***	−0.15***	−0.15***	−0.16***
	(0.02)	(0.02)	(0.02)	(0.02)	(0.02)
Exporter land locked	−0.11***	−0.12***	−0.06**	−0.07***	−0.10***
	(0.02)	(0.02)	(0.02)	(0.02)	(0.02)
Constant	−8.80***	−8.60***	−8.77***	−8.90***	−8.66***
	(0.15)	(0.15)	(0.15)	(0.15)	(0.15)
Observations	168,453	168,453	168,453	168,453	168,453
R-squared	0.52	0.53	0.53	0.53	0.53

Note: Each equation also included Importer's Ease of Doing Business Rank, Importer Energy Use, Exporter Energy Use, the log of knit imports into exporting country, the log of narrow materials inputs into the exporting country, the log of woven imports into the exporting country, and the log of yarn imports into the exporting country. n.a. = Not applicable.
***p<.01, **p<.05, *p<.1. Standard errors in parentheses.

a bathing suit should not be treated as equal and lumped into the same regression. There is, however, a problem with using product-level data. Using HTS codes it is possible to run a system of constrained regressions to solve for the elasticity of substitution. The downfall of this method is that there are holes throughout the data in the sense that different countries export different products. Estimating the system requires observations for prices from country A, Latin America, and China. In reality, product export overlap between the three countries is incomplete.

To work around the issue of incomplete product overlap, we employ a method used by Feenstra (1994) where the data are estimated in cross sections with shares (see table 3B.3). By holding China as the reference nation, we can obtain product-level elasticity estimates by employing the estimation in equation (3B.2).

$$Y_{i,t} = \beta_1 X_{i,t} + \beta_2 (X_{i,t})^2 + \mu_{i,t} \qquad (3B.2)$$

The dependent variable, $Y_{i,t}$ is given by equation (3B.3),

$$Y_{it} = (\Delta ln P_{i,t} - \Delta ln P_{k,t})^2, \qquad (3B.3)$$

where $P_{i,t}$ is the price of the product in country i in time t. $P_{k,t}$ gives the price of the same product in China in time t. The independent variable, $X_{i,t}$ is given by equation (3B.4),

$$X_{it} = (\Delta ln s_{i,t} - \Delta ln s_{k,t}), \qquad (3B.4)$$

where $s_{i,t}$ is the share of U.S. imports for that product that come from country i in time t, and $s_{k,t}$ is the share of U.S. imports for that product that come from China.

These estimations will generate hyperbolas of elasticity estimates whose intersections identify the elasticity of substitution, σ, so long as $\beta_1 > 0$. The elasticity of substitution is given by the calculation in equation (3B.5).

$$\rho = \frac{1}{2} + \left(\frac{1}{4} - \frac{1}{4 + \left(\beta_2^2 / \beta_1 \right)} \right)^{\frac{1}{2}}$$

$$\sigma = 1 + \left(\frac{2\rho - 1}{1 - \rho} \right) \frac{1}{\beta_2} \qquad (3B.5)$$

In practice, however, we estimate negative beta values, which are inconsistent with the theory. Restricting the analysis to the positive beta values may result in estimates that can be interpreted as estimates by holding the number of products constant so that new products do not emerge as substitutes. Whether a result of this interpretation or the fact that we drop negative beta estimates, the elasticity estimates are significantly higher than those estimated with the panel approach. They are somewhat similar in the sense that Cambodia's estimate is larger than

Table 3B.3 Feenstra (1994) Estimates

Bangladesh	16.98
Cambodia	21.39
India	20.47
Pakistan	31.62
Sri Lanka	18.23
Vietnam	18.05

Note: Results are the weighted averages over product using U.S. country import shares as weights. See text for complete details.

that for Bangladesh and India. The magnitudes, however, seem too large to be plausible. The elasticity estimates suggest that a 10 percent increase in China's prices would increase Pakistan's exports by 316.2 percent. By comparison, the system estimation estimates seem quite plausible.

While the two robustness exercises suggest that the system equation approach generates results that are relatively plausible, there are several directions for future work. In particular, it would be interesting to implement some of the advances to estimation techniques to our system. For example, McLaren and Zhao (2011) argue that share equations should be estimated using their specific functional forms. Kumbhakar and Tsionas (2011) suggest that it is important to derive the error structures explicitly and then estimate with the Multiplicative General Error Model (MGEM) Cost System. Thompson (1997) introduces an alternative measure for the elasticity of substitution that complements and is complemented by approaches of Mundra and Russel (2010), Christev and Featherstone (2009), and Blackorby and Russell (1981, 1989). Subsequent work should explore the robustness of the current results using these additional approaches.

Notes

1. Anecdotal evidence, such as Wonacott (2014), suggests that the slowdown represents the beginning of production shifts out of China.

2. These are presented as equation (3A.6) in annex 3A.

3. In microeconomics, the term *income effect* is used to describe the fact that, when prices fall, consumers can buy the same amount and have money left over. This leftover money is like additional income, which can then be spent on anything, including, in this case, apparel. If this "additional" money is spent on apparel and we did not control for the income effect, the income effect would confound the estimates of the substitution elasticity.

Bibliography

Agren, D. 2013. "Some Manufacturers Say 'Adios' to China." *USA Today*, March 18. http://www.usatoday.com/story/news/world/2013/03/18/manufacturing-mexico-china/1997883/.

Anderson, J. E., and E. van Wincoop. 2003. "Gravity with Gravitas: A Solution to the Border Puzzle." *American Economic Review* 93 (1): 170–92.

Binswanger, H. P. 1974. "A Cost Function Approach to the Measurement of Elasticities of Factor Demand and Elasticities of Substitution." *American Journal of Agricultural Economics* 56 (2): 377–86.

Blackorby, C., D. Primont, and R. R. Russell. 2007. "The Morishima Gross Elasticity of Substitution." *Journal of Productivity Analysis* 28 (3): 203–08.

Blackorby, C., and R. R. Russell. 1981. "The Morishima Elasticity of Substitution: Symmetry, Constancy, Separability, and Its Relationship to the Hicks and Allen Elasticities." *Review of Economic Studies* 48 (1): 147–58.

———. 1989. "Will the Real Elasticity of Substitution Please Stand Up? (A Comparison of the Allen/Uzawa and Morishima Elasticities)." *American Economic Review* 79 (4): 882–88.

Blackwell, J. L. 2005. "Estimation and Testing of Fixed-Effect Panel-Data Systems." *The Stata Journal* 5 (2): 202–07.

Broda, C., and D. Weinstein. 2006. "Globalization and the Gains from Variety." *Quarterly Journal of Economics* 121 (2): 541–85.

Christev, A., and A. Featherstone. 2009. "A Note on Allen-Uzawa Partial Elasticities of Substitution: The Case of the Translog Cost Function." *Applied Economics Letters* 16 (11): 1165–69.

Davis, G. C., and C. R. Shumway. 1996. "To Tell the Truth about Interpreting the Morishima Elasticity of Substitution." *Canadian Journal of Agricultural Economics* 44 (2): 173–82.

Feenstra, R. C. 1994. "New Product Varieties and the Measurement of International Prices." *American Economic Review* 84 (1): 157–77.

Gereffi, G. 1999. "International Trade and Industrial Upgrading in the Apparel Commodity Chain." *Journal of International Economics* 48 (1): 37–70.

Greenaway, D., A. Mahabir, and C. Milner. 2008. "Has China Displaced Other Asian Countries' Exports?" *China Economic Review* 19 (2): 152–69.

Hanson, G. H., and R. Robertson. 2010. "China and the Manufacturing Exports of Other Developing Countries." In *China's Growing Role in World Trade*, edited by Robert Feenstra and Shang-Jin Wei. Cambridge, MA: National Bureau of Economic Research.

Harrigan, J., and G. Barrows. 2009. "Testing the Theory of Trade Policy: Evidence from the Abrupt End of the Multifibre Arrangement." *Review of Economics and Statistics* 91 (2): 282–94.

Hicks, J. 1970. "Elasticity of Substitution Again: Substitutes and Complements." *Oxford Economic Papers* 22 (3): 289–96.

Kumbhakar, S. C., and E. G. Tsionas. 2011. "Stochastic Error Specification in Primal and Dual Production Systems." *Journal of Applied Econometrics* 26 (2): 270–97.

McLaren, K.R., and X. Zhao. 2011. "The Econometric Specification of Input Demand Systems Implied by Cost Function Representations." Draft, Monash University, Melbourne, Australia.

Mundra, K., and N. P. Russell. 2010. "Revisiting Elasticities of Substitution." Newark Working Paper 2010–007, Rutgers University, Camden, NJ.

Thompson, H. 1997. "Substitution Elasticities with Many Inputs." *Applied Mathematics Letters* 10 (3): 123–27.

Wonacott, P. 2014. "China Inc. Moves Factory Floor to Africa." *Wall Street Journal*, May 14. http://online.wsj.com/news/articles/SB10001424052702304788404579519631654112 5.

## PART 2

How Will Increased Apparel Production Affect Jobs?

CHAPTER 4

Market Responses to Higher Apparel and Textile Exports

Key Messages

- Our analysis of labor demand shows that the number of jobs created in response to higher demand for exports (output) in apparel is higher than in other sectors like agriculture.
- Our analysis of labor supply shows a definite (albeit small) wage premium for working in textiles and apparel versus agriculture, which would be particularly attractive for low-skilled women.
- If apparel wages remain higher than in sectors like agriculture, apparel holds the potential to increase female labor force participation, which, in turn, would be good for development.

Why Focus on Garments and Women?

South Asia could potentially pick the low-hanging fruit in the apparel sector and expand apparel exports as China's labor costs continue to rise and the growth rate of the Chinese market share in the global apparel sector continues to slow down. Even though South Asia is not as well positioned as its East Asian competitors, this study argues that under a business-as-usual scenario—that is, no dramatic changes in policy—South Asia could substitute for some of the Chinese exports. Specifically, a 10 percent price increase in China would increase U.S. imports from South Asia by 13–25 percent, compared to 37–51 percent for those from Southeast Asia (see chapter 3).

The author, Yevgeniya Savchenko, is grateful for comments provided by the core team and for substantive inputs from Raymond Robertson, Amir Sadeghi, and Jyotinder Kaur. Raymond Robertson advised on theoretical and empirical estimation, and provided estimations for table 4.3. Amir Sadeghi conducted the literature survey and the empirical estimation of labor demand section (figures 4.2, 4.5, 4.6, table 4.2, 4.4, 4.5, 4B.1, 4.B2, 4E.1, 4F.1, 4F.2), as well as producing tabulations using establishment-level data. Jyotinder Kaur conducted an analysis of the Garment Firms Survey in Bangladesh (Box 4.1) and produced tabulations using establishment-level data.

The apparel and textile sector appears to be a natural avenue for South Asia to create jobs, especially for women. The sector is quite labor intensive—even more so than textiles, which is more capital, skill, and scale intensive, although it does not require substantial capital investments. In addition, the region has an abundant labor endowment, giving it a comparative edge in labor-intensive sectors. It also has a particularly large pool of potential female workers, reflecting the fact that the region has one of the world's lowest female labor participation rates—only 32 percent, compared to 58 percent in Latin America and the Caribbean, 62 percent in Europe and Central Asia, and 67 in East Asia (World Bank 2014c). Furthermore, the apparel sector is female intensive, meaning that, when the sector expands, formal sector opportunities for women become increasingly available.

Good jobs for development in South Asia would boost gross domestic product (GDP) and reduce poverty—and there will be ever-greater pressure to create these jobs as India's population continues to grow at a rapid pace. We know that labor income is a key contributor to poverty reduction and shared prosperity; in some cases, we can attribute more than half of poverty reduction to rising labor income (Azevedo et al. 2013; World Bank 2014b). Bringing more women into the labor force would increase household labor income and strengthen the region's economic growth (Aguirre et al. 2012; Cuberes and Teignier 2012), contributing to poverty reduction. An increase in female labor force participation (LFP) and employment could have potential implications not only for earnings—and therefore for the reduction of monetary poverty—but also for strengthening the role of women in society and for improving household health and education outcomes (Afridi, Mukhopadhyay, and Sahoo 2012; Anderson and Eswaran 2009; Jensen 2012; Kabeer et al. 2013; Luke and Munshi 2011; Sivansankaran 2014).

The big question is what type of impact higher textile and apparel exports from South Asia will have on the region's labor market. As apparel exports represent a major share of total exports in most South Asian countries, and exports represent a major share of apparel production in South Asia—in Bangladesh, 75 percent of apparel output is exported[1]—one could expect that labor demand in the apparel sector would be mainly driven by exports. Thus, we first estimate by how much the expansion in the textile and apparel[2] sector would increase labor demand in the region—that is, how many new jobs firms would create in response to higher exports. On the supply side, we investigate how more jobs or higher wages would reshape the labor pool. In other words, to what extent (what economists call the labor supply "elasticity") higher expected labor income would draw more women into the labor force.

Our main results—which focus on Bangladesh, India, Pakistan, and Sri Lanka—show that on the demand side, using output as a proxy for exports, a 1 percent increase in apparel output is associated with a 0.3–0.4 percent increase in employment (both for men and for women) in Bangladesh, Pakistan, and Sri Lanka. India's values are lower, at a 0.14 percent increase in demand for male workers and a 0.08 percent increase in demand for female workers. These results for South Asia are consistent with labor demand elasticities found in the literature.

On the supply side, we find that a 1 percent increase in the expected wage increases the likelihood of women joining the labor force by between 16 percent in Pakistan and 89 percent in Sri Lanka. We also find that a wage premium exists in the apparel sector compared to agriculture that ranges from 8 to 27 percent, depending on the country—a premium that is even higher when only women are considered. However, this premium stopped rising with the end of the Multifibre Arrangement (MFA) in 2005, raising questions about whether the region can hold on to its competitive edge.

South Asia's Textile and Apparel Labor Market

How would higher textile and apparel exports affect South Asia's labor market? We set out to answer this question by first getting a fix on the key characteristics of the region's labor market—on both the demand and the supply sides—as represented by our four sample South Asia (SAR) countries: India, Bangladesh, Pakistan, and Sri Lanka. For our analysis, we drew on information at the establishment level, industry level, and country level. The establishment data (microdata) provide details on output, foreign sales, employment, wages, and exports. Given that industry export data use six-digit Harmonized System (HS) codes—and we needed to line up this information with firms in various industries—we changed the HS codes to International Standard Industrial Classification (ISIC) codes. The macrodata are collected from the International Monetary Fund's International Financial Statistics website and industry-level export data are collected from the United Nations COMTRADE website. On the supply side, we use mainly household and labor force surveys (see annex 4A for a detailed description of data sources).

Labor Productivity, Informality, and Size

Productivity in the textile and apparel industry is typically lower than average labor productivity in other manufacturing industries—consistent with its high labor intensity. Countries in the region exhibit different trends over time, except for Pakistan for which time series data are not available. In Bangladesh, labor productivity in textile and apparel has been increasing since 2001. India exhibits exactly the opposite trend with labor productivity declining since 2001. In Sri Lanka, the productivity increased before 2005—the end of the MFA—and has been declining afterward (figure 4.1).

We also see that, although the share of temporary employees working in the textile and apparel sector is lower than in other sectors, it has increased over the past decade—and this group could serve as a proxy for informality since firms typically do not provide temporary workers with benefits.[3] Although the share of temporary workers increased in manufacturing overall in both Bangladesh and India, it was consistently lower in textile and apparel than in other industries (see figure 4.2). In Bangladesh, the share of temporary workers in apparel increased from a negligible number to approximately 5 percent between 2001 and 2012, although in manufacturing overall it increased from 4 to 14 percent. In India,

Figure 4.1 Labor Productivity of Apparel Declined in Most Countries Post-MFA
(Average Output per Worker at Establishment Level by Industry and Year in 2012 US$)

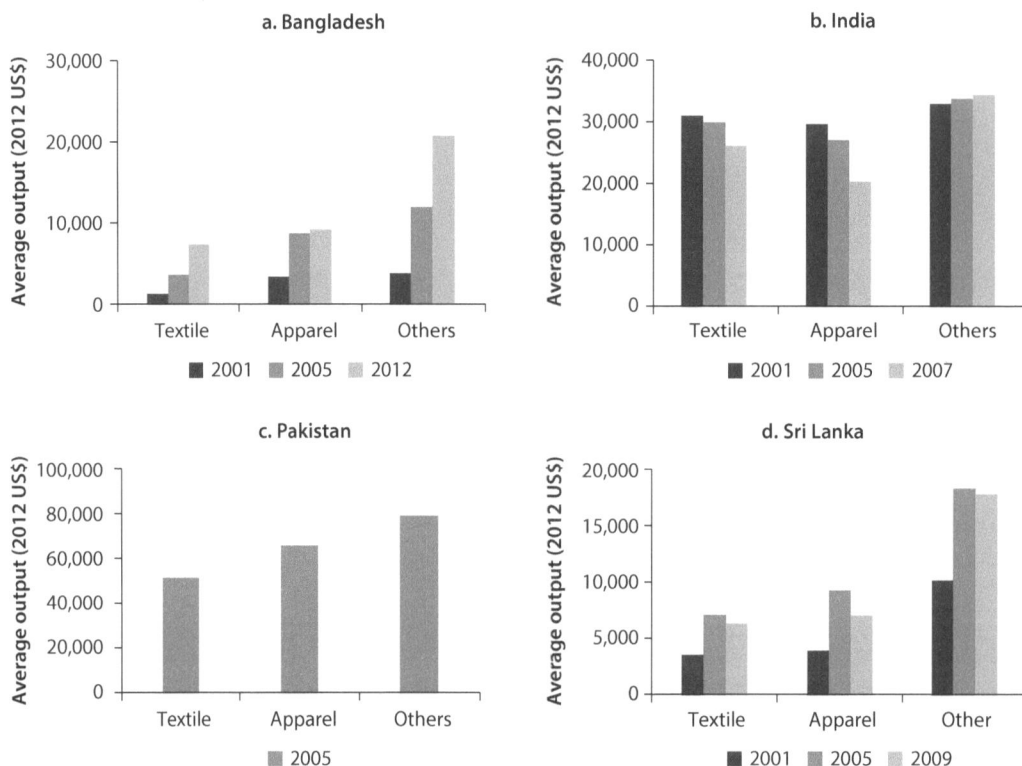

Source: World Bank calculations based on ASI (Annual Survey of Industries) and Census of Manufacturing Industries (CMI) establishment data, various years.
Note: To convert numbers into 2012 US$, first the current exchange rate was used to convert nominal values in local currency into nominal values in US$, then the numbers were deflated using 2012 US$ consumer price index (CPI).

the share of temporary workers in apparel increased from 8 to 10 percent between 2001 and 2011 (with a decrease from 13 to 10 percent between 2005 and 2011), but the overall share of temporary employment increased from 16 to 20 percent.

As for firm size, there are big differences among countries (annex 4B). Whereas in Bangladesh and Sri Lanka the majority of apparel firms are large, the majority in India and Pakistan are either small or medium. In addition, the male/female ratio in the apparel sector decreases with firm size in Bangladesh and Sri Lanka, but it goes up in India and Pakistan. However, in the textile sector, the male/female ratio goes up in all countries with the firm size. Finally, the permanent/temporary worker ratio increases with the firm size, which suggests that larger firms have the means to employ formal workers.

As for whether the exporting firms differ from those who are domestically oriented, unfortunately, the existing data are not very helpful. However, a World Bank survey of exporting apparel firms that was conducted in

Figure 4.2 Share of Temporary Workers Has Been Increasing over Time
(Share of Temporary Workers by Industry in Formal Manufacturing Firms)

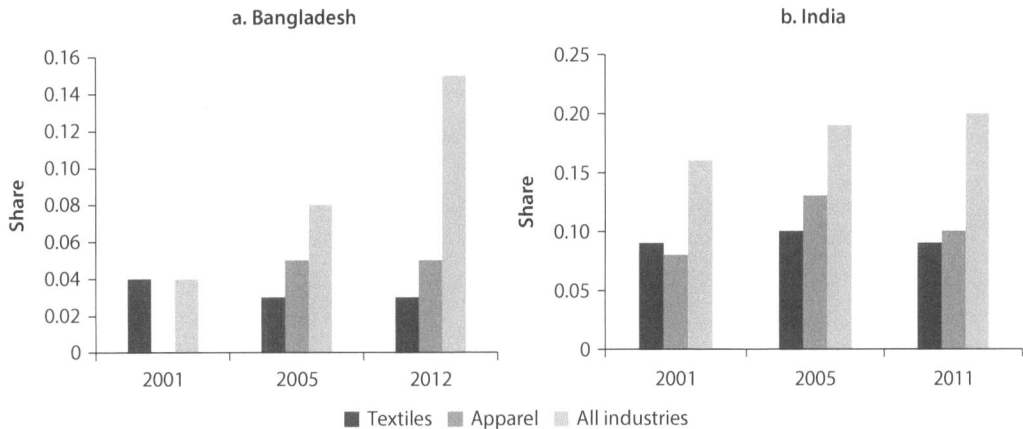

Source: World Bank calculations based on ASI (Annual Survey of Industries) and Census of Manufacturing Industries (CMI) establishment data, various years.

Bangladesh in 2011 allows us to characterize the sector as one that is made up of mostly large domestically owned firms, with a high level of female workers (box 4.1).

How Women Fare

South Asia is characterized by one of the lowest female LFP rates in the world—about 31.8 percent—which is almost two times lower than East Asia's 62.1 percent. However, the average masks great variations among the countries (figure 4.3). In Bangladesh, women are almost as likely to partici-pate in the labor force as in East Asia. Moreover, the female LFP was steadily increasing between 2000 (56.7 percent) and 2012 (60.2 percent). Although Pakistan's female LFP is the lowest in the region (25.4 percent in 2012), it has increased twofold from 1995. In Sri Lanka, the female LFP remained stable at about 40 percent during the period 1995–2012. In India, female LFP has been decreasing since 2005. Interestingly, India, Pakistan, and Sri Lanka have lower female LFP rates than expected for the countries at their respective per capita incomes (World Bank 2014a)—and it should be a major cause for concern given the increasing number of studies that underscore the vital role that women can play in raising economic growth and reducing poverty (see box 4.2).

Against this backdrop, perhaps not surprisingly, unemployment rates were higher for women (4.6 percent) than for men (3.3 percent) in 2012. We observed the largest differences in female and male unemployment rates in Pakistan (8.9 percent versus 4 percent) and Sri Lanka (7.4 percent versus 3.5 percent). The differences in Bangladesh and India were much smaller—5.2 versus 4 percent and 4 versus 3.1 percent, respectively.

Box 4.1 A Profile of Bangladeshi Apparel Exporters

The World Bank's 2011 Garment Firms Survey for Bangladesh, which focused on garment exporters, offers many insights into the makeup of this group. The key findings paint a picture of a European Union (EU)–focused sector that is female intensive and mostly domestically owned, with a number of export processing zones (EPZs). The survey included 1,018 woven garment firms (51 percent of these firms manufacture items such as pants and shirts) and knit-wear firms (52 percent of these firms produce items such as T-shirts and sweaters). It covered six broad geographical areas: Dhaka city, Chittagong city, Dhaka EPZ, Chittagong EPZ, the rural areas around Dhaka, and the urban areas around Dhaka.

The European Market and EPZs

For Bangladesh, the major market destination is the EU. For the sample as a whole, 58.9 percent of sales go to the EU whereas 33.5 percent go to the United States. Firms in most geographical locations tend to export more to the EU than to the United States, except for firms located in Chittagong city and Chittagong EPZ. Even though only a few firms are located in EPZs, they employ more workers and have higher sales than non-EPZ firms. Only 7 percent of sample firms are located in EPZs (3 percent in Dhaka and 4 percent in Chittagong). Although firms employing the most workers are mostly located in the Chittagong EPZ (with 2,022 workers per firm) and the least are in non-EPZ Dhaka city (with 663 workers per firm), the Dhaka EPZ firms have the largest sales (on average Tk 733.8 million), and Chittagong non-EPZ firms have the smallest sales (on average Tk 180.3 million).

Women and Domestic Ownership

In keeping with apparel sectors worldwide, the apparel sector in Bangladesh is female intensive (table B4.1.1). The average percentage of female workers employed per firm is 60.6 percent, with the highest female share in the two metro areas of Chittagong and Dhaka (63.7 percent) and the lowest share in the urban/suburban areas of Dhaka (56.8 percent). The wholly (100 percent) foreign-owned firms tend to have higher percentages of

Table B4.1.1 It Pays to Work for Foreign Firms
(Indicators across Ownership Type)

Ownership	Average female share (%)	Labor productivity 1	Labor productivity 2	Attrition rate (%)	Average wages (Tk per month)	Average benefits (Tk per month)	Average days of overtime per week
100% foreign owned	62.5	1,507.9	3,70,755.4	14.0	4,675.5	1,523.3	5.2
JV majority foreign owned	58.0	2,461.9	6,03,039.6	23.7	4,452.1	1,410.0	4.5
50-50 JV	59.1	2,789.5	6,51,494.1	17.3	5,645.1	1,270.6	4.2
100% locally owned	60.6	3,124.4	4,07,774.9	19.1	4,628.7	1,270.6	4.5

Source: World Bank calculations based on Bangladesh Garment Survey 2011.
Note: The attrition rate is defined as the number of people leaving the organization as a percentage of the total workforce at the end of the fiscal year. Labor productivity 1 is defined as the number of cloth pieces produced per worker per year. Labor productivity 2 is defined as sales in takas per unit worker per year. JV = Joint venture.

box continues next page

Box 4.1 A Profile of Bangladeshi Apparel Exporters *(continued)*

female workers, and these firms typically provide more benefits (such as health and childcare) than firms with other ownership patterns.

Most of the firms (about 91 percent) are domestically owned, with only 6 percent wholly foreign owned, and the rest being joint ventures between domestic and foreign entities. However, the majority of EPZ firms (65 percent) are wholly foreign owned. Foreign-owned firms have higher production volumes and better benefits than domestic firms. The average sales per firm for foreign-owned firms is Tk 600 million per year whereas that for wholly (100 percent) locally owned firms is about half this amount. Although the average wage provided by foreign-owned firms is not the highest, after accounting for benefits the compensation package is the highest for wholly foreign-owned firms. Foreign-owned firms also tend to have the lowest attrition rate at 14 percent compared to the 18.5 percent attrition rate for the sample as a whole and 19.1 percent for wholly (100 percent) domestically owned firms.

Figure 4.3 Still Lots of Room for Progress in Attracting Women Workers
(Percentage of female labor force participation, Age 15–64, 1995–2012)

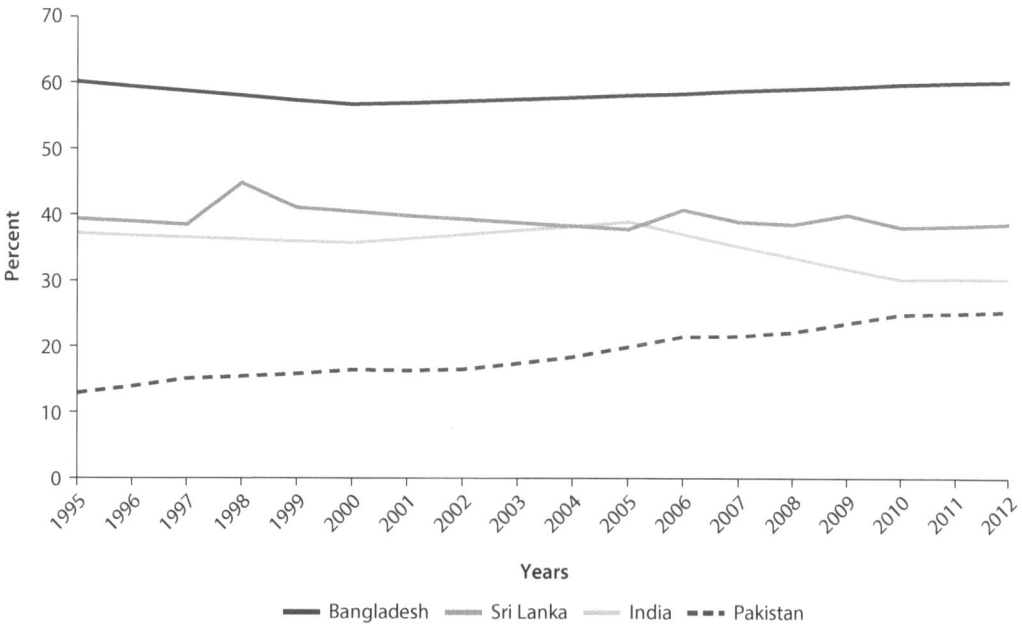

Source: World Development Indicators 2014.

Most women with jobs in South Asia work in agriculture, led by Pakistan (76 percent) and India (60 percent), with Sri Lanka only about 37 percent of women (figure 4.4). And both India and Pakistan (unlike Sri Lanka) have a higher proportion of women than men working in agriculture. Based on the experience of other countries—such as Mexico—a high proportion of women employed in agriculture could represent a potential workforce that is very likely to move to the apparel sector (Cardozo 2014).

Focusing in on the textile and apparel industry, its share of female employment is higher than in other manufacturing industries, ranging from 5 percent in Pakistan to 71 percent in Sri Lanka.[4] Although between 2001 and 2012 the share of female employment in apparel decreased from 61 to 52 percent in Bangladesh and from 26 to 18 percent in India, it remained stable in Sri Lanka (figure 4.5). We also see that the share of female employment in formal

---

Box 4.2 Why Focus on Women?

At the macroeconomic level, there is growing evidence that gender gaps in the labor market and low female labor force participation (LFP) rates have a major impact on the gross domestic products (GDP) of countries. One recent study finds that GDP per capita losses due to gender gaps in the labor market are as high as 27 percent in some regions (Cuberes and Teignier 2012). Another study estimates that raising the female LFP rates to country-specific male levels would raise the GDP in the United States by 5 percent, in Japan by 9 percent, in the United Arab Emirates by 12 percent, and in the Arab Republic of Egypt by 34 percent (Aguirre et al. 2012). A third study finds that countries with a comparative advantage in female labor–intensive goods are characterized by lower fertility (Do, Levchenko, and Raddatz 2014).

At the microeconomic level, some studies show that female LFP and employment is beneficial for a number of household indicators, including children's health and education and decision making about fertility and marriage.

- In India, a randomized experiment finds that an increase in labor market opportunities for women raised their LFP and their probability of going to school instead of getting married or having children, along with better nutrition and health investments for school-aged girls (Jensen 2012).
- Also in India, a recent study on women employed in the textile industry finds that those with a longer history of employment tended to delay marriage and have a lower desired fertility rate. Moreover, these effects had spillovers within the family—the younger sisters of women who worked in textiles also married later, and their younger brothers were less likely to drop out of school (Sivasankaran 2014).
- In Bangladesh, a study shows that the growth of the garments sector was associated with 0.27 percentage points increase in girls' school enrollment over 1983–2000—a more sizeable effect than a simultaneous supply side intervention of girls schooling subsidy (Heath and Mobarak 2012). Girls who live near a garment factory are 28 percent less likely to be married and 29 percent less likely to have given birth than those living in villages farther away from a factory.
- Also in Bangladesh, a recent study found that formally employed women had fewer children and possessed greater decision-making power over their own health expenses and formal savings (either through insurance or a bank account). (Kabeer et al. 2013).

box continues next page

Box 4.2 Why Focus on Women? *(continued)*

Figure B4.2.1 Working in Garments with Fewer Children
(Number of Children Ages 5 Years and Younger in a Household by Female Sector of Employment)

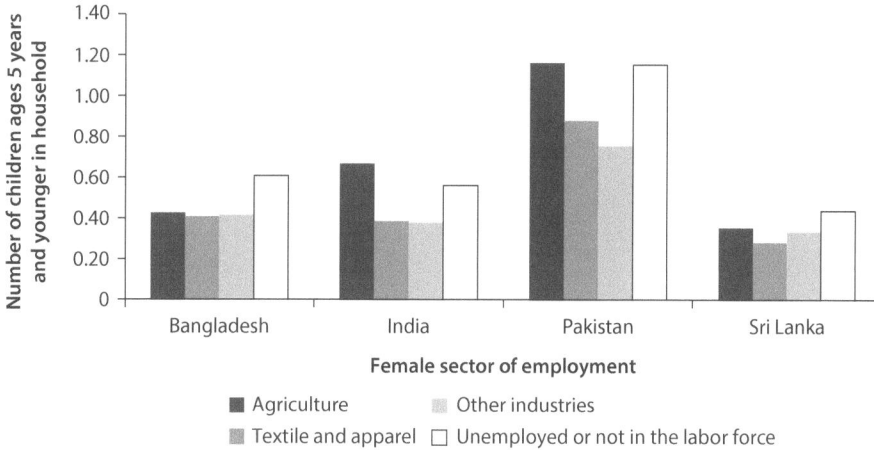

Female sector of employment

- Agriculture
- Other industries
- Textile and apparel
- Unemployed or not in the labor force

Source: World Bank estimation from household data.

Our own estimates confirm that South Asian households with women working, especially in the textile and apparel sector in India and Pakistan, tend to have fewer young children on average than women working in agriculture and women who are not in the labor force or are unemployed (figure B4.2.1). Also in Sri Lanka they spend almost twice as much (SLR 1,112) a month on education per student than households with women working in agriculture (SLR 657) (Sri Lanka household survey 2008).

Figure 4.4 Most Women Are Employed in Agriculture
(Percentage Distribution of Labor Force by Sector of Employment, 2012)

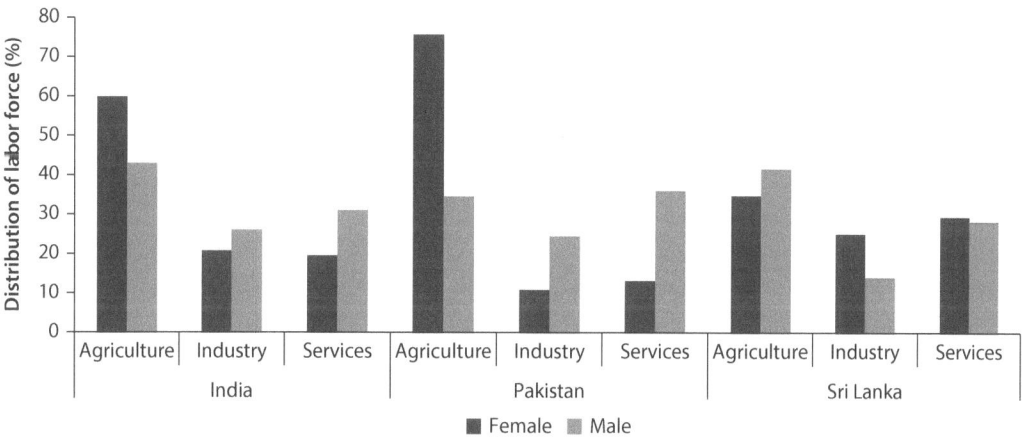

- Female
- Male

Source: World Development Indicators 2014.
Note: Data for Bangladesh were not available.

Stitches to Riches? • http://dx.doi.org/10.1596/978-1-4648-0813-5

Figure 4.5 Textile and Apparel Are the Most Female-Intensive Industries in South Asia
(Share of Female Employment by Industry in Formal Manufacturing Firms, Share)

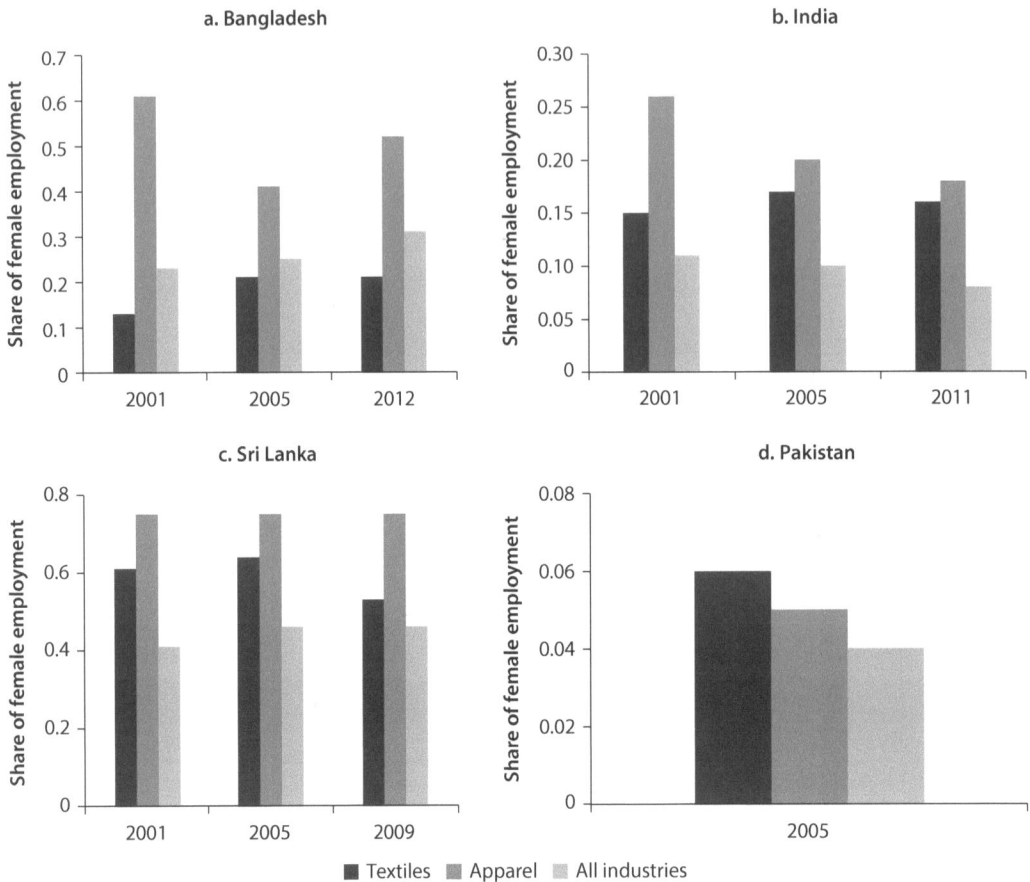

Textiles   Apparel   All industries

Source: World Bank calculations based on ASI (Annual Survey of Industries) and CMI establishment data, various years.

manufacturing increased over time in Bangladesh (from 23 to 31 percent) and Sri Lanka (from 41 to 46 percent), mostly driven by higher relative employment of women in the food and beverages industry. But in India the share of female employment in formal manufacturing declined (from 11 to 8 percent), possibly because women chose not to work as the country became wealthier. In Pakistan the share of female employment was the lowest in the region (4 percent).[5]

Similarly, the textile and apparel industry is the most female intensive—with women making up 71 percent of the workforce in Sri Lanka, 34 percent in Bangladesh, and 35 percent in India (table 4.1). Pakistan is the only country in South Asia where agriculture (35 percent) has a higher percentage of female workers than textiles and apparel (30 percent).[6] Additionally, in other industries

Table 4.1 Textiles and Apparel Has a Relatively High Share of Female Workers
(Share of Females, Earnings, and Average Years of Education by Sector, Various Years)

Industry	Share of females employed in each industry, percent	Monthly earnings, 2012 US$		Education, years	
		Women	Men	Women	Men
BANGLADESH (2010)					
Agriculture	8	29.22	58.88	3.05	1.38
Textiles and apparel	34	47.75	93.94	5.87	4.24
Other industries	12	79.07	108.01	5.87	5.92
INDIA (2010)					
Agriculture	31	54.22	106.07	3.58	6.48
Textiles and apparel	35	60.61	112.19	6.20	6.52
Other industries	14	212.68	235.79	8.47	9.13
PAKISTAN (2012)					
Agriculture	35	43.16	90.58	1.34	3.38
Textiles and apparel	31	46.96	125.43	3.33	6.48
Other industries	6	150.36	155.77	9.50	6.75
SRI LANKA (2012)					
Agriculture	37	65.55	90.19	7.05	7.35
Textiles and apparel	71	100.57	137.77	10.18	10.31
Other industries	27	138.48	147.47	10.60	9.51

Source: World Bank calculations based on household and labor force surveys.

across the region, the share of females in the workforce is substantially lower than in agriculture or apparel, varying from 6 percent in Pakistan to 27 percent in Sri Lanka. In general, women are less educated in South Asia then men, except in Sri Lanka. The most-educated women work in other industries, followed by textiles and apparel, then agriculture.

Labor Demand Analysis

Now that we have a good sense of South Asia's textile and apparel labor market, we can use this information to estimate how a higher demand for textile and apparel exports would affect the demand for labor overall and the specific types of workers needed. Although this study draws on the models already developed in the literature to estimate export elasticity of male and female labor demand, to our knowledge this is the first paper that uses South Asian data and focuses specifically on textiles and apparel.

To model labor demand, we modify the classic labor demand model (Hamermesh 1993) by controlling for structural differences in labor productivity related to the size of firms, capturing macro/global changes over time, and imposing the same cross-wage[7] elasticities (see annex 4C for details).

The following system of equations (4.1) is used to estimate the elasticities of labor demand:

$$\log\left(l_i^m\right) = \alpha_0^m + \alpha_1^m \log\left(w_i^m\right) + \alpha_2^m \log\left(w_i^f\right) + \alpha_3^m \log(y_i) + \alpha_4^m \, size_i + \alpha_5^m \, year + \varepsilon_i^m$$

$$\log\left(l_i^f\right) = \alpha_0^f + \alpha_1^f \log\left(w_i^m\right) + \alpha_2^f \log\left(w_i^f\right) + \alpha_3^f \log(y_i) + \alpha_4^f \, size_i + \alpha_5^f \, year + \varepsilon_i^f, \quad (4.1)$$

where labor input is heterogeneous with two types, male (l^m) and female (l^f). We assume that all factor prices, including wages for female (w_i^f) and male (w_i^m) workers, are exogenous. Also, we assume that all firms within an industry face the same prices for capital (r); in other words, none of the firms has a monopsony power in the input markets. As firms do not have a monopsony power and face the same price for capital inputs, we control for it using time dummies as a proxy. Time dummies would also capture macro and global changes over time that may not be necessarily controlled for by other variables in the model. Additionally, to control for structural differences in labor productivity related to size of firms and other inputs, we introduce an employment size dummy variable. The size dummies would also capture economies of scale that large firms might have compared to small and medium firms. Finally, we impose a symmetry constraint by assuming that cross-wage elasticity is the same in both equations, that is, $\alpha_2^m = \alpha_1^f$.

This model is similar in spirit to Grossman (1986), who proposes that intersectoral labor mobility is responsible for how import competition affects jobs.[8] His study is one of the first papers to look at how import competition impacts employment in the U.S. steel industry. It assumes that domestic steel is an imperfect substitute for imported steel and estimates the impact of the foreign price for steel on labor demand. The findings indicate that employment responds significantly to import competition and that wages are mostly unresponsive.

Our study follows nearly similar steps for building the model, although we focus on export rather than import competition. Along the same lines, Revenga (1997) studies the impact of trade liberalization on wages and employment in Mexico's manufacturing sector, and Currie and Harrison (1997) conduct a similar study for Morocco. Overall, as indicated in Rama (2003), the job-destruction and job-creation impact of trade is not yet conclusive—one of the gaps in the literature that this study tries to address by estimating the changes in male and female employment in response to potential changes in exports, with a focus on textile and apparel. In this model we use output as a proxy for exports, an assumption that seems reasonable given that, for most countries in the region, apparel firms are export oriented. Tables 4.2, 4.3, 4.4, and 4.5 present the results of the model estimations for different data subsamples in each country—all industries, textile only, and apparel only—under the business-as-usual scenario.[9]

Table 4.2 Labor Demand in Textiles and Apparel Is More Elastic Than in Other Sectors: Bangladesh
(Log Labor Demand Regressions Estimations for Male versus Female Workers, by Country, 2000 and 2010)

Bangladesh	All industries		Textile industry		Apparel industry	
	Male	*Female*	*Male*	*Female*	*Male*	*Female*
Log male wage	−0.137***	0.0268**	−0.348***	0.099***	−0.203***	0.144***
	(8.803)	(2.506)	(14.69)	(7.428)	(8.301)	(7.305)
Log female wage	0.027**	−0.179***	0.099***	−0.155***	0.144***	−0.324***
	(2.506)	(11.84)	(7.428)	(8.590)	(7.305)	(13.91)
Log output	0.230***	0.292***	0.407***	0.285***	0.311***	0.323***
	(45.48)	(45.04)	(41.44)	(23.83)	(41.73)	(45.63)
Small firm	−0.830***	−0.618***	−0.548***	−0.618***	−0.479***	−0.699***
	(40.47)	(23.39)	(15.18)	(13.76)	(10.76)	(16.53)
Large firm	0.636***	1.828***	0.374***	1.345***	0.669***	1.587***
	(28.81)	(64.25)	(8.497)	(24.46)	(17.96)	(44.81)
Constant	1.287***	0.099	1.373***	0.636***	−1.246***	−0.259
	(8.050)	(0.554)	(5.769)	(2.613)	(4.521)	(0.991)
Year dummy	Yes	Yes	Yes	Yes	Yes	Yes
Observations	10,656	10,656	3,278	3,278	5,228	5,228
R-squared	0.756	0.812	0.776	0.722	0.586	0.786

Z-statistics in parentheses; *** $p<0.01$, ** $p<0.05$, * $p<0.1$

Source: World Bank calculations using ASI (Annual Survey of Industries) establishment data of various years.
Note: Year 1998 and medium-size dummies are omitted. Years are 1995/96, 1997/98, 1999/2000, 2001/02, 2005/06, and 2012/13.

Wages and Labor Demand

Apparel labor demand is not very elastic. The labor demand curve in the textile and apparel sector is downward sloping—meaning that, as wages rise, fewer workers are demanded—and men and women are substitute labor inputs. Own-labor-wage elasticities in apparel and textile industries across all countries are negative, which is consistent with a downward sloping demand curve. In apparel a 1 percent increase in male wage is associated with a 0.06 percent (Sri Lanka) to 0.68 percent (Pakistan) decrease in male employment and a 0.01 percent (Sri Lanka) to 0.62 percent (Pakistan) decrease in female employment. The small size of this coefficient suggests that apparel labor demand across all the countries is not very elastic, with Sri Lanka having the lowest elasticity in the region. In textiles, the results are similar, except for in India where the change is bigger than in apparel for men and women.

Men and women are good substitutes. The cross-wage elasticities have a positive sign, which suggests that men and women are substitute factors across all industries including textiles and apparel—a 1 percent increase in male wage is associated with an increase in female employment in the range of 0.07 (0.09) percent in apparel (textiles) in Sri Lanka to 0.33 (0.28) percent in apparel (textiles) in Pakistan.[10] We also explore the importance of firm size in all countries. As expected, large firms have a more elastic—and

Table 4.3 Labor Demand in Textiles and Apparel Is More Elastic Than in Other Sectors: India
(Log Labor Demand Regressions Estimations for Male versus Female Workers, by Country, 2000 and 2010)

India	All industries		Textile industry		Apparel industry	
	Male	Female	Male	Female	Male	Female
Log male wage	−0.119***	0.001	−0.010***	−0.002	−0.120***	−0.030
	(9.595)	(0.228)	(2.814)	(0.0921)	(2.797)	(1.041)
Log female wage	0.001	−0.0754***	−0.002	−0.106***	−0.030	−0.139***
	(0.228)	(7.964)	(0.092)	(3.713)	(1.041)	(3.700)
Log output	0.158***	0.126***	0.137***	0.0772***	0.176***	0.172***
	(18.96)	(13.46)	(11.07)	(5.462)	(10.33)	(11.27)
Small firm	−0.390***	−0.395***	−0.555***	−0.541***	−0.568***	−0.506***
	(28.28)	(26.97)	(14.77)	(13.57)	(8.615)	(7.666)
Large firm	0.396***	0.440***	0.532***	0.557***	0.570***	0.651***
	(29.62)	(29.39)	(14.24)	(15.26)	(13.67)	(13.94)
Constant	1.604***		2.824***		2.231***	
	(13.13)		(10.10)		(6.379)	
Fixed effects	Yes		Yes		Yes	
Observations	156,102		25,388		12,630	
R-squared	0.146		0.170		0.228	

Z-statistics in parentheses; *** p<0.01, ** p<0.05, * p<0.1

Source: Calculations using ASI establishment data of various years.
Note: Each pair of male/female regression results was estimated as a single equation that included year dummy variables. Estimation (1) included industry dummy variables for textiles and apparel (separately) and their interactions with output. Year 1998 and medium-size dummy variables are omitted. Years are 1997/98–2007/08. All regressions also included firms-specific fixed effects.

small firms a less elastic—demand for both male and female workers than do medium-sized firms.

Output and Labor Demand

Textiles and apparel are more elastic than other sectors. There are great variations in labor demand elasticity with respect to output across different industries and countries. The elasticity varies from 0.13 percent in Pakistan to 0.26 percent in Sri Lanka for male labor demand and from 0.05 percent in Sri Lanka to 0.29 percent in Bangladesh for female labor demand. This suggests not only that labor demand is country specific but that it also probably depends on the industry composition in each country. The labor-output elasticities in the pooled industry group tend to be lower than those in textiles and apparel across all countries in South Asia. This supports the fact that textiles and apparel are labor-intensive industries, thus similar changes in output in textiles or apparel would lead to a larger change in labor demand in these sectors than in other industries.

Labor demand elasticity in apparel is similar across countries and gender in most of the South Asian countries. Our results show that a 1 percent increase in apparel output is associated with an increase in demand for male labor in a range between 0.31 percent (by moving from the mean of 48 percent to 48.3 percent)

Table 4.4 Labor Demand in Textiles and Apparel Is More Elastic Than in Other Sectors: Pakistan

(Log Labor Demand Regressions Estimations for Male versus Female Workers, by Country, 2000 and 2010)

Pakistan	All industries		Textile industry		Apparel industry	
	Male	Female	Male	Female	Male	Female
Log male wage	−0.540***	0.277***	−0.677***	0.277***	−0.676***	0.328***
	(33.47)	(21.14)	(11.89)	(5.231)	(17.23)	(9.855)
Log female wage	0.277***	−0.539***	0.277***	−0.653***	0.328***	−0.624***
	(21.14)	(39.23)	(5.231)	(12.91)	(9.855)	(18.66)
Log output	0.128***	0.108***	0.121***	0.115***	0.353***	0.336***
	(9.133)	(7.607)	(3.818)	(3.825)	(6.986)	(6.880)
Small firm	−0.690***	−0.681***	−0.957***	−0.838***	−0.439**	−0.355*
	(9.257)	(9.003)	(3.268)	(3.004)	(2.138)	(1.791)
Large firm	1.217***	1.224***	1.546***	1.465***	1.123***	1.097***
	(15.32)	(15.17)	(5.794)	(5.762)	(6.442)	(6.507)
Constant	3.053***	2.811***	3.615***	3.501***	0.824	0.729
	(17.32)	(15.89)	(5.875)	(5.980)	(1.390)	(1.277)
Year dummy	No	No	No	No	No	No
Observations	720	720	129	129	88	88
R-squared	0.780	0.711	0.692	0.644	0.813	0.837

Z-statistics in parentheses; *** $p<0.01$, ** $p<0.05$, * $p<0.1$

Source: World Bank calculations using Census of Manufacturing Industries (CMI) establishment data of 2005/06.
Note: Medium-size dummy is omitted. Year is 2005/06.

Table 4.5 Labor Demand in Textiles and Apparel Is More Elastic Than in Other Sectors: Sri Lanka

(Log Labor Demand Regressions Estimations for Male versus Female Workers, by Country, 2000 and 2010)

Sri Lanka	All industries		Textile industry		Apparel industry	
	Male	Female	Male	Female	Male	Female
Log male wage	−0.022***	0.081***	−0.050***	0.072***	−0.056***	0.094***
	(31.59)	(110.2)	(14.36)	(45.18)	(20.10)	(51.28)
Log female wage	0.081***	−0.034***	0.072***	−0.025***	0.094***	−0.014***
	(110.2)	(21.64)	(45.18)	(13.71)	(51.28)	(6.038)
Log output	0.264***	0.045***	0.249***	0.122***	0.380***	0.350***
	(81.53)	(9.567)	(29.15)	(13.63)	(44.20)	(45.53)
Small firm	−0.428***	−0.827***	−0.322***	−0.950***	−0.152***	−0.706***
	(28.08)	(39.08)	(6.967)	(19.62)	(3.336)	(19.38)
Large firm	0.629***	1.684***	0.953***	1.130***	0.666***	1.067***
	(42.07)	(80.59)	(18.97)	(21.44)	(16.52)	(29.74)
Constant	−2.689***	−1.322***	−1.571***	−0.478***	−4.757***	−3.627***
	(46.18)	(16.28)	(10.21)	(3.233)	(29.59)	(25.67)
Year dummy	Yes	Yes	Yes	Yes	Yes	Yes
Observations	20,027	20,027	3,410	3,410	4,401	4,401
R-squared	0.705	0.669	0.749	0.669	0.696	0.819

Z-statistics in parentheses; *** $p<0.01$, ** $p<0.05$, * $p<0.1$

Source: World Bank calculations using ASI establishment data of various years.
Note: year 1995 and medium-size dummies are omitted. Years are 1995–2009.

in Bangladesh and 0.38 percent in Sri Lanka (by moving the mean from 25 percent to 25.4 percent) and with an increase in demand for female labor in a range between 0.32 percent in Bangladesh (the move from the mean of 52 to 52.3 percent) and 0.35 percent in Sri Lanka (from mean of 75 percent to 75.3 percent). India's values are lower.[11] In India, a 1 percent increase in output is associated with a 0.14 percent increase in demand for male workers (by moving the mean from 82 to 82.14 percent) and with a 0.08 percent increase in demand for female workers (by moving the mean from 18 to 18.08 percent).

The textiles industry shows more elasticity for males than for females. Labor demand in textiles for male labor is more elastic than for female labor even though only India and Pakistan have a rich textile raw material base (for example, cotton). Our findings fit with the literature, which shows that the textiles industry tends to be less female intensive than the apparel industry. The output–male labor elasticity in textiles varies from 0.12 percent (Pakistan) to 0.41 percent (Bangladesh) and the output–female labor elasticity varies from 0.17 percent (India) to 0.29 percent (Bangladesh).

As for exports, in Bangladesh, the data allow us to differentiate between domestic and foreign sales. We find that the demand for female labor is more elastic in the apparel sector than the demand for male labor—a 1 percent increase in foreign sales is associated with a 0.04 percent increase in female labor and a 0.02 percent increase in male labor demand (figure 4.6).[12] Given that output-labor elasticities in Pakistan and Sri Lanka are similar in magnitude to those in Bangladesh, we could expect similar results for labor elasticities for foreign sales. Yet, in the Bangladesh textile sector, the demand for male labor is more elastic (0.04 percent) than the demand for female labor (0.03 percent).

Figure 4.6 Higher Apparel Demand Elasticity with Respect to Exports Bodes Well for Women

(Labor Elasticities in Bangladesh with Respect to a 1 Percent Change in Exports by Gender, Percent)

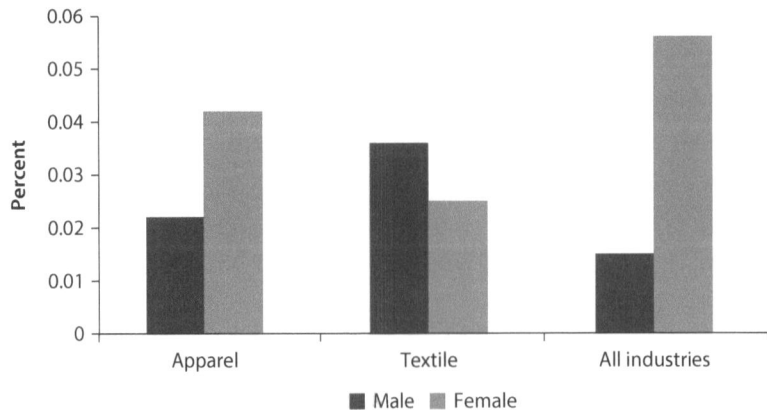

Source: World Bank calculations based on Bangladesh Establishment Surveys.
Note: Annex 4E provides detailed regression results.

Informality and Labor Demand

Labor-output elasticity is higher for permanent than for temporary workers.
In addition to investigating the changes in demand for labor by gender as a
response to changes in apparel exports, we would also like to understand the
effects of export changes on demand for formal and informal workers. We
could assume that a firm is deciding on a mix between two labor inputs such
as formal and informal labor. Informal workers could be proxied by temporary workers because typically firms do not have to provide temporary workers with benefits. Although hiring formal workers, proxied by permanent
employees, could be more expensive for a firm because it has to provide
permanent workers with benefits, the temporary workers could be less productive (Diaz-Mayans and Sanchez 2004). In Bangladesh and India[13] this
result holds for all industries as a whole, including textiles and apparel separately. This suggests that firms might consider it more profitable to hire
permanent and potentially more productive formal workers even if firms
have to pay higher wages rather than temporary and potentially less productive informal workers. In Bangladesh, the magnitudes of permanent labor–
output elasticity are higher for textiles and apparel than for all industries. In
India, however, these elasticities are about the same.

Wages matter more for textiles than apparel. In terms of own labor–wage
elasticities, Bangladesh and India do not behave in the same way. In India own
price elasticities are negative in the textile industry, implying that the demand
curves for both male and female are downward sloping. In Bangladesh, this is
true for permanent workers only; the demand curve for temporary workers is
upward sloping. In apparel, own price elasticities for permanent workers in
Bangladesh and India and temporary workers in Bangladesh are not statistically
different from zero, which could suggest that firms use other factors than the
wages in deciding on the permanent/temporary employee mix.

Labor Supply Analysis

Next, we turn to how higher exports in textiles and apparel might affect the
shape of the potential labor pool. To answer this question, we use standard
Mincer-type equations to establish whether a wage premium exists for working
in apparel (especially for women) rather than agriculture, which is a labor-
intensive low-skilled alternative. The reduced form of Mincer-type estimation
procedure is represented by equation (4.2) where W_i is wage of individual i;
age_i and age_i^2 are age and age squared; ind_{ji} is a set of industry of employment
dummies; $occup_{mi}$ is a set of occupation dummies; and ε_i are standard errors
(see details in annex 4D). We follow the Heckman two-step procedure to
account for selection (see details in annex 4D).

$$lnW_i = \beta_0 + \beta_1 age_i + \beta_2 age_i^2 + \beta_3 edu_i + \sum_j \delta_j ind_{ji} + \sum_m \lambda_m occup_{mi} + \varepsilon_i \qquad (4.2)$$

Then, following a classic labor supply model,[14] we explore whether expected higher wages—which could be induced by a greater availability of jobs in apparel in response to an increase in apparel exports—would attract more women into the labor force (see annex 4D for details on our methodology). Although Klasen and Pieters (2012) use India data to estimate the female labor supply, we believe that this is the first study to do this exercise for the region.

Wages and the Labor Supply

A persistent large female-male wage differential exists in the region. In 2012, women were paid between 31 percent (India) and 64 percent (Bangladesh) less than men holding other factors, such as education, age, occupation, and industry of employment, constant (table 4.6). The gap has been widening in all countries in South Asia since the mid-1990s, except in India and Sri Lanka where the gap narrowed between 2005 and 2012.

The wage premium for working in textile and apparel compared to agriculture has stopped rising after the MFA. Our results show that the premium rose until 2005 (when the MFA ended), but by 2010–2012 it narrowed (Sri Lanka) or was not statistically different from wages in agriculture (India and Pakistan). Only in Bangladesh did people working in textiles and apparel receive statistically significantly higher wages than in agriculture. These findings resonate with those in chapter 2 on trends in apparel exports. While Bangladesh and Pakistan have been increasing their global market share pre- and post-MFA, Sri Lanka and India have not done so. We also see that to the extent that these wage premiums existed, or still exist, it is the women who have benefited the most. The decline in those wage premiums might make the sector less attractive for women and have implications for female LFP.

Wages in urban areas for the overall population were higher than in rural areas. Indeed, the urban-rural wage differential ranged from 9.9 percent (Pakistan 2012) to 19.8 percent (Bangladesh 2010) (table 4.7). This differential was even higher for women than for men—for example, ranging from 10.3 percent in Bangladesh and Pakistan to 26.6 percent in India.

Table 4.6 Women Still Making Less Than Men in South Asia
(Female-Male Wage Gap Differential over Time, Percent)

	1995	2000	2005	2012
Bangladesh	n.a.	−58	−63	−64
India	−32	−33	−38	−31
Pakistan	−36	−40	−40	−45
Sri Lanka	−16	−32	−44	−41

Source: World Bank calculations using household and labor force surveys of different years.
Note: The wage gap differentials are calculated as follows: 100*(exp(β_f)1) where β_f is an estimated coefficient of the female dummy variable. Bangladesh—the last column is 2010; India—the first column is 1994, second is 2001, last is 2010; Pakistan—first column is 1996, second is 2001; Sri Lanka—first column is 1996, third is 2006. n.a. = Not applicable.

Table 4.7 City Workers Fare Better Than Rural Workers
(Urban-Rural Wage Differential over Time, Percent)

	1995	2000	2005	2012
Bangladesh	n.a.	26.0	10.5	19.8
India	19.4	21.5	19.6	18.6
Pakistan	12.7	15.3	12.0	9.9
Sri Lanka	27.6	26.4	17.4	15.3

Source: World Bank calculations using household and labor force surveys of various years.
Note: The wage gap differentials are calculated as follows: 100*(exp(β_f)1) where β_f is an estimated coefficient of the female dummy variable. Bangladesh—the last column is 2010; India—the first column is 1994, second is 2001, last is 2010; Pakistan—the first column is 1996, second is 2001; Sri Lanka—first column is 1996, third is 2006. n.a. = Not applicable.

Higher wages would draw more women into the labor force. We consider a classic static labor supply model (Blundell and MaCurdy 1999; Hausman 1980) the reduced form of which is represented by equations (4.3–4.4) (see detailed description of the model in annex 4D):

$$LFP_i = I\left(H_i \geq 0\right) \tag{4.3}$$

$$H_i = \beta_0 + \beta_1 lnW_i + \beta_2 N_i + \beta_3 X_i + \varepsilon_i \tag{4.4}$$

where LFP_i =1 if a person participates in the labor force, H_i represents hours worked, W_i is an individual hourly wage rate, X_i represents individual characteristics, and ε_i is an error term, which has a standard normal distribution.

We observe wages, W_i, only for those who participate in the labor force. Following Hausman (1980) and Klasen and Pieters (2012), we estimate a wage model using the Heckman-selection procedure (Heckman 1978) for which the selection correction equation includes age, age squared, years of education, and a series of dummies for marital status.

$$lnW_i = \beta_0 + \beta_1 age_i + \beta_2 age_i^2 + \beta_3 edu_i + \varepsilon_i \tag{4.5}$$

Using the estimates from equation (4.5), we predict $ln\hat{W}_i$ for the whole sample and estimate equations (4.3) and (4.4) in which X_i includes marital status, education, household size, education of household head, number of children between the ages of 0 and 5 and between the ages of 6 and 18, and the rural/urban location dummy.

The estimation results of the model described above suggest that an increase in LFP of women associated with an increase in expected wages was the highest in Sri Lanka, followed by Bangladesh, India, and Pakistan. Our results show that a 1 percent increase in expected wages is associated with an 89 percent increase in probability of female LFP in Sri Lanka, 31 in Bangladesh, 19 in India, and 16 in Pakistan.[15] These results are consistent with a very elastic labor demand. In many developing countries, including those in the sample SAR countries, the labor markets are characterized by surplus labor. This means that increases in labor demand would result in a very large increase in employment with a small

Table 4.8 Wages Still Matter, but They Matter Less
(Marginal Effects of Female Labor Participation with Respect to Log Expected Wage)

	1995	2000	2005	2012
Bangladesh	n.a.	1.646***	0.141***	0.306***
India	0.551***	0.426***	0.410***	0.189***
Pakistan	0.085***	0.194***	0.188***	0.163***
Sri Lanka	1.011***	0.939***	0.696***	0.892***

Source: World Bank calculations using household and labor force surveys of various years.
Note: Bangladesh—the last column is 2010; India—the first column is 1994, second is 2001, last is 2010; Pakistan—the first column is 1996, second is 2001; Sri Lanka—first column is 1996, third is 2006.
n.a. = Not applicable.

increase in wages. But we also found that, over the past decade, earnings have become a less important motivator for women to join the labor force (table 4.8).

Why might this be happening? One possible explanation is that for cultural reasons, especially in conservative societies, women are choosing not to join the labor force (see World Bank 2014a). Another reason is related to the U-shaped hypothesis, which suggests that there is a U-shaped relationship between female LFP and economic development (structural shifts in economic activity and changes to household labor supply and attitudes about women working outside the home) (Goldin 1995; Verick 2014). The female participation rates are the highest in poor countries (where women are engaged in subsistence activities), fall in middle-income countries (because of the transition of [mainly] men to industrial jobs), and increase in countries where female education levels are rising, fertility drops, and a growth in services opens up opportunities for women. Thus, as growth in South Asian countries accelerates and countries move to middle income status, women might drop out of the labor force because their spouses could support the whole family. More recent evidence from India suggests that these supply-side explanations may not capture the full story, and that declining female LFP may be partially explained by the collapse in the number of farming jobs without a parallel emergence of other employment opportunities considered suitable for women (Chatterjee, Murgai and Rama 2015). Other factors might be poor transportation to work, bad working conditions, and a lack of institutions for early childhood education.

Low-skilled women are typically more likely to increase their labor force participation compared to highly skilled women (figure 4.7). This suggests that the female labor supply curve is quite elastic, especially for low-skilled women. For example, a 1 percent increase in female wages is associated with a 94 percent increase in probability of low-skilled women being in the labor force as compared to a 62 percent increase in probability for high-skilled in Sri Lanka, 113 percent for low-skilled and 21 for high-skilled in Bangladesh, 24 for low-skilled and 12 for high-skilled in Pakistan. Only in India is the probability increase higher for high-skilled women (21) than for low skilled (12). Because apparel is a relatively low-skilled industry, employment opportunities in apparel that pay more than agriculture could potentially draw nonparticipating women into the labor force.

Encouragingly, international evidence suggests that textiles and apparel are a big draw for low-skilled women whose alternative is agriculture or the

Figure 4.7 Higher Wages Could Especially Draw Low-Skilled Women
(Marginal Effects of Female Labor Participation with Respect to Log Expected Wage by Skill Type, 2012 or Closest Year)

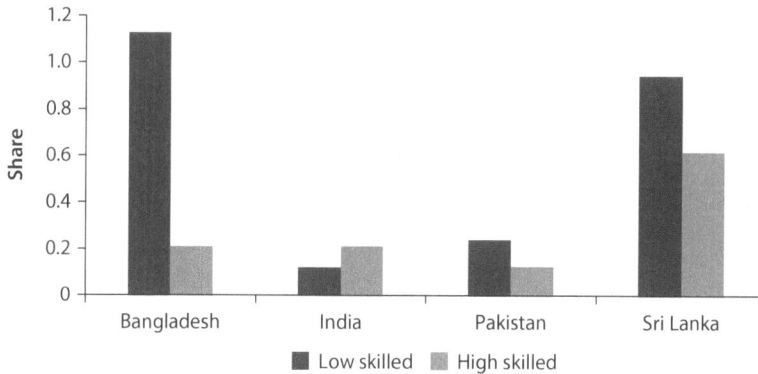

Source: World Bank calculations based on household and labor force surveys of various years.

informal sector. For example, a recent study on Mexico found that between 2005 and 2013 manufacturing was the main economic activity that attracted poor female workers from the agricultural sector (a probability between 4.05 percent and 13.43 percent) (figure 4.8). And, within manufacturing, about half of the women were employed in the textiles and apparel branch.

While the overall level of education decreases the probability of female labor force participation in all countries, education level boosts labor force participation for highly skilled but not low-skilled women. Our estimates suggest that an additional year of education decreases the probability of female LFP in South Asia in the range of 1 percent (India and Pakistan) to 7 percent (Sri Lanka) (figure 4.9). However, when we break this group down by skills, we find that more education draws highly skilled women into the labor force, although the opposite occurs with the low skilled. Furthermore, a more-educated head of a household is negatively associated with the probability of female LFP (see annex 4H for details). These findings are consistent with Klasen and Pieters (2012), who conclude that education becomes a pull factor drawing women at the highest education levels to the labor force. They are also consistent with the U-shaped female LFP hypothesis, which predicts that, as education levels improve and fertility rates fall, women are able to join the labor force in response to growing demand in the services sector (Verick 2014).

Whether women work also depends on location and family. Certainly, women living in urban areas are less likely to participate in the labor force than those in rural areas, and this generally holds for both highly skilled and low-skilled women. A possible explanation is that women in rural areas are driven by the economic necessity to join the labor force (Klasen and Pieters [2013] find similar effects in India). Single women are more likely to work than married, divorced, or widowed women—the main exceptions include divorced women in Bangladesh and India and widowed women (especially those who are low skilled) in Pakistan

Figure 4.8 From Agriculture to Textiles and Apparel in Mexico
(Probability of Transitioning from Agriculture to Other Economic Sectors)

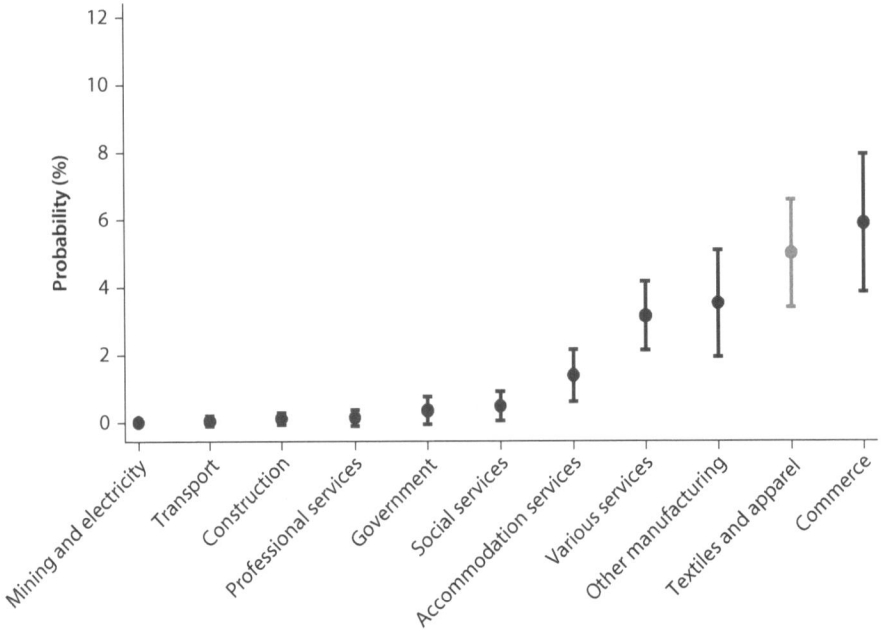

Source: ENOE (2005–2013) processed by the World Bank.
Note: The sample is restricted to women in Mexico who were employed in the primary sector and reported living in a labor-poor rural household during the initial period. The upper and lower bounds were computed using one standard deviation from the average probability of transiting to a specific sector.

Figure 4.9 More Education Especially Motivates Highly Skilled Women
(Marginal Effects of Female Labor Participation with Respect to Education by Skill Type, 2012 or the Closest Year)

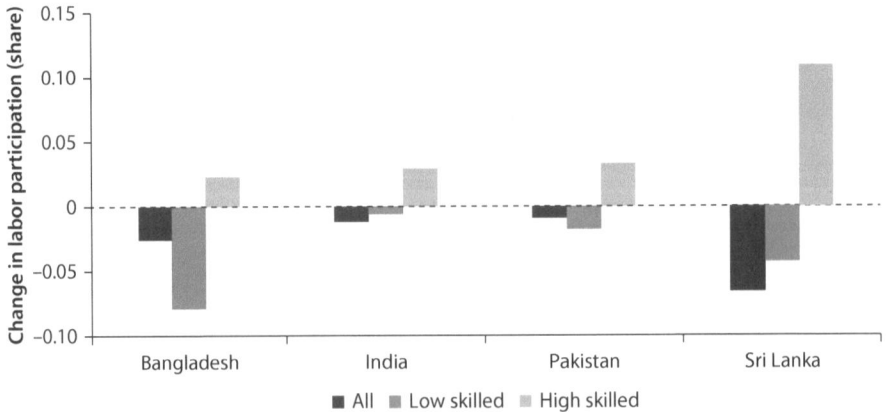

Source: World Bank calculations based on household and labor force surveys of various years.

and to some extent in Bangladesh. Finally, the larger the household size (that is, the higher the number of children), the more likely it is that women will not join the labor force in Pakistan and Sri Lanka, although the opposite is true in India and the results are mixed in Bangladesh (see annex 4H for details).

Matching More Jobs with Workers

In our attempt to answer how higher textile and apparel exports will trigger more job creation and reshape the labor force—especially by sharply boosting the share of women in the labor force, which in South Asia is relatively low—we have undertaken a careful analysis of the region's labor market dynamics.

On the demand side, we find that elasticity with respect to exports is larger in textile and apparel exports than in other industries. In other words, the textile and apparel sector has a larger potential than other industries for job generation in response to an increase in exports. The magnitude of labor demand elasticities for the majority of South Asian countries, except for India where elasticities are lower, is in line with what is found in the literature. We also find that the export elasticity of labor demand in this sector is higher for female workers relative to male workers, which suggests that women are more likely to benefit from the jobs that are generated.

On the supply side, we show that female labor, especially low-skilled labor, is very responsive to higher wages. The magnitudes of the coefficients are consistent with those found in other studies, for example Klasen and Pieters (2013). In South Asia, wage premiums exist for working in textiles and apparel compared to agriculture, which means that, if countries in the region generate more jobs in this sector, they could potentially increase the expected wages for women and, consequently, raise their LFP. We find that wage premiums in the textile and apparel industry compared to agriculture have declined after the end of the MFA in South Asia. If this trend continues, the firms might find it difficult to attract workers into this section.

We are now in a position to tackle a key objective of this report: estimating the potential number of jobs that South Asia could generate through greater apparel exports as China's prices rise. That will be the focus of the next chapter, along with exploring what the findings of this report mean for policy makers.

Annex 4A: Data Description

Labor Demand

This study requires a dataset with establishment-level, industry-level, and country-level information. The establishment data (microdata) are necessary because we needed the most detailed output, foreign sales, employment, and wage data to estimate reliable industry-specific coefficients. As explained in the theoretical foundation section, we also needed the most disaggregated industry

---

The section on labor demand was prepared by Amir Sadeghi.

Stitches to Riches? • http://dx.doi.org/10.1596/978-1-4648-0813-5

export data for our estimations. We required a GDP deflator and information on the consumer price index and exchange rate to deflate the nominal variables and change the U.S. dollar export values to local currency. Furthermore, industry export data use six-digit HS codes. To line up this information with firms in various industries, we changed the HS codes to ISIC codes. The macrodata are collected from the International Monetary Fund's International Financial Statistics website and industry-level export data are collected from the United Nations (UN) COMTRADE website.

The establishment data for each of our sample countries—India, Bangladesh, Pakistan, and Sri Lanka—come from that country's Bureau of Statistics and are not freely available. For India, we use ten rounds of the Annual Survey of Industries (ASI) (1997/98–2007/08). Our ASI data are panel data; however, when country-specific data are pooled, we could not maintain the panel feature of the India data and, therefore, we demeaned the India data before merging them with data from other countries. For Pakistan, we were able to obtain only the 2005/06 round from the census of manufacturing industries.[16] The Sri Lanka ASI spans the period 1995–2009 and is cross-sectional. For Bangladesh, we use the Survey of Manufacturing Industries (SMI) for 1995/96, 1997/98, 1999/2000, 2001/02, 2005/06, and 2012/13. These data are also cross-sectional. Since the establishment data are not harmonized, and the data for each country come from a different source, some of the data do not include information about temporary workers. For the same reason, some of the data do not have survey weights. Also the firms in the Indian panel have various weights over time.

Another issue with the establishment data was that each country used different industry codes. Although all four countries adopted ISIC codes to classify their economic activities, ISIC has different revisions. To merge different years of data, we used concordance tables available from the UN Statistics Division.[17] The final version of data used for this study came from four-digit ISIC Rev.3.1. Based on the ISIC Rev. 3.1 specification that the manufacturing sector comes under the range of 15–37 two-digit codes, we determined that any firm outside of this range is a mistake and deleted it. Furthermore, we assumed all of the datasets we used contained only formal firms, those with ten or more employees. Thus, all firms that have fewer than ten employees are also deleted.

Labor Supply

This section uses mainly household and labor force surveys. Household and labor force surveys provide information about individual labor market outcomes (LFP, employment, and earnings), education, and other individual and household-level variables. These surveys are available for the following years: Bangladesh—Household Income and Expenditure Survey (HIES) 2000, 2005, and 2010; India—National Sample Survey (NSS) employment and unemployment (schedule 10 and 10.2) 1993–1994, 1999–2000, 2004–2005, 2007–2008, and 2009–2010; Pakistan—Labor Force Surveys (LFS) 1995–2012; and Sri Lanka—Labor Force Surveys (LFS) 1995–2002, 2004, 2006, 2008, 2011, and 2012. Additionally, we supplement these data with World Development Indicators.

Annex 4B: Firm Distribution, Male/Female, and Permanent/Temporary Employment Ratios by Industry and Size

Table 4B.1 Firm Distribution by Size

	a. Bangladesh					b. India			
	Small	Medium	Large	Total		Small	Medium	Large	Total
Textile	87.34	5.63	7.03	100	Textile	63.24	14.12	22.64	100
	46.31	20.36	15.09	38.05		6.67	8.56	11.3	7.61
Apparel	28.98	6.92	64.09	100	Apparel	54.29	17	28.71	100
	6.41	10.44	57.37	15.86		1.61	2.9	4.03	2.14
Others	73.62	15.79	10.59	100	Others	73.36	12.32	14.32	100
	47.28	69.2	27.54	46.09		91.72	88.54	84.67	90.24
Total	71.76	10.52	17.72	100	Total	72.18	12.56	15.26	100
	100	100	100	100		100	100	100	100

	c. Sri Lanka					d. Pakistan			
	Small	Medium	Large	Total		Small	Medium	Large	Total
Textile	66.77	11.52	21.7	100	Textile	48.38	11.91	39.71	100
	25.02	9.21	11.11	17.03		14.57	24.27	39.36	20.75
Apparel	17.11	13.82	69.08	100	Apparel	46.93	19.33	33.74	100
	8.28	14.25	45.63	21.98		3.47	9.68	8.22	5.1
Others	49.68	26.73	23.59	100	Others	76.13	9.07	14.8	100
	66.7	76.54	43.26	61		81.96	66.05	52.43	74.16
Total	45.43	21.3	33.27	100	Total	68.89	10.18	20.93	100
	100	100	100	100		100	100	100	100

Source: World Bank calculations using ASI (Annual Survey of Industries) and CMI (Census of Manufacturing Industries) establishment data of various years.

Table 4B.2 Average Male, Female, and Temporary Workers, by Industry and Size

	a. Male/female employment ratio				b. Permanent/temporary employment ratio			
Bangladesh	Industry/size	Small	Medium	Large	Industry/size	Small	Medium	Large
	Textile	3.5	4.1	7.8	Textile	3.1	7.1	31.2
	Apparel	2.7	2.8	0.5	Apparel	5.9	22.2	75.9
	Others	3.3	6.3	12.9	Others	1.8	3.6	6.8
India	Industry/size	Small	Medium	Large	Industry/size	Small	Medium	Large
	Textile	2.3	3.9	27.6	Textile	2.9	3.3	10.3
	Garment	4.0	6.4	5.2	Garment	2.5	2.1	3.7
	Others	2.7	5.6	19.5	Others	1.7	1.8	2.9
Sri Lanka	Industry/size	Small	Medium	Large				
	Textile	1.2	1.4	2.5				
	Apparel	1.1	0.9	0.4				
	Others	4.1	4.9	7.7				
Pakistan	Industry/size	Small	Medium	Large				
	Textile	6.0	7.5	29.7				
	Garment	4.9	3.8	27.0				
	Others	4.2	6.5	27.2				

Source: World Bank calculations using ASI (Annual Survey of Industries) and CMI (Census of Manufacturing Industries) establishment data of various years.

Annex 4C: Labor Demand Model and Empirical Estimation Strategy

This section provides a theoretical foundation for the reduced-form equation system we used for our estimations. We consider a standard labor-demand model (Hamermesh 1993) and assume that a firm has the production function seen in equation (4C.1):

$$y = f(z), \tag{4C.1}$$

where z is a nonnegative vector of input levels, $f(\cdot)$ represents a production technology, and y represents the amount of output. A firm can reach its maximum profit by minimizing its costs, which is referred to as the dual problem. Defining $w \gg 0$ as the vector of input prices, the constrained cost-minimization problem takes the form seen in equation (4C.2):

$$\min_{z \geq 0} w \cdot z \ s.t. \ f(z) \geq y, \tag{4C.2}$$

where the constraint is to keep output at a constant level while the cost of input is minimized. The first-order conditions from the cost minimization problem above are used to derive a *cost function c(w,y)*. Assuming that the derived cost function is differentiable, Shephard's lemma proposes that the demand for input z is a derivative of the cost function with respect to input z's price (labor wage in our model) as seen in equation (4C.3):

$$z(w,y) = \nabla_w c(w,y), \tag{4C.3}$$

where $z(w,y)$ is known as a *conditional factor demand function* because the derived factor demand depends on the amount of output, y.

Assume that each product is produced using two inputs—labor (*l*) and capital (*k*)—and that the labor input is heterogeneous with two types—male (*l^m*) and female (*l^f*). After taking logs, the reduced-form system of equations for heterogeneous labor demand for firm i is equation (4C.4):

$$\log(l_i^j) = \alpha_0^j + \alpha_1^j \log(w_i^m) + \alpha_2^j \log(w_i^f) + \alpha_3^j \log(r) + \alpha_6^j \log(y_i), \tag{4C.4}$$

where $j \in (m, f)$, r, is the price for capital. We assume that all factor prices, including wages for female and male workers, are exogenous.[18] Also, we assume that all firms within an industry face the same prices for capital (r); in other words, none of the firms has a monopsony power in the input markets.

As firms do not have a monopsony power and face the same price for capital inputs, we control for it using a time dummy as a proxy. Time dummies would also capture macro and global changes over time that may not be necessarily controlled for by other variables in the model. Additionally, to control for structural differences in labor productivity related to size of firms and other inputs,

---

This annex was prepared by Amir Sadeghi.

we introduce an employment size dummy variable.[19] The size dummies would also capture economies of scale that large firms might have compared to those that are small and medium. Finally, we impose a symmetry constraint by assuming that cross-wage elasticity is the same in both equations, that is, $\alpha_2^m = \alpha_1^f$. As a result, the following system of equations (4C.5 and 4C.6) is used to estimate the elasticities of labor demand:

$$\log\left(l_i^m\right) = \alpha_0^m + \alpha_1^m \log\left(w_i^m\right) + \alpha_2^m \log\left(w_i^f\right) + \alpha_3^m \log\left(y_i\right)$$

$$+ \alpha_4^m \, size_i + \alpha_5^m \, year + \varepsilon_i^m \tag{4C.5}$$

$$\log\left(l_i^f\right) = \alpha_0^f + \alpha_1^f \log\left(w_i^m\right) + \alpha_2^f \log\left(w_i^f\right) + \alpha_3^f \log\left(y_i\right)$$

$$+ \alpha_4^f \, size_i + \alpha_5^f \, year + \varepsilon_i^f \tag{4C.6}$$

We estimate the system of equations (4C.5 and 4C.6) using the seemingly unrelated regressions (SUR) method introduced by Zellner (1962) for each country separately.[20] In India, where panel data are available, we also include firm-level fixed effects into the SUR estimation.

Annex 4D: Labor Supply Model

We consider a classic static labor supply model (Blundell and MaCurdy 1999; Hausman 1980) and assume that individuals have a quasi-concave utility function:

$$U\left(C_i, L_i, X_i\right) \tag{4D.1}$$

In equation (4D.1) C_i, L_i, and X_i are an individual's i consumption, leisure hours, and vector of individual attributes. Utility is maximized subject to a budget constraint seen in equation (4D.2)

$$C_i = N_i + W\left(T - L_i\right), \tag{4D.2}$$

in which W is an hourly wage rate, N_i is a nonlabor income (asset income and other unearned income), T is the total time available, and a single consumption good is taken as a numeraire. The first-order conditions in equations (4D.3) and (4D.4) take the form

$$U_c\left(C_i, L_i, X_i\right) = \lambda_i \tag{4D.3}$$

$$U_L\left(C_i, L_i, X_i\right) \geq \lambda_i W, \tag{4D.4}$$

in which λ_i is a marginal utility of income. If the inequality in (4D.4) strictly holds, then the individual is not working, and $T = L_i$. The wage, W_R, such that

$U_L(C_i, L_i, X_i) = \lambda_i W_R$, is the reservation wage below which the individual will not work.

The reduced form of a labor-force participation decision can be specified as

$$LFP_i = I(H_i \geq 0) \tag{4D.5}$$

$$H_i = \beta_0 + \beta_1 lnW_i + \beta_2 N_i + \beta_3 X_i + \varepsilon_i, \tag{4D.6}$$

in which $LEP_i = 1$ if a person participates in the labor force, $H_i = T - L_i$, and represents hours worked, and ε_i is an error term, which has a standard normal distribution.

We observe wages, W_i, only for those who participate in the labor force. Following Hausman (1980) and Klasen and Pieters (2012), we estimate a wage model using the Heckman-selection procedure (Heckman 1978) for which the selection correction equation includes age, age squared, years of education, and a series of dummies for marital status.

$$lnW_i = \beta_0 + \beta_1 age_i + \beta_2 age_i^2 + \beta_3 edu_i + \varepsilon_i \tag{4D.7}$$

Using the estimates from equation (4D.7), we predict $ln\hat{W}_i$ for the whole sample and estimate equations (4D.5) and (4D.6) in which X_i includes marital status, education, household size, education of household head, number of children between the ages of 0 and 5 years and between the ages of 6 and 18, and the rural/urban location dummy. This estimation would make it possible to assess how much LFP could be affected by a change in the expected reservation wage.

To estimate the apparel wage premiums, we use a Mincer-type estimation procedure as described by equation (4D.8) by including industry and occupation dummies. We follow the Heckman two-step procedure, as described above, to account for selection:

$$lnW_i = \beta_0 + \beta_1 age_i + \beta_2 age_i^2 + \beta_3 edu_i + \sum_j \delta_j ind_{ji} + \sum_m \lambda_m occup_{mi} + \varepsilon_i. \tag{4D.8}$$

Annex 4E: Log Labor Demand Regressions Estimations for Male versus Female Workers with Foreign and Domestic Output, Bangladesh

Table 4E.1 Log Labor Demand Regressions, Male versus Female Workers

Bangladesh Variables	All industries		Textile industry		Apparel industry	
	Male	Female	Male	Female	Male	Female
Log male wage	−0.031*	0.074***	−0.143***	0.035**	−0.020	0.277***
	(1.781)	(6.477)	(5.473)	(2.368)	(0.626)	(10.85)
Log female wage	0.074***	−0.066***	0.035**	−0.063***	0.277***	−0.144***
	(6.477)	(4.336)	(2.368)	(3.408)	(10.85)	(4.975)

table continues next page

Table 4E.1 Log Labor Demand Regressions, Male versus Female Workers *(continued)*

Bangladesh Variables	All industries		Textile industry		Apparel industry	
	Male	Female	Male	Female	Male	Female
Log output, domestic	0.006***	−0.004*	0.0259***	0.010***	−0.009***	−0.005**
	(3.758)	(1.932)	(8.084)	(2.827)	(3.882)	(2.228)
Log output, foreign	0.015***	0.056***	0.036***	0.025***	0.022***	0.042***
	(6.944)	(27.44)	(11.98)	(7.465)	(7.157)	(14.07)
Small firm	−1.097***	−0.804***	−1.086***	−0.995***	−0.670***	−0.716***
	(49.42)	(29.74)	(27.17)	(21.78)	(11.62)	(12.83)
Large firm	0.938***	1.733***	0.957***	1.774***	1.063***	1.998***
	(36.40)	(55.21)	(19.18)	(31.11)	(24.05)	(46.71)
Constant	2.555***	2.173***	3.724***	2.531***	0.556	1.116***
	(13.71)	(11.16)	(13.37)	(10.09)	(1.375)	(2.867)
Year dummy	Yes	Yes	Yes	Yes	Yes	Yes
Observations	9,323	9,323	3,112	3,112	4,211	4,211
R-squared	0.706	0.793	0.678	0.685	0.480	0.729

Source: World Bank calculations using ASI (Annual Survey of Industries) establishment data of various years.
Note: Year 1995 and medium size dummies are omitted.
Z-statistics in parentheses; *** $p<0.01$, ** $p<0.05$, * $p<0.1$.

Annex 4F: Log Labor Demand Regressions Estimations for Permanent versus Temporary Workers, by Country

Table 4F.1 Log Labor Demand Regressions, Permanent versus Temporary Workers, Bangladesh

Bangladesh Variables	All industries		Textile industry		Apparel industry	
	Permanent	Temporary	Permanent	Temporary	Permanent	Temporary
Log perm wage	−0.315***	−0.0128	−0.258***	0.0313	−0.0595	−0.0347
	(11.61)	(0.684)	(9.480)	(1.480)	(0.727)	(0.650)
Log temp wage	−0.0128	−0.0790***	0.0313	0.195***	−0.0347	0.00350
	(0.684)	(3.401)	(1.480)	(5.786)	(0.650)	(0.0383)
Log output	0.187***	0.154***	0.392***	0.164***	0.323***	0.105***
	(24.26)	(19.07)	(37.52)	(12.11)	(18.32)	(3.813)
Small firm	−0.853***	−0.856***	−0.746***	−0.605***	−0.898***	−0.0911
	(25.24)	(23.69)	(14.87)	(9.326)	(8.247)	(0.528)
Large firm	1.152***	0.248***	0.551***	0.604***	1.146***	0.536***
	(27.79)	(5.589)	(8.960)	(7.617)	(11.88)	(3.512)
Constant	3.269***	1.483***	−0.343	−2.169***	−0.434	0.803
	(13.97)	(6.979)	(1.001)	(5.166)	(0.514)	(0.855)
Observations	5,695	5,695	2,004	2,004	726	726
R-squared	0.627	0.351	0.814	0.465	0.799	0.150

Source: World Bank calculations using ASI (Annual Survey of Industries) establishment data of various years.
Note: Z-statistics in parentheses; *** $p<0.01$, ** $p<0.05$, * $p<0.1$.

Table 4F.2 Log Labor Demand Regressions, Permanent versus Temporary Workers, India

India	All industries		Textile industry		Apparel industry	
Variables	Permanent	Temporary	Permanent	Temporary	Permanent	Temporary
Permanent wage	−0.0554***	0.101***	−0.151***	−0.0573***	0.0516	0.0473
	(13.21)	(23.05)	(6.756)	(2.657)	(1.295)	(1.203)
Temporary wage	0.0333***	−0.177***	0.0747***	−0.190***	0.0726***	−0.229***
	(15.07)	(76.39)	(6.407)	(16.88)	(3.371)	(10.81)
Output	0.225***	0.132***	0.260***	0.113***	0.230***	0.128***
	(121.4)	(67.92)	(33.09)	(14.92)	(13.15)	(7.407)
1.size, small	−0.554***	−0.932***	−0.562***	−0.797***	−0.315***	−0.779***
	(72.43)	(116.5)	(15.68)	(23.10)	(4.411)	(11.08)
3.size, large	0.958***	0.987***	1.084***	0.935***	1.035***	1.048***
	(119.4)	(117.5)	(30.98)	(27.74)	(16.71)	(17.17)
Constant	−1.521***	−0.246***	−2.419***	−1.940***	0.104	−1.077**
	(34.01)	(5.254)	(9.996)	(8.324)	(0.221)	(2.327)
Observations	97,501	97,501	6,245	6,245	1,485	1,485
R-squared	0.621	0.618	0.578	0.524	0.490	0.581

Source: World Bank calculations using ASI (Annual Survey of Industries) establishment data of various years.
Note: Year 1995 and medium-size dummies are omitted.
Z-statistics in parentheses; *** $p<0.01$, ** $p<0.05$, * $p<0.1$.

Annex 4G: Log Wage Regressions Estimations by Country

Table 4G.1 Log Wage Regressions, Bangladesh

	2000 lw1	2005 lw1	2010 lw1	2000 lw1	2005 lw1	2010 lw1
Variables	All			Women only		
Female	−0.871***	−0.984***	−1.018***			
	(0.054)	(0.067)	(0.048)			
Age, years	0.060***	0.101***	0.078***	0.002	0.037**	0.038***
	(0.005)	(0.006)	(0.004)	(0.013)	(0.016)	(0.011)
Age squared	−0.001***	−0.001***	−0.001***	−0.000	−0.000	−0.000**
	(0.000)	(0.000)	(0.000)	(0.000)	(0.000)	(0.000)
Education, years	0.049***	0.059***	0.048***	0.092***	0.113***	0.087***
	(0.002)	(0.002)	(0.002)	(0.009)	(0.008)	(0.006)
Urban dummy	0.231***	0.100***	0.181***	0.161**	0.214***	0.098**
	(0.020)	(0.021)	(0.016)	(0.064)	(0.069)	(0.048)
Textiles and apparel	0.092*	−0.010	0.171***	0.293**	−0.557***	0.305**
	(0.052)	(0.052)	(0.049)	(0.148)	(0.192)	(0.148)
Mills ratio	0.085*	0.516***	0.371***	−0.185**	0.068	0.073
	(0.051)	(0.061)	(0.045)	(0.078)	(0.086)	(0.061)
Constant	7.366***	6.063***	6.747***	8.373***	7.235***	7.153***
	(0.138)	(0.173)	(0.118)	(0.565)	(0.526)	(0.469)
Occupation, dummies	Yes	Yes	Yes	Yes	Yes	Yes
Industry, dummies	Yes	Yes	Yes	Yes	Yes	Yes
Observations	22,209	20,803	33,780	11,051	9,886	17,419

Source: World Bank calculations using household data of various years.
Note: Omitted industry is agriculture; standard errors in parentheses. lw1 = log wage.
*** $p<0.01$, ** $p<0.05$, * $p<0.1$.

Table 4G.2 Log Wage Regressions, India

Variables	1994 lw1	2001 lw1	2005 lw1	2010 lw1	1994 lw1	2001 lw1	2005 lw1	2010 lw1
	All				Women only			
Female	−0.384***	−0.405***	−0.478***	−0.375***				
	(0.013)	(0.010)	(0.013)	(0.020)				
Age, years	0.052***	0.054***	0.060***	0.055***	0.038***	0.045***	0.060***	0.068***
	(0.002)	(0.002)	(0.002)	(0.003)	(0.004)	(0.003)	(0.004)	(0.007)
Age squared	−0.001***	−0.001***	−0.001***	−0.000***	−0.000***	−0.000***	−0.001***	−0.001***
	(0.000)	(0.000)	(0.000)	(0.000)	(0.000)	(0.000)	(0.000)	(0.000)
Education, years	0.049***	0.051***	0.058***	0.061***	0.050***	0.057***	0.068***	0.090***
	(0.001)	(0.001)	(0.001)	(0.001)	(0.002)	(0.002)	(0.002)	(0.003)
Urban dummy	0.177***	0.195***	0.179***	0.171***	0.136***	0.183***	0.196***	0.236***
	(0.009)	(0.007)	(0.008)	(0.009)	(0.018)	(0.015)	(0.017)	(0.021)
Textiles and apparel	0.323***	0.222***	0.352***	−0.050	0.481***	0.295***	0.476***	−0.157
	(0.036)	(0.027)	(0.037)	(0.038)	(0.080)	(0.084)	(0.120)	(0.138)
Mills ratio	0.016	0.032**	0.074***	0.014	0.078***	0.124***	0.148***	0.128***
	(0.017)	(0.013)	(0.018)	(0.023)	(0.023)	(0.019)	(0.025)	(0.033)
Constant	6.679***	7.018***	6.635***	6.414***	6.354***	6.709***	6.082***	5.647***
	(0.066)	(0.050)	(0.072)	(0.107)	(0.124)	(0.109)	(0.145)	(0.244)
Occupation, dummies	Yes	Yes	Yes	Yes	Yes	Yes	Yes	Yes
Industry, dummies	Yes	Yes	Yes	Yes	Yes	Yes	Yes	Yes
Observations	330,629	346,081	346,229	272,725	167,460	178,231	182,909	141,489

Source: World Bank calculations using household data of various years.
Note: Omitted industry is agriculture; standard errors in parentheses. lw1 = log wage.
*** $p<0.01$, ** $p<0.05$, * $p<0.1$.

Table 4G.3 Log Wage Regressions, Pakistan

Variables	1996 lw1	2001 lw1	2005 lw1	2012 lw1	1996 lw1	2001 lw1	2005 lw1	2012 lw1
	All				Women only			
Female	−0.444***	−0.508***	−0.518***	−0.603***				
	(0.124)	(0.075)	(0.097)	(0.093)				
Age, years	0.051***	0.065***	0.052***	0.052***	0.078***	0.061***	0.070***	0.080***
	(0.010)	(0.007)	(0.008)	(0.008)	(0.011)	(0.009)	(0.010)	(0.008)
Age squared	−0.001***	−0.001***	−0.001***	−0.001***	−0.001***	−0.001***	−0.001***	−0.001***
	(0.000)	(0.000)	(0.000)	(0.000)	(0.000)	(0.000)	(0.000)	(0.000)
Education, years	0.028***	0.031***	0.037***	0.027***	0.060***	0.074***	0.070***	0.076***
	(0.002)	(0.001)	(0.002)	(0.001)	(0.007)	(0.007)	(0.006)	(0.006)
Urban dummy	0.120***	0.142***	0.113***	0.094***	0.053	0.113***	0.159***	0.101***
	(0.026)	(0.017)	(0.020)	(0.015)	(0.053)	(0.044)	(0.035)	(0.035)
Textile and apparel	0.073**	0.103***	0.082***	−0.020	0.105	0.221**	0.209**	0.142
	(0.031)	(0.026)	(0.022)	(0.022)	(0.115)	(0.110)	(0.095)	(0.106)
Mills ratio	−0.024	0.018	−0.002	0.049	0.498***	0.416***	0.390***	0.418***
	(0.114)	(0.072)	(0.097)	(0.090)	(0.100)	(0.079)	(0.093)	(0.084)

table continues next page

Table 4G.3 Log Wage Regressions, Pakistan *(continued)*

Variables	1996 lw1	2001 lw1	2005 lw1	2012 lw1	1996 lw1	2001 lw1	2005 lw1	2012 lw1
	All				Women only			
Constant	8.332***	7.845***	8.018***	8.420***	6.329***	6.524***	6.572***	6.166***
	(0.311)	(0.199)	(0.248)	(0.240)	(0.384)	(0.335)	(0.365)	(0.322)
Occupation, dummies	Yes	Yes	Yes	Yes	Yes	Yes	Yes	Yes
Industry, dummies	Yes	Yes	Yes	Yes	Yes	Yes	Yes	Yes
Observations	68,232	64,789	119,333	128,118	33,366	31,552	59,006	62,873

Source: World Bank calculations using household data of various years.
Note: Omitted industry is agriculture; standard errors in parentheses. lw1 = log wage.
*** $p<0.01$, ** $p<0.05$, * $p<0.1$.

Table 4G.4 Log Wage Regressions, Sri Lanka

Variables	1996 lw1	2000 lw1	2006 lw1	2012 lw1	1996 lw1	2000 lw1	2006 lw1	2012 lw1
	All				Women only			
Female	−0.169***	0.389***	−0.577***	−0.527***				
	(0.053)	(0.073)	(0.067)	(0.032)				
Age, years	0.030**	0.095***	0.114***	0.089***	0.039***	0.048***	0.059***	0.059***
	(0.013)	(0.017)	(0.014)	(0.006)	(0.010)	(0.013)	(0.012)	(0.006)
Age squared	−0.000*	−0.001***	−0.001***	−0.001***	−0.000***	−0.001***	−0.001***	−0.001***
	(0.000)	(0.000)	(0.000)	(0.000)	(0.000)	(0.000)	(0.000)	(0.000)
Education, years	0.039***	0.043***	0.038***	0.045***	0.033***	0.038***	0.036***	0.037***
	(0.003)	(0.004)	(0.004)	(0.002)	(0.005)	(0.006)	(0.006)	(0.004)
Urban dummy	0.244***	0.234***	0.160***	0.142***	0.257***	0.252***	0.203***	0.162***
	(0.018)	(0.026)	(0.029)	(0.013)	(0.032)	(0.041)	(0.051)	(0.023)
Textile and apparel	0.192***	0.189***	0.304***	0.275***	0.294***	0.116	0.568***	0.409***
	(0.037)	(0.050)	(0.048)	(0.025)	(0.071)	(0.086)	(0.087)	(0.047)
Mills ratio	−0.127	0.352**	0.477***	0.378***	−0.041	0.187*	−0.014	0.100**
	(0.102)	(0.149)	(0.133)	(0.053)	(0.068)	(0.097)	(0.089)	(0.045)
Constant	8.816***	7.203***	6.869***	7.465***	8.613***	8.063***	7.663***	8.218***
	(0.288)	(0.423)	(0.358)	(0.162)	(0.259)	(0.362)	(0.335)	(0.192)
Observations	40,593	40,139	47,292	41,680	21,508	20,425	24,781	22,159

Source: World Bank calculations using household data of various years.
Note: Omitted industry is agriculture; standard errors in parentheses. lw1 = log wage.
*** $p<0.01$, ** $p<0.05$, * $p<0.1$.

Annex 4H: Probit Model Estimation of Female Labor Force Participation, Marginal Effects

Table 4H.1 Estimation of Female Labor Force Participation, Bangladesh

	2000 lf	2005 lf	2010 lf	2000 lf	2005 lf	2010 lf	2000 lf	2005 Lf	2010 lf
Variables	All			Low skilled			High skilled		
Predicted log wage	1.646***	0.141***	0.306***	0.454***	0.076***	1.126***	0.196***	0.411***	0.208***
	(0.214)	(0.020)	(0.027)	(0.095)	(0.026)	(0.086)	(0.075)	(0.067)	(0.029)
Years of school	−0.174***	−0.007***	−0.026***	−0.050***	−0.007***	−0.079***	0.033**	0.011	0.023**
	(0.023)	(0.002)	(0.003)	(0.010)	(0.003)	(0.006)	(0.013)	(0.013)	(0.009)
Urban	−0.175***	0.028***	−0.007	−0.014	0.041***	−0.067***	−0.114**	−0.238***	−0.055*
	(0.025)	(0.007)	(0.006)	(0.015)	(0.006)	(0.008)	(0.048)	(0.048)	(0.032)
Married	−0.189***	−0.040***	−0.076***	−0.214***	−0.028**	−0.086***	−0.005	−0.085*	−0.021
	(0.014)	(0.012)	(0.012)	(0.016)	(0.012)	(0.011)	(0.056)	(0.050)	(0.040)
Divorced	0.185***	0.250***	0.144***	0.153***	0.236***	0.109***		0.032	0.075
	(0.035)	(0.045)	(0.027)	(0.034)	(0.046)	(0.024)		(0.185)	(0.123)
Widowed	0.021	0.126***	0.010	−0.028	0.135***	0.047***	0.211	−0.119	−0.107**
	(0.019)	(0.028)	(0.012)	(0.018)	(0.030)	(0.012)	(0.194)	(0.093)	(0.054)
HH size	−0.018***	−0.022***	−0.020***	−0.019***	−0.026***	−0.015***	−0.024**	0.008	−0.016**
	(0.003)	(0.002)	(0.002)	(0.003)	(0.002)	(0.002)	(0.012)	(0.009)	(0.008)
Education of HH head	−0.004***	−0.005***	−0.004***	−0.005***	−0.004***	−0.004***	−0.008*	−0.001	−0.003
	(0.001)	(0.001)	(0.001)	(0.001)	(0.001)	(0.001)	(0.005)	(0.004)	(0.003)
# of kids 0–5 years	0.011*	0.008	0.005	0.012**	0.014***	−0.005	0.064	−0.056*	−0.017
	(0.006)	(0.005)	(0.004)	(0.006)	(0.005)	(0.004)	(0.039)	(0.029)	(0.024)
# of kids 6–18 years	0.015***	0.009***	0.011***	0.017***	0.015***	0.005*	0.023	−0.028	−0.003
	(0.004)	(0.003)	(0.002)	(0.004)	(0.003)	(0.002)	(0.019)	(0.018)	(0.014)
Observations	11,076	9,916	17,419	10,564	9,129	16,237	511	787	1,182

Source: World Bank calculations using household data of various years.
Note: Low skilled = less than 12 years of education (less than high school), omitted marital status is never married; standard errors in parentheses. lf = labor force dummy.
*** p<0.01, ** p<0.05, * p<0.1.

Table 4H.2 Estimation of Female Labor Force Participation, India

Variables	All				Low skilled				High skilled			
	1996 lf	2001 lf	2005 lf	2012 lf	1996 lf	2001 lf	2005 lf	2012 Lf	1996 lf	2001 lf	2005 lf	2012 lf
Predicted log wage	0.551***	0.426***	0.410***	0.189***	0.593***	0.526***	0.642***	0.121***	0.492***	0.268***	0.241***	0.211***
	(0.010)	(0.007)	(0.006)	(0.004)	(0.012)	(0.011)	(0.011)	(0.008)	(0.016)	(0.009)	(0.008)	(0.008)
Years of school	-0.059***	-0.045***	-0.042***	-0.012***	-0.064***	-0.053***	-0.052***	-0.006***	0.023***	0.021***	0.026***	0.029***
	(0.001)	(0.001)	(0.001)	(0.001)	(0.001)	(0.001)	(0.001)	(0.001)	(0.003)	(0.002)	(0.002)	(0.002)
Urban	-0.262***	-0.282***	-0.272***	-0.161***	-0.278***	-0.327***	-0.338***	-0.144***	-0.178***	-0.145***	-0.183***	-0.177***
	(0.003)	(0.003)	(0.003)	(0.002)	(0.003)	(0.004)	(0.003)	(0.003)	(0.011)	(0.009)	(0.007)	(0.007)
Married	-0.100***	-0.091***	-0.100***	-0.033***	-0.098***	-0.082***	-0.098***	0.046***	-0.245***	-0.197***	-0.186***	-0.123***
	(0.005)	(0.004)	(0.004)	(0.004)	(0.005)	(0.005)	(0.005)	(0.004)	(0.013)	(0.011)	(0.010)	(0.009)
Divorced	0.143***	0.156***	0.159***	0.246***	0.150***	0.165***	0.155***	0.337***	0.002	0.051	0.172***	0.249***
	(0.016)	(0.015)	(0.015)	(0.020)	(0.016)	(0.015)	(0.016)	(0.022)	(0.068)	(0.051)	(0.054)	(0.049)
Widowed	-0.075***	-0.089***	-0.090***	-0.007	-0.072***	-0.078***	-0.086***	0.086***	-0.031	-0.063***	-0.010	0.028
	(0.005)	(0.005)	(0.005)	(0.006)	(0.006)	(0.006)	(0.006)	(0.008)	(0.027)	(0.021)	(0.024)	(0.020)
HH size	-0.019***	-0.022***	-0.020***	-0.007***	-0.019***	-0.021***	-0.019***	-0.004***	-0.006***	-0.013***	-0.018***	-0.012***
	(0.001)	(0.001)	(0.001)	(0.001)	(0.001)	(0.001)	(0.001)	(0.001)	(0.002)	(0.002)	(0.002)	(0.002)
Education of HH head	-0.016***	-0.014***	-0.014***	-0.009***	-0.017***	-0.016***	-0.014***	-0.009***	-0.011***	-0.009***	-0.014***	-0.010***
	(0.000)	(0.000)	(0.000)	(0.000)	(0.000)	(0.000)	(0.000)	(0.000)	(0.001)	(0.001)	(0.001)	(0.001)
# of kids 0–5 years	0.017***	0.022***	0.018***	0.008***	0.016***	0.020***	0.015***	-0.006***	0.008	0.009	0.020***	0.017***
	(0.002)	(0.002)	(0.002)	(0.002)	(0.002)	(0.002)	(0.002)	(0.002)	(0.007)	(0.005)	(0.006)	(0.005)
# of kids 6–18 years	0.011***	0.014***	0.016***	0.002**	0.015***	0.017***	0.018***	0.002*	-0.021***	-0.011***	-0.001	-0.009***
	(0.001)	(0.001)	(0.001)	(0.001)	(0.001)	(0.001)	(0.001)	(0.001)	(0.004)	(0.003)	(0.003)	(0.003)
Observations	168,831	178,893	188,180	142,161	154,612	159,377	165,638	115,789	14,219	19,516	22,542	26,372

Source: World Bank calculations using household data of various years.

Note: Low skilled = less than 12 years of education (less than high school), omitted marital status is never married; standard errors in parentheses. lf = labor force dummy.

*** p<0.01, ** p<0.05, * p<0.1.

Table 4H.3 Estimation of Female Labor Force Participation, Pakistan

Variables	All				Low skilled				High skilled			
	1996	2001	2005	2012	1996	2001	2005	2012	1996	2001	2005	2012
	lf	lf	lf	lf	lf	lf	lf	lf	lf	lf	lf	lf
Predicted log wage	0.085***	0.194***	0.188***	0.163***	0.034***	0.270***	0.234***	0.238***	0.181***	0.219***	0.200***	0.124***
	(0.010)	(0.011)	(0.008)	(0.007)	(0.010)	(0.018)	(0.015)	(0.013)	(0.037)	(0.030)	(0.017)	(0.013)
Years of school	-0.002*	-0.014***	-0.014***	-0.009***	-0.003***	-0.021***	-0.019***	-0.018***	0.009**	0.007	0.006*	0.033***
	(0.001)	(0.001)	(0.001)	(0.001)	(0.001)	(0.001)	(0.001)	(0.001)	(0.004)	(0.006)	(0.004)	(0.003)
Urban	-0.004	-0.048***	-0.122***	-0.133***	0.003	-0.060***	-0.114***	-0.131***	-0.047	-0.010	-0.182***	-0.110***
	(0.006)	(0.007)	(0.004)	(0.003)	(0.006)	(0.007)	(0.004)	(0.003)	(0.051)	(0.045)	(0.023)	(0.016)
Married	-0.051***	-0.100***	-0.087***	-0.086***	-0.041***	-0.100***	-0.076***	-0.087***	-0.103***	-0.198***	-0.196***	-0.151***
	(0.006)	(0.007)	(0.006)	(0.005)	(0.006)	(0.008)	(0.006)	(0.006)	(0.025)	(0.027)	(0.017)	(0.014)
Divorced	0.039***	-0.052***	-0.045***	-0.062***	0.039***	-0.048***	-0.044***	-0.055***	0.025	-0.118**	-0.103***	-0.121***
	(0.010)	(0.006)	(0.007)	(0.006)	(0.009)	(0.005)	(0.007)	(0.006)	(0.082)	(0.047)	(0.030)	(0.026)
Widowed	0.134***	0.026	0.111***	0.092***	0.140***	0.018	0.118***	0.090***	0.355	-0.130	0.277*	-0.009
	(0.048)	(0.031)	(0.031)	(0.028)	(0.049)	(0.029)	(0.032)	(0.029)	(0.329)	(0.109)	(0.162)	(0.084)
HH size	0.000***	0.000***	0.003***	0.001***	0.000***	0.000***	0.003***	0.002***	-0.000***	0.000	-0.001	0.001
	(0.000)	(0.000)	(0.000)	(0.000)	(0.000)	(0.000)	(0.000)	(0.000)	(0.000)	(0.000)	(0.001)	(0.001)
Education of HH head	-0.000***	-0.000***	-0.001***	-0.000***	-0.000***	-0.000***	-0.001***	-0.000***	-0.000	-0.000***	-0.001***	-0.001***
	(0.000)	(0.000)	(0.000)	(0.000)	(0.000)	(0.000)	(0.000)	(0.000)	(0.000)	(0.000)	(0.000)	(0.000)
# of kids 0–5 years	-0.000***	-0.000***	-0.004***	-0.003***	-0.000***	-0.000***	-0.005***	-0.004***	-0.000	-0.000	0.007***	0.001
	(0.000)	(0.000)	(0.001)	(0.001)	(0.000)	(0.000)	(0.001)	(0.001)	(0.000)	(0.000)	(0.002)	(0.002)
# of kids 6–18 years	-0.000***	-0.001***	-0.004***	-0.003***	-0.000***	-0.001***	-0.004***	-0.003***	0.001***	0.000	0.002	0.000
	(0.000)	(0.000)	(0.000)	(0.000)	(0.000)	(0.000)	(0.000)	(0.000)	(0.000)	(0.000)	(0.002)	(0.002)
Observations	33,374	31,554	59,013	62,881	31,472	29,464	54,038	56,225	1,902	2,090	4,975	6,656

Source: World Bank calculations using labor force data of various years.

Note: Low skilled = less than 12 years of education (less than high school), omitted marital status is never married; standard errors in parentheses. lf = labor force dummy.

*** $p<0.01$, ** $p<0.05$, * $p<0.1$.

Table 4H.4 Estimation of Female Labor Force Participation, Sri Lanka

Variables	All				Low skilled				High skilled			
	1996 lf	2000 lf	2006 lf	2012 lf	1996 lf	2000 lf	2006 lf	2012 lf	1996 lf	2000 lf	2006 lf	2012 lf
Predicted log wage	1.011***	0.939***	0.696***	0.892***	0.734***	1.455***	1.038***	0.944***	0.606***	0.561***	0.432***	0.616***
	(0.035)	(0.030)	(0.018)	(0.024)	(0.057)	(0.078)	(0.054)	(0.052)	(0.046)	(0.041)	(0.023)	(0.035)
Years of school	-0.078***	-0.074***	-0.066***	-0.066***	-0.060***	-0.090***	-0.078***	-0.043***	0.019	0.055***	0.027**	0.109***
	(0.003)	(0.003)	(0.002)	(0.002)	(0.004)	(0.005)	(0.004)	(0.003)	(0.018)	(0.014)	(0.012)	(0.010)
Urban	-0.362***	-0.374***	-0.289***	-0.209***	-0.302***	-0.477***	-0.387***	-0.226***	-0.247***	-0.242***	-0.169***	-0.151***
	(0.009)	(0.009)	(0.008)	(0.008)	(0.013)	(0.013)	(0.010)	(0.010)	(0.024)	(0.022)	(0.019)	(0.019)
Married	-0.255***	-0.243***	-0.238***	-0.165***	-0.158***	-0.191***	-0.136***	0.079***	-0.268***	-0.198***	-0.273***	-0.227***
	(0.011)	(0.011)	(0.010)	(0.011)	(0.012)	(0.013)	(0.012)	(0.009)	(0.031)	(0.027)	(0.021)	(0.023)
Divorced	-0.231***	-0.256***	-0.207***	-0.086***	-0.172***	-0.227***	-0.161***	0.181***	-0.309***	-0.264***	-0.301***	-0.141***
	(0.010)	(0.012)	(0.012)	(0.014)	(0.012)	(0.013)	(0.015)	(0.018)	(0.065)	(0.058)	(0.043)	(0.046)
Widowed	-0.067**	-0.112***	-0.111***	0.010	0.041	-0.045	-0.006	-0.272***	-0.157	-0.177	-0.148	-0.087
	(0.028)	(0.030)	(0.026)	(0.025)	(0.032)	(0.033)	(0.029)	(0.027)	(0.137)	(0.120)	(0.094)	(0.080)
HH size	-0.001	-0.010***	-0.012***	-0.005**	-0.002	-0.014***	-0.017***	-0.000	0.028***	0.015**	0.005	0.005
	(0.002)	(0.002)	(0.002)	(0.003)	(0.002)	(0.003)	(0.003)	(0.003)	(0.006)	(0.006)	(0.006)	(0.006)
Education of HH head	-0.001	-0.008***	-0.011***	-0.009***	-0.001	-0.010***	-0.013***	-0.007***	-0.001	-0.007***	-0.011***	-0.009***
	(0.001)	(0.001)	(0.001)	(0.001)	(0.001)	(0.001)	(0.001)	(0.001)	(0.002)	(0.003)	(0.002)	(0.003)
# of kids 0–5 years	-0.008	-0.008	-0.033***	-0.045***	-0.016***	-0.012*	-0.035***	-0.093***	-0.033*	-0.017	-0.039***	-0.033**
	(0.006)	(0.007)	(0.006)	(0.006)	(0.006)	(0.007)	(0.007)	(0.007)	(0.019)	(0.017)	(0.014)	(0.014)
# of kids 6–18 years	-0.000	0.000	-0.005	-0.025***	0.008**	0.013***	0.013***	-0.032***	-0.064***	-0.048***	-0.040***	-0.044***
	(0.003)	(0.003)	(0.004)	(0.004)	(0.003)	(0.004)	(0.004)	(0.004)	(0.011)	(0.009)	(0.009)	(0.009)
Observations	21,553	20,457	24,802	22,166	18,834	16,930	19,637	16,956	2,719	3,527	5,165	5,210

Source: World Bank calculations using labor force data of various years.

Note: Low skilled = less than 12 years of education (less than high school), omitted marital status is never married; standard errors in parentheses. lf = labor force dummy.

*** p<0.01, ** p<0.05, * p<0.1.

Notes

1. While the establishment survey used in this analysis does not provide us with export data for other countries, the consultations with industry experts suggest that, in most South Asian countries, exports represent a majority of total apparel production.

2. Because export volume is highly correlated with output volume, we proxy exports by the total output.

3. We have information on temporary and permanent workers only in Bangladesh and India.

4. An important consideration for female employment in textiles and apparel is that women do not stay in this sector for a long time. According to anecdotal evidence, the length of employment for women in apparel is 5–10 years. Although we are not able to observe with our data what happens to women after they leave the apparel sector, this topic could be an area of future research.

5. Unfortunately, we do not have a time series for Pakistan.

6. Note also that there is a considerable difference between the share of females employed in textiles and apparel when comparing household (30 percent) and establishment (5 percent) data. Unfortunately, we cannot explain why the data give such different estimates.

7. Cross-wage elasticity is modeled as elasticity of male (female) employment with respect to change in female (male) wage.

8. Regarding the intersectoral reallocation of labor, Seddon and Wacziarg (2001) and Levinsohn (1999) provide further readings.

9. The industrial classification is according to the International Standard Industrial Classification, UN Statistics Division.

10. In India the results were not statistically different from zero.

11. The magnitude in Indian results is smaller because we use panel data to estimate the model and include firm-level fixed effects in the estimation.

12. Note that the magnitude of labor-output elasticities in Bangladesh is much lower when one differentiates between foreign and domestic sales as opposed to looking at the total output. This could be caused by the fact that not all firms that report on total output answer the questions about foreign and domestic sales.

13. Unfortunately, the data cover permanent and temporary workers only for Bangladesh and India. We estimate the model as described in equation (4.2), but consider temporary and permanent workers as two labor inputs (see annex 4F).

14. The literature on the female labor supply is extensively researched and established. Becker (1965, 1973, 1974) published seminal pieces on this topic and developed a framework for the analysis. The classic female labor supply model was developed by Hausman (1980) and further advanced by Blundell and MaCurdy (1999).

15. While we acknowledge that there are substantial differences in labor force participation response between the countries, we are not trying to answer the question of why these differences exist in this study. Cultural differences could be one of the potential explanations, but further study is needed to address this question in more detail.

16. The Pakistan establishment data have only total wage information while our analysis is based on gender-separated wage information. To retain Pakistan in the paper, we had to generate female-to-male wage ratios using a same-year labor force survey.

17. http://unstats.un.org/unsd/cr/registry/regdnld.asp?Lg=1.

18. The wage exogeneity assumption is based on the assumption that neither workers nor firms have the power to determine wages (the competiveness assumption). Dropping the outliers in terms of the amount of output and number of employees ensures that the sample does not violate the competitiveness assumption.

19. Employment size is defined as small (10–50 employees), medium (50–100), and large (100+).

20. Industry data for all countries, except Pakistan, provide the sampling weight that is used in estimations.

Bibliography

Afridi, Farzana, Abhiroop Mukhopadhyay, and Soham Sahoo. 2012. "Female Labour Force Participation and Child Education in India: The Effect of the National Rural Employment Guarantee Scheme." Discussion Paper 6593, Institute for the Study of Labor, Bonn, Germany.

Aguirre, De Anne, Leila Hoteit, Christine Rupp, and Karin Sabbagh. 2012. *Empowering the Third Billion: Women and the World of Work in 2012.* New York: Booz & Co.

Anderson, S., and M. Eswaran. 2009. "What Determines Female Autonomy? Evidence from Bangladesh." *Journal of Development Economics* 90 (2): 179–91.

Ayyagari, M., A. Demirgüç-Kunt, and V. Maksimovic. 2011. *Small vs. Young Firms across the World: Contribution to Employment, Job Creation, and Growth.* Washington, DC: World Bank.

Azevedo, Joao Pedro, Gabriela Inchauste, Sergio Olivieri, Jaime Saavedra, and Hernan Winkler. 2013. "Is Labor Income Responsible for Poverty Reduction? A Decomposition Approach." Policy Research Working Paper WPS 6414, World Bank, Washington, DC.

Becker, G. S. 1965. "A Theory of the Allocation of Time." *The Economic Journal* 75 (299): 493–517.

———. 1973. "A Theory of Marriage: Part I." *Journal of Political Economy* 81 (4): 813–46.

———. 1974. "A Theory of Social Interactions." NBER Working Paper 74, National Bureau of Economic Research, New York.

Blackwell, J. L. 2005. "Estimation and Testing of Fixed-Effect Panel-Data Systems." *The Stata Journal* 5 (2): 202–07.

Blundell, R., and T. MaCurdy. 1999. "Labor Supply: A Review of Alternative Approaches." *Handbook of Labor Economics* 3: 1559–695.

Cardozo, Diego. 2014 (forthcoming). "Exploring Labor Transitions for Rural Poor Female Workers in Mexico."

Chatterjee, Urmila, Murgai, Rinku, and Martin Rama. 2015. "Job Opportunities along the Rural-Urban Gradation and Female Labor Force Participation in India." Policy Research Working paper 7412, World Bank, Washington, DC.

Cuberes, D., and M. Teignier. 2012. "Gender Gaps in the Labor Market and Aggregate Productivity." SEPR Working Paper 2012017, University of Sheffield, Department of Economics, Sheffield, UK.

Currie, J., and A. Harrison. 1997. "Trade Reform and Labor Market Adjustment in Morocco." *Journal of Labor Economics* 15 (3): S44–71.

Diaz-Mayans, Maria Angeles, and Rosario Sanchez. 2004. "Temporary Employment and Technical Efficiency in Spain." *International Journal of Manpower* 25 (2): 181–94.

Do, Q. T., A. A. Levchenko, and C. E. Raddatz. 2014. "Comparative Advantage, International Trade, and Fertility." Policy Research Working Paper 6930, World Bank, Washington, DC.

Feenstra, R. C., and G. H. Hanson. 1997. "Foreign Direct Investment and Relative Wages: Evidence from Mexico's Maquiladoras." *Journal of International Economics* 42: 371–94.

Fukunishi, T., and T. Yamagata, eds. 2014. *The Garment Industry in Low-Income Countries: An Entry Point of Industrialization.* Basingstoke, UK: Palgrave Macmillan.

Goldin, C. 1995. "The U-Shaped Female Labor Force Function in Economic Development and Economic History." In *Investment in Women's Human Capital and Economic Development*, edited by T. P. Schultz, 61–90. Chicago: University of Chicago Press.

Grossman, G. M. 1986. "Imports as a Cause of Injury: The Case of the U.S. Steel Industry." *Journal of International Economics* 20: 201–23.

Hamermesh, D. 1993. *Labor Demand.* Princeton, NJ: Princeton University Press.

Harrison, A., and G. Hanson. 1999. "Who Gains from Trade Reform? Some Remaining Puzzles." *Journal of Development Economics* 59: 125–54.

Hasan, R., D. Mitra, and K. Ramaswamy. 2007. "Trade Reforms, Labor Regulations, and Labor Demand Elasticities: Empirical Evidence from India." *The Review of Economics and Statistics* 89 (3): 466–81.

Hausman, J. A. 1980. "The Effect of Wages, Taxes, and Fixed Costs on Women's Labor Force Participation." *Journal of Public Economics* 14 (2): 161–94.

Heath, Rachel, and A. Mushfiq Mobarak. 2012. "Does Demand or Supply Constrain Investments in Education? Evidence from Garment Sector Jobs in Bangladesh." Unpublished manuscript.

Heckman, J. J. 1978. "A Partial Survey of Recent Research on the Labor Supply of Women." *The American Economic Review* 68 (2): 200–07.

Jensen, Robert. 2012. "Do Labor Market Opportunities Affect Young Women's Work and Family Decisions? Experimental Evidence from India." *Quarterly Journal of Economics* 27 (2): 753–92.

Kabeer, Naila, Ragui Assaad, Akosua Darkwah, Simeen Mahmud, Hania Sholkamy, Sakiba Tasneem, Dzodzi Tsikata, amd Munshi Sulaiman. 2013. *Paid Work, Women's Empowerment and Inclusive Growth: Transforming the Structures of Constraint.* UN Entity for Gender Equality and the Empowerment of Women.

Klasen, S., and J. Pieters. 2012. "Push or Pull? Drivers of Female Labor Force Participation during India's Economic Boom." IZA paper 6395, Institute for the Study of Labor, Bonn, Germany.

———. 2013. "What Explains Low Female Labor Force Participation in Urban Areas?" IZA paper 7597, Institute for the Study of Labor, Bonn, Germany.

Levinsohn, J. 1999. "Employment Responses to International Liberalization in Chile." *Journal of International Economics* 47: 321–44.

Lichter, A., A. Peichl, and S. Lichter. 2013. "Exporting and Labor Demand: Micro-level Evidence from Germany." IZA Discussion Paper 7494, Institute for the Study of Labor, Bonn, Germany.

Lopez -Acevedo, G., and R. Robertson, eds. 2012. *Sewing Success? Employment, Wages, and Poverty Following the End of the Multi-fibre Arrangement.* Washington, DC: World Bank.

Luke, Nancy, and Kaivan Munshi. 2011. "Women as Agents of Change: Female Income and Mobility in India." *Journal of Development Economics* 94 (1): 1–17.

Mas-Colell, A., M. D. Whinston, and J. R. Green. 1995. *Microeconomic Theory*. Oxford: Oxford University Press.

Rama, M. 2003. *Globalization and Workers in Developing Countries*. Washington, DC: World Bank.

Revenga, A. 1997, July. "Employment and Wage Effects of Trade Liberalization: The Case of Mexican Manufacturing." *Journal of Labor Economics* 15 (53): S20–43.

Rodrick, D. 1997. *Has Globalization Gone Too Far?* Washington, DC: Institute for International Economics.

Seddon, J., and R. Wacziarg. 2001. *Trade Liberalization and Intersectoral Labor Movements*. Stanford GSB Working Paper 1652.

Sivasankaran, Anitha. 2014. "Work and Women's Marriage, Fertility and Empowerment: Evidence from Textile Mill Employment in India." Harvard University Job Market Paper.

Verick, Sher. 2014. "Female Labor Force Participation in Developing Countries." *IZA World of Labor* 2014: 87.

World Bank. 2012. *More and Better Jobs in South Asia*. Washington, DC: World Bank.

———. 2014a. *Gender Equality and Shared Prosperity in South Asia—What Will It Take?* Washington, DC: World Bank.

———. 2014b. *Global Monitoring Report 2014/2015: Ending Poverty and Sharing Prosperity*. Washington, DC: World Bank.

———. 2014c. *World Development Indicators*. Washington, DC: World Bank.

Zellner, A. 1962. "An Efficient Method of Estimating Seemingly Unrelated Regressions and Tests for Aggregation Bias." *Journal of the American Statistical Association* 57 (2): 348–68.

## PART 3

What Role Can Policy Play in Increasing Apparel Exports and Jobs?

## CHAPTER 5

Policies to Foster Apparel Exports and Jobs

Key Messages

- For South Asia to expand apparel exports and jobs, it needs to adopt policies to increase market access, ease import barriers (notably for manmade fibers), improve export logistics, and facilitate foreign investment.
- If it fails to do so—and fails to do so quickly—it risks losing out on a huge opportunity to create good jobs for development given China's rising apparel prices.
- For the U.S. market, our analysis shows that a 10 percent increase in Chinese prices could boost employment in South Asia by up to 9 percent, even without changed policies, so better policies would be a major plus. For the European Union market, Sri Lanka and India would benefit, although Pakistan and Bangladesh would not.

How Policies Fit In

So far this report has shown that South Asia's apparel sector exhibits significant potential to increase apparel exports and jobs, although in the current situation Southeast Asia stands to capture more displaced production as apparel prices rise in China. For South Asia—including our sample "SAR countries" of Bangladesh, India, Pakistan, and Sri Lanka—to become more competitive, it needs to improve its performance in areas that matter most to global buyers (see chapter 2). All the SAR countries (with the exception of Sri Lanka) generally appear to be cost competitive. But they are inhibited by too great a concentration in cotton products, even though the industry is increasingly moving toward manmade fiber products (MMF). And they lag behind Southeast Asia in quality,

The authors, Atisha Kumar, Stacey Frederick, and Raymond Robertson, are grateful for comments provided by the core team and for substantive inputs from Cornelia Staritz.

input availability (like synthetic fibers), lead times (the time between placing and receiving an order), reliability, and social compliance.

If the situation persists—that is, if no new policies are set up and implemented to alter the picture—a 10 percent increase in China's prices would mean an increase in SAR exports of between 13 and 25 percent (depending on the country)—compared to a gain for Southeast Asia of between 37 and 51 percent (see chapter 3). This gap matters greatly because textiles and apparel have a larger potential than other sectors to create jobs in response to increased exports, especially for women (see chapter 4). The industry accounts for 14.6 percent of total exports in South Asia and is also one of the largest employers of female workers.

Within South Asia, there are tremendous differences in product mix and quality, level of policy involvement, and design and implementation strategies. Each country specializes in different types of products—for example, Bangladesh and Pakistan largely produce a narrow range of basic cotton garments, India also concentrates on cotton but in a broader range of product categories, whereas Sri Lanka produces more synthetics and specializes in higher-value intimate apparel (see chapter 2).

With respect to policies, all South Asian countries have adopted measures to promote the apparel sector in view of the Multifibre Arrangement (MFA) phaseout in 2005. Government policies in the region typically focus on tax and duty exemption, finance facilities for technology upgrading through capital investments (like TUFS [the Technology Upgradation Funds Scheme]), and skill development, clustering, and export promotion measures. Sri Lanka has had the most effective initiatives in apparel, with the Joint Apparel Association Forum (JAAF)—the industry association—playing an important role in coordinating stakeholders. In the other countries, coordination between stakeholders is limited. More recently, India's "Make in India" initiative proposes policies related to the manufacturing sector, and "Textiles and Garments" are included as key industries in this initiative.

Are South Asia's policy efforts sufficient? What more could be done? This chapter attempts to answer these questions by pulling together the material developed in earlier chapters. We start by estimating how many new jobs South Asia might hope to create if the status quo continues. Then we explore how policies are linked to the stages of production in textiles and apparel, which policies matter most for this industry, how South Asia performs in these areas, and the key hurdles that need to be tackled to give the region a greater competitive edge.

Our key finding is that with respect to jobs, all four of the SAR countries exhibit significant employment generation potential as represented by elasticities of employment to Chinese prices. Bangladesh and Pakistan have the highest potential to increase jobs (in percentage terms) for exports to the U.S. markets, and Sri Lanka is the big winner with respect to European Union (EU) markets. To increase jobs, it is imperative and urgent for the SAR economies to enact supporting policies. We find that, although reform priorities vary by country, most countries would benefit from increasing market access, easing barriers to the import of inputs such as MMFs, and facilitating foreign investment.

Predicting Job Effects in South Asia

Throughout this report we have assumed that higher Chinese prices will boost the demand for apparel from South Asia and that firms in South Asia will respond by creating jobs. We have also assumed that more jobs will enhance welfare (as opposed to simply leave the level of welfare unchanged) because workers will be drawn from either the informal sector or agriculture, both of which pay lower wages than apparel exporting firms. In other words, apparel exporters face a relatively elastic supply curve, especially in the short run because there is a large pool of temporary workers.

But how many new jobs will the increased demand translate into? To answer that question, we combine two elasticity estimates—(i) the responsiveness of South Asian apparel exports to an increase in Chinese prices (from chapter 3, table 3.5) and (ii) the responsiveness of employment to apparel output (from chapter 4, table 4.3)—for both males and females in the U.S. and EU markets. That is,

$$\%\Delta Employment = \varepsilon_{xp}\varepsilon_{Ex}. \tag{5.1}$$

This is correct because

$$\frac{\%\Delta Exports}{\%\Delta Prices}. \tag{5.2}$$

and

$$\varepsilon_{Ex}\frac{\%\Delta Employment}{\%\Delta Exports}, \tag{5.3}$$

such that, when multiplied, we get

$$\frac{\%\Delta Employment}{\%\Delta Prices}. \tag{5.4}$$

For the U.S. market, we find that a 10 percent increase in Chinese apparel prices would increase apparel employment in Pakistan for males by 8.93 percent—by far the biggest winner followed by Bangladesh (4.22 percent) and India (3.32 percent) (table 5.1, panels a and b). The gains for Sri Lanka are less than 1 percent, but it is important to keep in mind that the estimates in table 5.1 are for exports to the United States only. The story is much the same for females. In India, the gains in employment for females are small (2.51 percent) because of the small employment estimate for India. Overall, because apparel hires relatively more females to begin with, the expected total number of women working in apparel would increase more than the number of men working in apparel.

For the EU market, the most striking result is the large difference in the predicted employment gains for Sri Lanka, whose elasticity is very high (table 5.1, panels c and d). The results suggest that a 10 percent increase in Chinese apparel prices would increase Sri Lankan male apparel employment by 8.55 percent, followed by India (4.30 percent), but Bangladesh and Pakistan would experience small decreases because their trade estimates do not suggest that they are close substitutes for Chinese apparel products in the EU market. For females, the results are qualitatively similar in that employment in Sri Lanka now would appear to increase by 7.87 percent, whereas the other countries are predicted to have a small change. Again, the exception might be India. If China's prices to the EU increase by 10 percent, India could have a 3.26 percent increase in female employment.

Table 5.1 For the U.S. Market, Pakistan and Bangladesh Are the Big Winners, Whereas Sri Lanka Is for the EU

Panel a: Male employment responses for exports to United States

Country	Elasticity of exports to prices (ε_{xp})	Elasticity of jobs to exports (ε_{Ex})	Elasticity of jobs to prices $\left(\dfrac{\%\Delta Employment}{\%\Delta Prices}\right)$
Bangladesh	1.358*	0.311***	**0.422**
India	1.462*	0.176***	0.332
Pakistan	2.531*	0.353***	**0.893**
Sri Lanka	0.024	0.380***	0.009

Panel b: Female employment responses for exports to United States

Country	ε_{xp}	ε_{Ex}	$\dfrac{\%\Delta Employment}{\%\Delta Prices}$
Bangladesh	1.358*	0.323***	**0.439**
India	1.462*	0.172***	0.251
Pakistan	2.531*	0.336***	**0.850**
Sri Lanka	0.024	0.350***	0.008

Panel c: Male employment responses for exports to the EU

Country	ε_{xp}	ε_{Ex}	$\dfrac{\%\Delta Employment}{\%\Delta Prices}$
Bangladesh	−0.238	0.311***	−0.074
India	1.895*	0.176***	**0.430**
Pakistan	−0.060	0.353***	−0.021
Sri Lanka	2.249*	0.380***	**0.855**

Panel d: Female employment responses for exports to the EU

Country	ε_{xp}	ε_{Ex}	$\dfrac{\%\Delta Employment}{\%\Delta Prices}$
Bangladesh	−0.238	0.323***	−0.077
India	1.895*	0.172***	**0.326**
Pakistan	−0.060	0.336***	−0.020
Sri Lanka	2.249*	0.350***	**0.787**

Source: Chapters 3 (table 3.5) and 4 (table 4.3) of this report.
Note: *** $p<.01$, ** $p<.05$, * $p<.1$. The elasticities reported here are for a 1 percent increase in prices of Chinese apparel. The ratios denoted in bold highlight high values of the elasticity of jobs to prices.

Although the estimates for the U.S. and EU markets, which together account for about half of global apparel imports, are not necessarily small, they are smaller than those predicted for Southeast Asia. They suggest that demand for apparel in the United States and the EU is elastic in the sense that the imports increase by a higher percentage than the drop in prices—consistent with Harrigan and Barrows (2009), who show a large U.S. import response to falling Chinese prices at the end of the MFA in 2005. We do not have the employment elasticities for the Southeast Asian countries, but using the mean of the estimates from the South Asian countries above suggests that the gains would be even larger in Southeast Asia. One possible reason for the different expected job effects arises from the fact that the trade elasticities of these two regions may differ because of Southeast Asia's apparel-friendly policies, particularly with respect to low tariffs and attracting investment.

How Policies and Processes Interact in Apparel

Government policies apply to varying degrees at the different stages of apparel production and distribution in the industry. The goal of this exercise is to draw conclusions about *which policies* come into play at *what stage* of the production process. Overall, policies need to be aligned with the general dynamics of the global apparel industry (discussed in chapter 2), particularly the sourcing strategies of buyers. South Asian (and other) countries are trying to expand production at a time when global buyers are streamlining sourcing strategies to reduce the cost and complexity of their supply chains by focusing on large and more capable core suppliers. This results in fewer suppliers and countries. However, opportunities for expansion still exist because of rising wages in China and other existing players, the expansion of emerging consumer markets, particularly in Asia, and the stated desire of buyers to diversify sourcing from China.

On the production side, as illustrated in figure 5.1, government policies play a critical role at each of the four stages of the apparel supply chain: (1) production of fibers, (2) production of textiles (yarn and fabric), (3) production of apparel, and (4) distribution and sales.

Along each of the four stages of figure 5.1, government policies shape the apparel industry and firms in significant ways. However, each policy, though beneficial for apparel firms, may have an economic or social cost. Waiving of import duties on certain fibers (such as MMFs) may lead to increased imports of the fibers—but it also may mean a movement away from other types of fibers (such as cotton), which may adversely affect the latter group. Note that the focus of this chapter will be on stages 2 and 3.

Market Orientation

At the fiber and textile production stages, policies vary greatly depending on whether the objective is to develop capabilities domestically or to facilitate imports. For imports, the two critical policies are trade (such as waiving import duties, which may lead to higher production) and industrial (which affects the

Figure 5.1 Policies Matter at Each Stage of the Apparel Production and Supply Chain

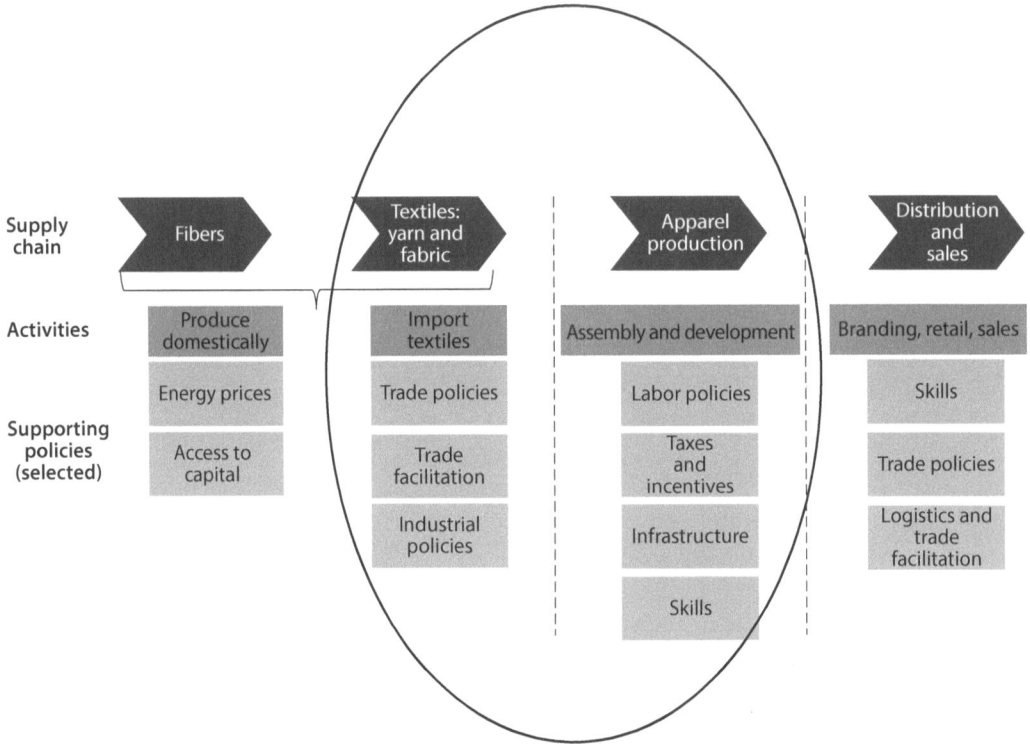

bureaucracy and time required to import) (Birnbaum 2013). For domestic production, the key policies relate to infrastructure (such as fuel price subsidies, which would lower energy rates) and the availability of capital to purchase machinery. Producers also need workers with knowledge of how to operate machinery and conduct tests on quality, and developing these skills often comes through learning via foreign investors with global operations in the textile industry or textile training programs.

The next stage, which centers on the final assembly and development of apparel products, requires supportive industrial and labor policies. Regarding labor, competitive wage levels and social compliance are vital for attracting new investors. Of course, national minimum wage laws play a key role in a firm's margins and competitiveness. Important areas for industrial policy relate to efficient infrastructure (lead times), corporate taxes, exchange rates, and incentives for foreign investment. As firms move beyond basic assembly, a more skilled labor force is needed with experience in customer management, sourcing, and manipulating design software and equipment.

The final stage, which revolves around distributing and selling final apparel products to consumers, necessitates policies that focus on developing a workforce with soft skills in these areas (especially knowledge-intensive capital) and providing access to new end markets and buyers. To diversify exports, trade policies that reduce the import tariffs faced in end market countries are also important. In addition, customs clearance procedures can determine firms' delivery times to global buyers.

Actors

All of these government policies primarily facilitate outcomes for three main sets of actors in the global, export-oriented apparel industry.

The first is composed of *global buyers* primarily headquartered in the United States and the EU: the apparel brand owners and retailers. As the lead firms in the chain, they make the ultimate decision on which firms and countries to source from. Whereas buyers take both firm- and country-specific factors into account, it is the firm-level factors that matter most, and which we will turn to shortly (see chapter 2). As for the key country-level criteria, these include political stability, labor policy and compliance, and transportation and communication infrastructure—all areas that can indirectly impact a buyer's reputation or directly impact buyers' ability to communicate with suppliers. Country-specific factors are also important in making an initial impression on global buyers. After all, a negative reputation or lack of awareness of the capabilities in a country reduces the likelihood of buyers looking at a certain country for suppliers. In this sense, these factors play an important role as an "entry bar" for consideration.

The second group consists of *apparel manufacturers and intermediaries* who assemble the final garment, coordinate the purchase of inputs, and ship the final product to buyers. Producers are far more concerned with the policy environment as it will either facilitate or hinder their ability to meet buyers' demands. Policies that enable producers to lower costs and diversify in terms of products and end markets include wage levels, workforce capabilities, trade preferences in end markets, and import tariffs on yarn and fabric. Compliance is largely related to labor policies, and lead times and reliability are affected by infrastructure and production efficiency.

The third group is composed of supporting *national stakeholders* that provide services and implement policies to help develop the country's industrial sector. It includes industry associations, unions, and government agencies responsible for export promotion, attracting investment, and developing industrial policies (see annex 5A for a list of key supporting stakeholders in each SAR country).

How does this policy mapping along different stages of the supply chain apply to South Asia's apparel industry? We begin by identifying the factors on which apparel buyers place the most weight, an exercise that was carried out in chapter 2 of this report. The results, based on buyers' surveys, show that buyers care foremost about product availability (that is, the ability to produce a diverse range of products that matches demand), along with cost, short lead times and reliability, and compliance.[1]

The next step is to rank the four SAR countries' performance in these areas and benchmark them against their main Southeast Asian competitors, an analysis that was performed in chapter 2. The results indicate that overall, the Southeast Asian countries and China are outperforming the South Asian countries on the non-cost-related factors important to global buyers, although South Asian countries remain competitive with respect to cost. That said, there are tremendous variations within South Asia.

- Bangladesh is one of the lowest countries in terms of price in nearly every major product category. At present, this appears to make up for the issues in meeting buyers' desired criteria in other areas with respect to compliance, quality, and reliability.
- India, like China, has midrange unit values compared to competitors despite buyers' perceptions of having comparatively higher prices. Where they differ, however, is across all other criteria, with India ranking among the bottom in all categories including productivity, product diversity, and lead times.
- Pakistan offers low prices in most product categories, but like India does not perform well in other areas (especially reliability and stability). Further, it is almost entirely dependent on cotton products, which means the country lacks product diversity.
- Sri Lanka's prices are higher than those of competitors in all major product categories, but the country is viewed positively in other areas, notably compliance and stability.

Outside the region, Cambodia offers low unit values, and its performance in other areas is generally average or acceptable. Indonesia offers low to moderate unit values across all product categories and has a positive image across other indicators. Vietnam's rank by unit values varies across product categories, although it delivers in all other non-cost-related areas as the first- or second-ranked country. China, like Vietnam, ranks among the top two countries in all non-cost criteria considered to be important when choosing a sourcing partner, and China's unit values are in the middle of the range of countries (see chapter 2).

Key Policies Relevant to South Asia's Apparel Industry

Armed with these results, we can now identify the main policy areas that affect factors deemed important by buyers, and determine how the SAR countries compare to competing countries in each area. Overall, our findings underscore the need to take a closer look at relevant trade, labor, industrial, and infrastructure policies. In particular, SAR countries exhibit high average most-favored nation (MFN) tariffs on textiles (except Sri Lanka) and poor logistics performance relative to Southeast Asia (figure 5.2 and table 5.2).

Policies Impacting Cost and Product Diversity
Trade and Investment Policies
Trade policies important to cost include (i) foreign import tariffs that SAR countries face for their final product exports and (ii) the import tariffs SAR countries impose on textile inputs. Investment policies, particularly those governing foreign investment, also play an important role in access to capital.

Figure 5.2 South Asia Has Higher Tariffs and Ranks Worse Than Southeast Asia in Logistics Performance

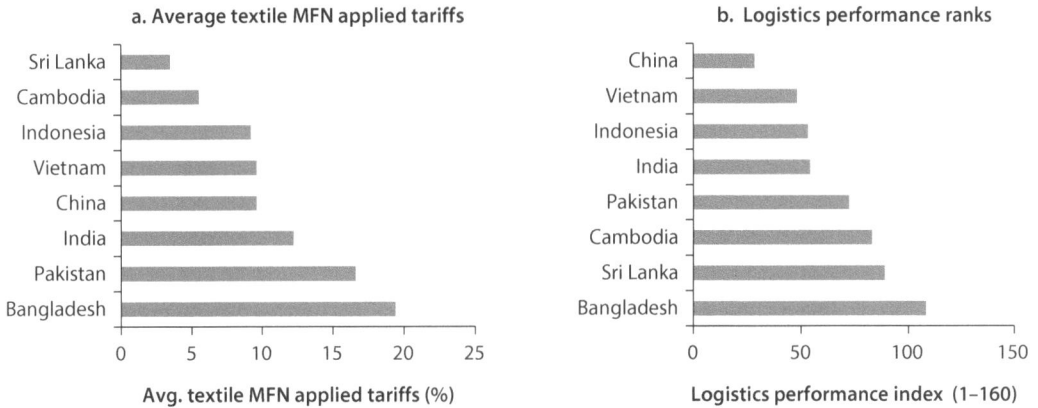

a. Average textile MFN applied tariffs

b. Logistics performance ranks

Source: Textile Import Tariffs: WTO, UNCTAD, and ITC 2014. Logistics Performance Index (LPI) Rank: Logistics Performance Index, World Bank.
Note: Textiles include yarn, fabric, and textile products, but not apparel. MFN = most-favored nation.

Table 5.2 Room for Rethinking Labor, Trade, and Industrial Policies

Factor/ country	Cost				Lead time and reliability		Compliance
Policy area	Trade			Labor	Industrial/infrastructure		Labor
Benchmark indicator	Apparel market access preferences	Textile import tariffs	Import tariff reduction policies	Min. wages	Logistics Performance Index (LPI) rank	Trading across borders (doing business) rank	National compliance initiative (if any)
China	4	4	EPZ	8	28	98	Chinese social compliance (CSC) 9000P
Cambodia	1	2	EPZ	3	83	124	Better work (2001)
Indonesia	3	3	DD	7	53	62	Better work (2011)
Vietnam	2	4	EPZ, DD	5	48	75	Better work (2009)
Bangladesh	1	8	DD, BWH	1	108	140	Accord & alliance (2013); Better work (2014)
India	2	6	DD	4	54	126	—
Pakistan	3	7	DD	6	72	69	—
Sri Lanka	3	1	—	2	89	108	Garments without guilt (2006)

Sources: Apparel Market Access Preferences: based on data in table 5A.3 in annex 5A. Textile Import Tariffs: WTO, UNCTAD, and ITC 2014. Import Tariff Reduction Policies: section below on "Import Tariffs and Tariff Reduction Schemes for Exporters." Minimum wages: chapter 2 of this report. Logistics Performance Index (LPI) Rank: Logistics Performance Index, World Bank. National Compliance Initiative: compiled by World Bank.
Note: Textiles include yarn, fabric, and textile products, but not apparel. Light grey cells are best, dark gray cells are worst, gray cells are in the middle. Textile import tariffs rank from lowest (best) to highest (worst). Minimum wages rank from lowest to highest. World Bank Logistics Performance Indicators (2014), 160 countries ranked, with 1 being the highest. World Bank Doing Business Indicators: 189 countries are ranked, with 1 being the highest. National compliance initiative: WRAP (Worldwide Responsible Accredited Production) and SAI Global Compliance are also both very active in China and India. (1) = GSP beneficiary; LDC-EBA duty-free access to EU; (2) = GSP beneficiary; reduced tariffs in EU, plus FTAs with other key end markets; (3) = GSP beneficiary, but limited FTAs; (4) = non-GSP beneficiary in most countries and limited FTAs; BW = bonded warehouses; DD = duty drawback; EBA = everything but arms; EPZ = export processing zones; FTA = free trade agreement; GSP = generalized system of preferences; LDC = least-developed country; — = Not available.

Preferential end market access: Given the relatively high tariffs applied to apparel products in developed countries compared to other manufactured goods, trade preferences shape how countries fare in the global apparel industry. Indeed, they determine the number and volume of orders a firm receives.

For the U.S. and EU markets, tariffs vary considerably for different product categories, with MFN tariffs averaging 12.8 and 10.1 percent for knitted and woven apparel in the United States and 11.7 and 11.3 percent for the EU (WTO 2013). These are high compared to the overall simple average MFN applied tariffs (on all products) of 3.4 and 5.5 percent in the United States and the EU, respectively (WTO, UNCTAD, and ITC 2014).

As a least-developed country (LDC), Bangladesh enjoys duty-free access under the "Everything but Arms (EBA)" scheme. Pakistan had GSP (generalized system of preferences) status until the end of 2013, but since January 2014 has received duty-free access via the GSP+ scheme, which has increased buyer interest and exports to the EU. Sri Lanka had GSP+ benefits until 2010 but now enjoys only the 20 percent general GSP duty reduction. India has GSP status for apparel but not textiles. The U.S. GSP does not cover tariff reductions for apparel, so all countries face average MFN tariffs.

For the Japanese market, the average MFN rate for apparel is 9.05 percent, although all SAR and Southeast Asian benchmark countries (Cambodia, Indonesia, and Vietnam, or "SEAB countries") receive some form of preferential access. For example, India and Bangladesh face zero tariffs because of the Free Trade Agreement and GSP-LDC schemes, respectively (WTO 2013). China, Indonesia, Pakistan, Sri Lanka, and Vietnam are all GSP beneficiaries and receive reduced tariff rates of 3.94 percent for 19 items under Japan's current GSP scheme or, in the case of the Southeast Asian countries, benefit from the ASEAN (Association of Southeast Asian Nations) agreement. As LDCs, Bangladesh and Cambodia have duty-free access under all other major GSP schemes (including Australia, Canada, New Zealand, Norway, the Russian Federation, Switzerland, and Turkey). India, Pakistan, and Sri Lanka also figure among the beneficiary countries in several GSP lists. It is important to keep in mind, however, that reduced duty rates are subject to meeting rules of origin requirements (see table 5A.3 in annex 5A for more details).

Import tariffs and tariff reduction schemes: A large proportion of apparel firms in SAR countries use material inputs or supplies of foreign origin, including MMFs. However, their own high tariffs and import barriers often prevent firms from obtaining these inputs, which limits their competitiveness in the global market. For example, China's consumption of synthetic fabrics is 10 times that of India (Jordan, Kamphuis, and Setia 2014). Although domestic backward linkages are important from a value added and competitiveness perspective (especially for lead times), no country will produce *every* type of yarn and fabric needed to maintain a competitive apparel export portfolio. Hence, imports of textile inputs remain an important factor in establishing a diverse product mix.

Within South Asia, the level of these tariffs and barriers varies greatly. Sri Lanka has zero duties on textile imports, while in the other three SAR countries relatively high tariffs prevail compared to Southeast Asian (China and SEAB) competitors (table 5.3). Furthermore, in India, additional domestic taxes and duties are also levied, with MMFs facing a 10 percent excise tax (whereas cotton is not taxed). This is particularly problematic for MMF fabric that is produced only to a limited extent locally. India also imposes high antidumping duties against China, the Republic of Korea, Indonesia, and other major producers of synthetic fibers, which often exceed 17 percent (above $500 per ton in absolute terms).

India's and Pakistan's apparel export associations have put liberalizing input import regimes at the top of their "wish lists."[2] In Pakistan, the government announced a rationalization of tariffs in the context of the Textile Policy 2009–14 to facilitate the availability of inputs (MINTEX 2012). In India, although the Ministry of Textiles proposed a "fiber neutral" policy to eliminate the differential tariffs between cotton and MMFs in 2011/12, the policy has not yet been enacted.

Even if a country imposes high import tariffs, there are various schemes that can be used to eliminate, reduce, or refund tariffs for exporters—such as duty drawback systems, bonded warehouses, or export processing zones (EPZs) (box 5.1). Although EPZs have been established in all four SAR countries, they do not play an important role in the apparel industry in terms of output and employment. Duty drawback schemes for exporters work well in Bangladesh, but in India—and even more so Pakistan—there are obstacles to using them (Jordan, Kamphuis, and Setia 2014; Nabi and Hamid 2013). For example, in India, qualitative information highlights that a large amount of paperwork may be required to prove that the stock of imports is used entirely for exports.

Table 5.3 South Asia Has Higher Import Tariffs Than Southeast Asia
(Percent)

Product category	Bangladesh (%)	India (%)	Pakistan (%)	Sri Lanka (%)	Cambodia (%)	China (%)	Indonesia (%)	Vietnam (%)
Yarn								
Cotton (5203–5207)	5–10	10	5–25	0	0	5–6 (2)	5	5
MMF (5401–5406/ 5501–5511)	5–25	10 (1)	0–10	0	0	5	0–5	0–5
Woven fabric								
Cotton (5208–5212)	25	10 (1)	15–25	0	7	10–14	10–15	12
MMF (5407–5408/ 5512–5516)	25	10–12.5 (1)	15	0–15	7	10–18	10–15	12
Knit Fabric (60)	25	10 (1)	20–25	0	7	10–12	10	12
MFN Avg. Applied	19.4	12.2	16.6	3.5	5.5	9.6	9.2	9.6
Duties (2014) Textiles		12.9				8.5		

Source: OTEXA 2014. Data on average MFN applied tariffs are from WTO, UNCTAD, and ITC 2014.
Note: Textiles include yarn, fabric, and textile products, but not apparel. (1) = Certain products are also subject to specific rupees per unit duty rates. (2) = Tariff rate quotas allow for imports of cotton and wool in limited quantities at reduced duties, ranging from 1 percent to 9 percent. Imports exceeding set quota levels are assessed at a much higher rate of duty. (3) = The MFN average applied duties are the average of the average tariffs in each category and are not weighted by imports. (4) = Tariffs on wool, silk, and vegetable fibers are omitted given their small share of the overall apparel export market compared to cotton and MMF. MFN = most-favored nation; MMF = manmade fiber.

Box 5.1 South Asia's Schemes to Reduce Import Tariffs for Exporters

Bangladesh:

- *Bonded warehouses.* Manufactured goods exporters can import raw materials and inputs—which are kept in the bonded warehouse—without paying duties and taxes. The required amount of inputs is released when exporters submit evidence of production for exports. This facility applies to exporters of apparel and specialized textiles, providing they export at least 70 percent of their output (ILO 2013a).
- *Duty drawback.* Manufactured goods exporters are given a refund of customs duties and sales taxes paid on the imported raw materials that are used in producing those exported goods. Exporters can also obtain drawbacks on the value added tax on local inputs used in production (ILO 2013a).
- *Cash subsidy.* This scheme, introduced in 1986, is mainly used by exporters of textiles and apparel who choose not to use bonded warehouse or duty drawback facilities and whose inputs are procured locally. Exporters can use this incentive to offset input tariffs. The cash subsidy ranges from 10 to 15 percent and is granted on the free on board (FOB) export value. A drawback of this system is that exporters have incentives to overinvoice exports (World Bank 2013b).
- *Export processing zones (EPZs).* Import tariffs on exported goods are eliminated in these special customs areas. Bangladesh has eight EPZs, with apparel firms constituting a large share of jobs and investment; however, EPZ exports represent a small share of the country's total apparel exports (less than 10 percent).

India:

- *DBK (drawback) system.* Duty is paid up front, and exporters apply for a drawback. Problems arise, however, because the drawback is calculated on the cost of materials less the amount of duty paid—and no drawback on trim items is permitted. Furthermore, tariffs plus additional import duties of 25–30 percent make FOB prices for garments uncompetitive (Birnbaum 2013).
- *Advance license scheme (ALS).* No duty is paid on imports used in export products, but procedures are extremely difficult and any error results in serious problems (Birnbaum 2013; National Stakeholders 2014).
- *EPZs:* There are 199 operational EPZs, of which seven are specialized in textiles and apparel.

Pakistan:

- *Duty and tax remission for export (DTRE).* The scheme enables postexport remission of duties and taxes. It is viewed by exporters as complex and time consuming, which discourages imports of manmade fiber (MMF) inputs and orders (Nabi and Hamid 2013).
- *EPZs:* There are nine EPZs that have been formally set up, of which Karachi is the only successful one.

Sri Lanka:

- *EPZs:* There are nine EPZs, but they are mostly located in urban areas.

What are the implications of the high import tariffs and duties, particularly with respect to inputs such as MMFs? In India, historical protection of the cotton industry and high tariffs on MMFs have skewed the export composition toward cotton garments. About 32 percent of the global apparel market is made up of synthetic fiber garments, yet India accounts for only 2 percent. In addition, India's apparel exports are heavily concentrated in the global spring/summer season, which affects capacity use because it leads to apparel factories operating only six and a half months annually relative to the global average of nine months (Jordan, Kamphuis, and Setia 2014). In contrast, Sri Lanka's low import tariffs contribute to a more diverse export portfolio in terms of fiber type. Thus, reducing tariffs on foreign inputs and easing the passage of these inputs may boost volume and improve both the composition of exports and overall efficiency.

Further, there are issues with respect to the domestic production of MMFs upstream in the value chain. Purified terephthalic acid (PTA) is a critical raw material required to produce polyester or synthetic fibers. But in India only two large firms produce this chemical, with the largest one owning 79 percent of production capacity. If a domestic industry is to grow, import barriers must be lowered and more support given to firms to produce these inputs (Jordan, Kamphuis, and Setia 2014).

Trade agreements: South Asia has one of the most restrictive trade regimes globally—ahead only of Sub-Saharan Africa on the World Bank's Overall Trade Restrictiveness index (Rama 2014). One way to reduce import tariffs is with regional, bilateral, and multilateral trade agreements. In theory, these agreements are less preferable than unilateral reductions in tariffs and duties because they may lead to trade diversion (that is, when trade is diverted from a more efficient producer to a less efficient one). But, given the political economy landscape and difficulties in achieving unilateral reductions and policies, they are a viable second-best solution to facilitate forward and backward linkages between two or more countries.

At this point, South Asia continues to be one of the least integrated regions in terms of intraregional trade as a share of total trade—accounting for less than 10 percent in 2012. Its most important trade agreement is the South Asian Free Trade Area (SAFTA), but there is little progress in its implementation given political tensions, particularly between India and Pakistan. Furthermore, asymmetries between SAR countries are high, with India accounting for the large majority of production, consumption, and trade. Despite some growth in textile trade from India to Bangladesh and, to a lesser extent, Sri Lanka, one cannot speak of a regional value chain.

In contrast, the Southeast Asian competitors are part of ASEAN, which was formed in 1967. It has negotiated additional trade agreements and, hence, zero or reduced tariffs with other key textile suppliers and apparel end markets, including Australia, China, Japan, and Korea.

Foreign investment: The role of foreign direct investment (FDI) in Asia's apparel exports has differed greatly within and among subregions (box 5.2). Whereas some countries initially relied on foreigners, others did not. Historically,

Box 5.2 Using FDI to Make Inroads into Textile and Apparel Markets

Whereas barriers to entry into apparel manufacturing are low in terms of capital, technology, and skill levels, gaining access to U.S. and EU buyers can be quite difficult. For that reason, ties to Asian foreign investment have played an important role in the growth trajectory of apparel exports over the past several decades.

All of the top Asian apparel exporters—except India and Pakistan—grew thanks to FDI or factories with owners of foreign descent. This can largely be explained by the well-established structure of production and distribution networks that has characterized the global apparel export industry since the 1970s. U.S. and European buyers purchase from intermediaries and multinational manufacturers based in China; Hong Kong SAR, China; Korea; and Taiwan, China, who have textile and apparel investment and sourcing ties throughout Asia. These firms started outsourcing and offshoring production during the MFA to take advantage of quota preferences and lower operating costs. Today these decisions are driven by market access preferences and favorable investment incentives.

Currently, Southeast Asian countries have an advantage over South Asia in capturing some of China's production that is destined for the United States and the EU-15 because these countries are part of existing production networks. This connection is important because buyers evaluate suppliers on their ability to supply products across multiple product categories. Buyers are looking at not just what is made at one factory but what the vendor is capable of supplying on a global level.

Looking ahead, whereas India and Pakistan have managed to maintain their positions as top exporters without FDI, they may need to attract it to make deeper inroads into the U.S. and EU markets, particularly given buyers' desire to reduce the number of firms they work with directly. South Asia is in a good position to expand to the EU-15—and is already exporting more there—because of duty-free benefits granted to Bangladesh and recently Pakistan (now, because of GSP+ benefits, Pakistan is on China's list of target FDI countries as part of its "go out" development strategy to encourage firms to invest overseas).

South Asia is also well situated to capitalize on emerging end markets because of the dominance of domestic ownership. But to succeed, it must create stronger ties with Argentina, Australia, Brazil, Canada, China, the Russian Federation, Saudi Arabia, and the United Arab Emirates on forward linkages. This means (i) preferable tariffs for its apparel exports, (ii) knowledge on how the retail industry operates (in these countries), and (iii) relationships with brand owners and retailers that have large market shares in these emerging end markets.

---

foreign investment has played a key role in the initial setup of the apparel industry in Bangladesh and Sri Lanka but not in India and Pakistan.

- In Bangladesh, the Bangladesh Export Processing Zone Authority (BEPZA) was set up in1983 to promote foreign and local investment. The initial foreign investment—especially from Korea—was vital for the industry's development, for access not just to capital but also to technology and knowledge. Also helpful were quota advantages and market access preferences. Bangladesh has followed a path most similar to that of Southeast Asia, although it has now managed to shift from FDI to domestic ownership by using industrial policies that require domestic participation and access to finance.

- In Sri Lanka, the industry was initiated by U.S. foreign investors who quickly established joint ventures with local entrepreneurs.
- In India and Pakistan, domestic ownership dominates. One reason why is that India was restricted by quotas during the MFA and thus was not a target for quota-hopping East Asian investors. Other reasons include initial restrictions on foreign ownership and an overly complex legal system that would be difficult for a foreigner to navigate alone. Thus, firms are responsible for establishing relationships with buyers *and* backward linkages to fabric and yarn on their own.

In contrast, the Southeast Asian countries developed with significant support from foreign investment. Prior to the MFA and its predecessors, U.S. and EU-15 buyers originally started sourcing from apparel manufacturers in East Asia (China; Hong Kong SAR, China; Korea; and Taiwan, China). But as East Asia's production declined because of rising production costs and quotas, its firms set up facilities in China and later Southeast Asia (Cambodia, Indonesia, and Vietnam). The fact that these firms already had relationships with U.S. and EU buyers facilitated the transfer of orders and exports to these countries. While investing in apparel firms in nearby countries, the East Asian countries also became leading producers of textiles to supply these factories. Domestic branch plants, however—especially in Cambodia and Vietnam—have a limited ability to develop independent forward linkages to buyers.

Currently, FDI is formally allowed in all SAR countries, but obstacles remain in India and Pakistan. Sri Lanka has had liberal FDI policies, whereas it was restricted in the other countries until the mid-2000s (Aggarwal 2005; Sahoo, Nataraj, and Dash 2014). In Bangladesh, as well, there has historically been support to attract increased foreign investment since the 1980s. However, even in Bangladesh, challenges to attracting foreign investment remain. For instance, Samsung, a multinational manufacturer of electronics, was initially interested in investing in Bangladesh but could not follow through because of issues with acquiring land in EPZs. Boosting investor confidence should remain a high priority in Bangladesh. In India and Pakistan, 100 percent FDI is formally possible, but in practice there are still challenges due to the number of authorities involved and the specific conditions or permits required. For example, India allows 100 percent FDI in the textile sector under the automatic route (that is, without any prior approval), and the Ministry of Textiles has recently set up FDI Cell to attract FDI. However, the textiles sector is not one of the top sectors receiving FDI in the country, and no explicit policy exists to attract FDI to apparel.

Labor Policies
Labor policies, especially policies governing wage levels, play a critical role in shaping costs. Overall, South Asia's minimum wages are lower than those of its

Southeast Asian competitors and China, giving it a competitive edge (table 5.2). Bangladesh's rise as an apparel powerhouse is in large part due to its low wages. India and Pakistan's wage rates remain some of the lowest among the major apparel-exporting nations. Sri Lanka also has a low minimum wage; but, unlike the other SAR countries, it has relatively high labor costs for the region due in part to a smaller, more highly skilled workforce. Indeed, our interviews with Sri Lankan apparel firms show that they feel that they are not competitive relative to Bangladesh largely because of their higher wages.[3] In Sri Lanka, 41.5 percent of total employment is concentrated in the services sector, which has a higher average wage.

Within each country's apparel sector, there are also big variations in pay. In Bangladesh, wages are higher inside EPZs than outside them. Wage rates also vary by skill level—averaging $21 per month for an apprentice, $38 per month for an unskilled worker, $45 per month for a semiskilled worker, and up to $60 per month for a skilled worker as of 2010 (World Bank 2013b). In India, there are also significant variations in wage rates among states.

However, South Asia's overall labor wage advantage may not be sustainable for economic and social compliance reasons. In Bangladesh, wages have not kept up with inflation, and since the Rana Plaza and Tazreen factory fire incidents, there has been global pressure to raise the wage rates. In India, rapidly rising living costs in current hubs of apparel manufacturing may reduce the future available labor pool, including from migration. Already, factory owners report an average of 16–18 percent annual wage and mandatory benefit increases (Birnbaum 2013).

Against this backdrop, South Asian countries will need to find ways to boost productivity to maintain competitiveness. Overall, productivity levels in South Asia remain lower than in China and Vietnam. In India, labor productivity is almost one-third the level in China in the apparel sector.

A key way to increase productivity is by reforming labor regulations, such as those governing hiring and firing and number of hours worked. One study finds that India's stringent labor regulations result in lower output, employment, investment, and productivity in the formal manufacturing sector (Besley and Burgess 2004). The Apparel Export Promotion Council (AEPC) in India contends that India's strict laws governing number of overtime hours worked—50 hours per quarter—are tougher than what the International Labour Organization (ILO) mandates and lead to lower productivity and underuse of capacity. Indian firms also cite limitations on overtime (and female adolescents' working hours) imposed by the Factories Act (1948) as a key barrier to growth. Another issue is job termination: India's Industrial Dispute Act (1947) requires state involvement in firing decisions when the firm size exceeds 100 employees. Given that most exporting firms exceed this threshold, firms are opting to use other means of introducing flexibility in their use of labor, such as contract workers to avoid permanent employment. This leads to high turnover and the need to retrain workers, which is a drag on productivity.

That said, some studies question that stringent labor policies are a major constraint. For example, in a follow-up survey of 17 large textile firms in India, Bloom et al. (2012) find that firms cited that labor regulations did not hinder them from adopting a set of "good" management practices. However, this suggests only that labor regulations may not be a critical issue, not that they do not constrain productivity at all.

Another component of labor policies that affects productivity is skills training, given that investing in skills at different stages of the apparel value chain can lead to higher efficiency and lower costs. In Sri Lanka, human resources and skill development are a key component of its policies (National Stakeholders 2014). Apparel-specific training institutes build on the country's high general education level, with education free from kindergarten to the university level for the majority of the population. In India, there is a vast network of educational institutions focused on textiles and apparel. In 2010, a major government-led skill development program was announced, and in 2014 a Ministry of Skill Development and Entrepreneurship was created, consolidating all training programs. But in Pakistan and Bangladesh, a great deal more needs to be done (Nabi and Hamid 2013; World Bank 2013b). Pakistan has made little progress on a previously announced skills scheme. However, large firms report that they carry out in-house training for most of their workers (Nabi and Hamid 2013). Bangladesh adopted a National Skill Policy in 2011; but, overall, policies to enhance skills are not coordinated. A variety of skill enhancement programs centered around the industry associations, with limited coordination and with a focus on "on-the-job" training, remain in place (UNCTAD 2014).

Policies to Shorten Lead Times
Policies to Support Spatial Development
Clustering strategies, with industrial parks or EPZs, are a way to reduce lead times by co-locating multiple steps in the chain and providing one-stop resources for common procedures. But they also are being used by many South Asian countries to tackle other objectives. In India and Pakistan, these strategies serve as a way to tackle systematic infrastructure problems.

- India's policy on industrial parks tries to provide better infrastructure in a concentrated way, although so far only a small share of firms benefit from these initiatives (Saleman and Jordan 2013). In 2005, the government announced the Scheme for Integrated Textile Parks (SITP) to consolidate individual units in a cluster and provide state-of-the-art infrastructure to local and international manufacturers. SITP was created by merging two schemes initiated in 2002 (the Apparel Parks for Exports Scheme and the Textile Center Infrastructure Development Scheme). There are now 27 operational parks and 13 more have been approved (TEXMIN 2015). And investments in the EPZs have an export focus (Aggarwal 2007, 2010).
- Pakistan is trying a similar approach with the support of Textile and Garment Cities (launched in 2004) to provide key infrastructure and common facilities,

but the long-awaited clusters have only recently begun to make much progress (Flanagan 2014b) (MINTEX 2012). To date, only two garment cities (one each in Faisalabad and Lahore) are operational. The Karachi Garment City and Pakistan Textile City are still contending with numerous problems (litigation; nonsupply of gas, water, and electricity; and lack of funding), but Karachi is slated to be developed on a fast-track basis (MINTEX 2015).

In Sri Lanka and Bangladesh, clustering strategies are used to further social policy.

- Sri Lanka is promoting industrial relocation of the apparel industry to handle labor shortages. It recently tried to tap into the more remote and war-torn areas in the north and east with incentives for apparel investments, although few plants have opened because of poor transportation networks and lack of workers with apparel sewing machine operator experience (National Stakeholders 2014). But the 200 Garment Factories program has shown that, from a social standpoint, female workers benefit from working in factories located close to their villages.
- Bangladesh is trying to move unsafe production units to formal clusters, in response to the Rana Plaza disaster (World Bank 2013b). Recent interviews with Bangladeshi firms show that relocating ready-made garment factories to an EPZ can benefit the firms in many ways, including on the social front (see box 5.3). For example, male workers in Bangladesh are attracted to EPZs because of the contract security (Zohir 2001a), and EPZs have been found to attract additional female workers (Zohir 2001b). Many of the issues high-lighted are applicable to the other SAR countries.

For China, strategically located cluster development has been a key feature in developing the textile and apparel industry—with apparel concentrated in the coastal regions. Indeed, in 2006, the provinces with the highest production capacity were Guangdong (27 percent), Zhejiang (19 percent), Jiangsu (18 percent), Shangdong (13 percent), and Fujian (6 percent)—and their combined total output constituted 83 percent of China's total apparel output. As an added benefit, textile production is also concentrated on the coast in Zhejiang and Jiangsu provinces. Clusters within these regions also tend to be specialized in particular types of products (FBIC 2007).

So far, China has favored the coastal areas for apparel for a variety of reasons: (i) these were China's traditional locations for its apparel industry as well as for upstream industries such as the textile industry and synthetic fiber industry; (ii) there are more qualified workers in the coastal areas than in the rest; (iii) China's earliest Economic Development Zones—which have attracted foreign investment since the mid-1980s—were located in the coastal areas of Shenzhen, Zhuhai, Haikou, Ningbo, Shanghai, Dalian, Qingdao, and Xiamen; (iv) the coastal areas have high population densities, with residents who tend to have higher disposable income, a better education, and greater fashion

Box 5.3 Relocating to a Bangladeshi Industrial Zone

Over the past few decades, the sporadic rise of ready-made garment factories in Bangladesh has taken place without adherence to a global compliance regime. As a result, policy makers are debating ways to improve the situation—including encouraging firms to relocate to an industrial zone. A recent World Bank study (2015) aimed at examining the costs and benefits of such a move suggests that over time the relocation should pay off. It was conducted through interviews with medium-sized firms in Dhaka city that employ 500–2,000 workers—of whom, on average, about 90 percent are women. It found the following:

Key costs of relocation to a zone include (i) buying land or renting factory premises; (ii) moving or buying equipment; (iii) transporting inventory, raw materials, and equipment; (iv) halting and shifting production; (v) rebranding, logistics of a new address, and printing business cards and letterheads; and (vi) financing relocation expenses for workers or severance packages.

Key benefits of relocation to a zone include (i) design of a zone with improved infrastructure and adequate transportation facilities; (ii) location of zone with good connections to ports; (iii) clustering of businesses for ease of access for buyers; and (iv) greater efficiency with necessary facilities (such as bonded warehouse, wet/dry facilities, banks, and services).

Short-, medium-, and long-term payoffs

As for whether the benefits outweigh the costs, the study found the following:

- In the *short run* (first 6 months) of the relocation process, the payoffs to firms may not be tangible. But buyers would view relocated firms as compliant with global standards in terms of safety and providing workers' rights. This may in turn attract additional orders and buyers, although it would take at least a year. This increase in orders may offset the cost of relocation (including halting production and cost of land).
- In the *medium term* (2–4 years), the zone's enhanced goods and on-time delivery of finished products may attract additional buyers, which could increase profits and make up for the relocation costs.
- In the *long run*, not only will the factories be more competitive but the industry may also converge to the standards as implemented in the zone. It is expected that the additional efficiency, along with increased profits and orders, will help factories break even on the costs incurred and eventually make net profits.

consciousness, thereby leading to huge market potential; and (v) logistics infrastructure is generally better developed in the coastal regions, making the areas attractive to foreign investors (FBIC 2007).

However, as costs to operate in the coastal regions increase, apparel firms are being encouraged by national and local government incentives to relocate either within the province to less-developed areas, further inland to other less-developed provinces, or to other lower-cost Asian countries (FBIC 2007; Zhu and Pickles 2014).

Policies to Support a Domestic Textile Industry

All SAR countries have policies in place to support backward linkages to the textile sector. India and Pakistan have historically applied an integrative approach toward the textile and apparel industry given their strong textile base, focusing in particular on textiles and cotton. In both countries, domestic and foreign inputs are treated differently, as reflected in trade policy (like import tariffs on textiles, particularly natural fiber based) and domestic industrial policies, including the policy bias against MMFs (Jordan, Kamphuis, and Setia 2014; Nabi and Hamid 2013).

India has made the most progress with its technology missions on Cotton and Technical Textiles (Tewari and Singh 2010). Bangladesh achieved considerable success in establishing backward linkages in the knit segment with a set of policies that included cash subsidies for apparel exports made from locally produced yarn and fabrics and conditional FDI policies (World Bank 2005). Sri Lanka still imports most of its textile needs, despite some policy initiatives to support textile production.

Technology upgrading also holds enormous potential, which is why it is being so aggressively pursued. TUFS, a major element in India's textile and apparel strategy, has helped modernize the industry by providing capital investment support for modernizing technology (for example, a 10 percent investment subsidy and a 5 percent interest rate reduction). A similar policy was launched in Pakistan, although results have been mixed, with firms citing implementation issues and high interest rates (Nabi and Hamid 2013; National Stakeholders 2014). Although there are no TUFS or similar schemes in Bangladesh and Sri Lanka, capital investments are supported (Raihan and Razzaque 2007). Sri Lanka has been especially successful in upgrading technology and processes.

Another important issue is energy costs and reliability—notably the challenges of inadequate supply and frequent power outages, with many apparel and textile firms operating stand-alone fossil-fuel-powered electricity units, which increase production time and costs. The costs and availability of energy are particularly important for the textile sector, but less so for apparel, which is primarily labor intensive rather than capital intensive. In Bangladesh, on-grid costs range from $0.07 to $0.10 per kWh (kilowatt-hour), but off-grid generating costs are as high as $0.26 per kWh (World Bank 2013a).[4] In Pakistan, the textile industry has also suffered for lack of adequate infrastructure facilities, especially in the Punjab province (Lahore) where approximately 65 percent of the industrial units are located (MINTEX 2015). In India, the extent of the problem varies across regions. In Sri Lanka, interviews reveal that, although large firms view energy costs as high, they do not perceive energy as a major constraint.

Beyond the actual high costs of energy, it is also expensive—in both monetary and nonmonetary terms—just to set up the initial electrical connection. Bangladesh has the highest cost of securing electricity (as a proportion of its per capita incomes) in South Asia (figure 5.3). It takes Bangladeshi firms almost 4,000 percent of per capita income to get electricity, and it takes 428 days for a standardized warehouse in Bangladesh to get electricity, well above the 115 days in Vietnam.

Figure 5.3 Bangladesh Has the Highest Bill for Securing Electricity

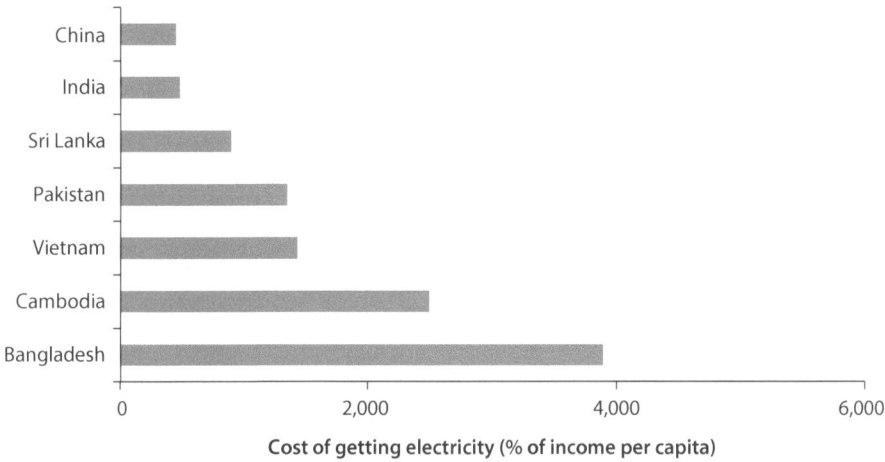

Cost of getting electricity (% of income per capita)

Source: Doing Business 2015, World Bank.
Note: Cost is recorded as a percentage of the economy's income per capita and exclusive of value added tax. All the fees and costs associated with completing the procedures to connect a warehouse to electricity are recorded, including those related to obtaining clearances from government agencies, applying for the connection, receiving inspections of both the site and the internal wiring, purchasing material, getting the actual connection works, and paying a security deposit.

Provision of Infrastructure

Infrastructure—particularly transport, logistics, and customs—is a highly problematic issue in most SAR countries. The World Bank Logistics Performance Index, which shows SAR performing well below China and its SEAB competitors (except Cambodia), underscores the need for taking a close look at relevant trade, labor, industrial, and infrastructure policies (table 5.2).

In Bangladesh, inefficiencies at the Chittagong port remain a problem, although the currently executed extension of Dhaka–Chittagong highway should ease congestion. The government has also taken several measures to facilitate customs and further automate customs processes (World Bank 2013a).

In India and Pakistan, transportation infrastructure is the most important issue, given that both countries are large (in terms of land area) and that the largest geographic concentrations of firms are inland rather than near major ports. In India, the condition of roads, railways, and ports is problematic. In addition, there are significant regulatory barriers (such as check posts) involved in internal traffic (Jordan, Kamphuis, and Setia 2014). The government aims to address these systemic infrastructure issues through the cluster approach. India has introduced a risk management system for customs; however, firms report that implementation is lagging and, hence, still demand electronic transactions.[5] The establishment of the Pakistan Land Port Authority aimed to make land ports more efficient and responsive to security issues, smuggling, and human trafficking. Although customs procedures are reformed and automated, there is still room for further improvements (Nabi and Hamid 2013; WTO 2008).

Although Sri Lanka ranks low in the economy wide Logistics Performance Index (LPI) rankings, it has solid supporting infrastructure as compared to the other SAR countries for the apparel industry. Interviews with buyers and the apparel association, along with numerous empirical studies, highlight that Sri Lanka's transportation and logistics networks helped facilitate the development of the apparel industry. The recent "hub" concept, which foresees a key role for Sri Lanka in the transshipment business and related public investment in ports and railways, is expected to benefit the industry (JAAF 2011). That said, infrastructure does present a challenge and will need to be developed to expand production into the more remote areas to the north and east (National Stakeholders 2014).

Policies to Improve Compliance

Buyers are increasingly paying more attention to labor standards and firms' compliance levels, especially following a number of fires and deaths in textile and apparel facilities. In Bangladesh, in the aftermath of the Rana Plaza and Tazreen factory fire incidents, buyers have come under additional global pressure to ensure adequate health and safety conditions for workers. Recently, Bangladesh passed a labor law that allows employees to form labor unions without factory owner approval—and, in 2014, there were more than 120 registered garment trade unions as compared to only three in 2012–13.[6] This type of internal pressure from groups such as labor unions will help increase monitoring of compliance to health and safety standards (box 5.4).

In India, firms are often able to avoid monitoring by staying small. The processing industry is dominated by small units, and compliance with environmental regulations is particularly low within these firms (Jordan, Kamphuis, and Setia 2014). Reforming labor regulations on firm size may indirectly improve compliance because, once firms are larger and registered, they will be easier to monitor. In Pakistan, a major challenge is political stability and safety (Global Apparel Buyers 2014). Many buyers will not travel to Pakistan because of security concerns, so domestic firms often travel to Dubai to meet them, which makes sourcing complicated (National Stakeholders 2014).

In recent years, South Asian countries—with Sri Lanka leading the pack—have ratified a number of ILO conventions on labor conditions like workers' safety. Interviews with firms in Sri Lanka highlight the importance they place on safety and enforcing the no child labor policy. However, in some cases across South Asia, despite formal adoption of labor standards and international conventions, in practice compliance may be lacking. Studies of the ILO's Better Work program highlight that the highest rates of noncompliance across countries globally are with respect to paid leave, social security, employee benefits, inaccurate payments, and insufficient wage information (ILO 2014). Policies to improve monitoring and to penalize noncompliance could help improve the situation.

Thoughts on Policies to Help Reposition South Asia

What can South Asia do to improve competitiveness in apparel? For South Asia to expand apparel exports and employment, it needs to improve its performance

Box 5.4 Bangladesh Takes Steps to Boost Compliance

In Bangladesh, wages and working conditions have long been a source of concern in the apparel sector. This is evidenced by the frequent strikes and labor unrest following the Rana Plaza disaster in April 2013—the single worst incident in the history of the apparel industry, which killed about 1,200 people—and other incidents such as the fire at Tazreen Fashions in November 2012. In response to these incidents, the industry—in collaboration with the government, foreign buyers, and development partners—has agreed on several policy measures to improve factory safety and social compliance.

One recent initiative is the Accord on Fire and Building Safety in Bangladesh (the "Accord")—signed by mostly European apparel buyers along with two global trade unions—a legally binding agreement between buyers and unions in which companies commit to conducting independent inspections and developing stronger worker-management committees in factories. It also includes financial obligations by buyers to help suppliers pay for safety upgrades (Anner, Bair, and Blasi 2013; Gifford and Ansett 2014). Another recent initiative is the essentially voluntary Alliance for Bangladesh Worker Safety (the "Alliance"), largely backed by North American buyers. Together these two initiatives cover nearly half of the country's total factories (1,600 factories for the Accord, and 600 for the Alliance).

These initiatives are a positive step, but they have also been criticized for focusing primarily on large firms and on fire and building safety rather than other major labor issues. To cover the remaining firms, the government and representatives from local employers' and workers' organizations have signed an integrated National Tripartite Plan of Action (NTPA) under the guidance of the International Labour Organization (ILO). In addition, a "Better Work" program for the ready-made garment industry has also been announced. The success of these programs will be a challenge, as it will require major changes and financing. It is estimated that about half of the country's apparel factories—mostly small and medium-sized firms that depend on subcontracting from large factories—will have difficulty adopting international standards and may be forced to close (ADB 2014).

in areas that matter most to global buyers. All the SAR countries (with the exception of Sri Lanka) generally appear to be cost competitive. But they are inhibited by too great a concentration on cotton products, even though the industry is increasingly moving toward MMF products. And they lag behind Southeast Asia in quality, input availability (like synthetic fibers), lead times (the time between placing and receiving an order), reliability, and social compliance (table 5.4).

If the situation persists—that is, no policies are set up and implemented to alter the picture—this report has estimated that a 10 percent increase in China's prices would mean an increase in South Asian exports of between 13 and 25 percent—well below the estimated gain for Southeast Asia of between 37 and 51 percent.

With respect to policies, all South Asian countries have adopted measures to promote the apparel sector in view of the MFA phaseout in 2005. Government policies in the region typically focus on tax and duty exemption, and finance facilities for technology upgrading through capital investments (like TUFS) and skill development, clustering, and export promotion measures. Sri Lanka has had the most effective initiatives in apparel, with JAAF—the industry association—playing an important role in coordinating stakeholders. In the other countries, coordination between stakeholders is limited. More recently, India's "Make in India" initiative proposes policies related to the manufacturing sector, and "Textiles and Garments" are included as key industries of this initiative.

Even so, our analysis shows that most South Asian countries would benefit significantly from easing barriers to the import of inputs and facilitating market access and foreign investment. The top reform priorities include increasing market access, removing barriers to access to MMFs, and attracting more foreign investment (box 5.5). Thus, it is imperative for South Asian economies to quickly design and implement policies to capture more apparel production and employment as wages rise in China, or they risk losing out on a huge opportunity to create good jobs for development.

Table 5.4 South Asia is Less Competitive Than Southeast Asia in Non-cost Areas
(Country Comparison: Non-Cost-Related Factors Impacting Performance)

		Buyers' perceptions of:			
Country	Quality		Lead time & reliability		Social compliance & sustainability
China	●	1	●	1	▲ 3
Bangladesh	●	5	●	5	● 6
India	●	6	●	6	● 5
Vietnam	●	2	●	2	● 2
Cambodia	▲	4	▲	4	▲ 4
Indonesia	▲	3	▲	3	● 1

Source: Chapter 2 of this report.
Note: Based on buyers and stakeholders' surveys conducted for this study. Countries were ranked from 1 to 6 on each factor, with 1 being the best and 6 being the worst. Ranks for quality and lead time/reliability are the same, so only one line is visible. Green indicates top two countries (factor is not an issue); Orange is for the middle two countries (indicates caution); Blue is used for the bottom two ranking countries (factor is an issue).

Box 5.5 Possible Strategic Steps for South Asia's Apparel Sector

India

As the benchmarking revealed, India currently has midrange unit values but low productivity, product diversity, and lead times. Our elasticity estimates reveal that a 10 percent increase in Chinese prices to the EU can increase male employment by 4.3 percent and female employment by 3.26 percent. Given these potential gains and the current situation in India, the following policies could help India increase apparel exports:

- Reduce tariffs and import barriers to ease access to manmade fibers (MMFs).
- Provide incentives (like lower excise taxes) to develop a domestic MMF industry.
- Promote foreign investment for apparel and take advantage of market access to emerging markets.

box continues next page

Box 5.5 Possible Strategic Steps for South Asia's Apparel Sector *(continued)*

Bangladesh

Along almost every apparel product category, the benchmarking highlights that Bangladesh has the lowest prices. However, it performs poorly in the areas of compliance, quality, and reliability, which are important in attracting foreign investment. Bangladesh also stands to gain a lot in terms of jobs from additional apparel exports—a 10 percent increase in Chinese prices to the United States would lead to an increase of over 4 percent each in male and female employment. Thus, Bangladesh could benefit from the following policies:

- Adopt policies to attract more foreign direct investment (FDI) to ensure access to buyers and additional capital.
- Reduce import barriers to MMF.
- Ensure policies to improve compliance are enforced (such as better safety conditions in EPZs).

Sri Lanka

Sri Lanka's apparel prices are higher than those of competitors in most product categories, and its product portfolio is largely made up of higher-value, niche products. Sri Lanka stands to gain a lot from increasing its apparel exports, particularly to the EU market. Elasticity estimates highlight that a 10 percent increase in Chinese apparel prices could increase Sri Lankan male employment by 8.55 percent and female employment by 7.87 percent. Thus, Sri Lanka could benefit from the following policies:

- Enter into more trade agreements to help diversify end markets and export destinations for existing products (such as activewear and intimate apparel).
- Attract foreign investment, which remains at 2 percent of gross domestic product (GDP) five years after the end of armed conflict.
- Expand into new products such as formal wear and high-end outerwear that require higher skills, and position as regional apparel and textile trade hub taking advantage of infrastructure and location.

Pakistan

Despite low prices in most apparel product categories, Pakistan lags competitors in reliability. It also remains highly concentrated in cotton products. Pakistan also stands to gain a lot of jobs from the apparel sector. A 10 percent increase in Chinese prices to the United States would increase Pakistan's male employment by 8.93 percent and female employment by 8.5 percent. Pakistan should enhance apparel competitiveness by diversifying its product offerings away from cotton and improving its lagging indicators. Thus, it could benefit from the following policies:

- Reduce barriers on imports to ease access to MMF.
- Adopt policies to reduce red tape and increase transparency to close gap with South Asian countries whose textile and apparel industries are located primarily on the coast.
- Take advantage of market access to emerging markets, and improve road infrastructure.

Annex 5A: Examples of Key Policies and Stakeholders in South Asia

Table 5A.1 SAR Countries—Examples of Key Textile- and Apparel-Specific Policies in South Asia

Country	Bangladesh	India	Pakistan	Sri Lanka
		Policy focus area		
Midterm strategies	National Coordination Council (NCC)	National Textile Policy 2000	Textile Vision 2005, incl. Technology Upgradation Fund	Five-Year Strategy (2002)
	Post-MFA Action Program (PMAP)	Technology Upgradation Fund Scheme (1999)	National Textile Policy 2009–2014	Hub Concept (2010)
		Technology Missions on Cotton (2000), Non-Cotton Fibers and Yarns (2010)	Textile Policy 2014–2019 (draft)	
		Vision, Strategy & Action Plan for Indian Textiles & Apparel 2024 (draft)		
Cluster policies		Scheme for Integrated Textile Parks (2005)	Garment/Textile Cities (mid-2000s)	
		Mega clusters for handlooms, power looms, handicrafts (2008)		
Social and environmental compliance	Better Work in Textiles & Garments (2010)	Integrated Skill Development Scheme (ISDS) (2010)	Textile Garment Skill Development Board (2006)	Garments without Guilt (2007)
	Promotion of Social and Environmental Standards in Industry (2010)	Driving Industry Towards Sustainable Human Capital Advancement (DISHA) (2011)		
	National Tripartite Plan of Action (NTPA) (2013)	Integrated Processing Development Scheme (IPDS) (2013)		
	Better Work (2013—announced)			
	Accord and Alliance (2013)			
	Sustainability Pact (2013)			

Source: Updated from Frederick and Staritz 2012.
Note: SAR = South Asian sample countries—Bangladesh, India, Pakistan, and Sri Lanka.

Table 5A.2 Key Stakeholders in South Asia by Type of Policy Function

Country	Bangladesh	India	Pakistan	Sri Lanka
Trade policy	Ministry of Commerce (MoC), National Board of Revenue (NBR)	Ministry of Commerce and Industry (MoCI)	Ministry of Commerce (MoC), Ministry of Industry and Production (MoIP), National Tariff Commission (NTC), Engineering Development Board (EDB)	Ministry of Industry and Commerce (MoIC)
Industrial policy	MoC, Ministry of Textile and Jute (MoTJ), NBR, Ministry of Industry (MoI)	MoCI, Ministry of Textiles (TEXMIN)	MoC, MoIP Ministry of Textile Industry (MINTEX), NTC, EDB, Small & Medium Enterprises Development Authority (SMEDA)	MoIC
FDI/export promotion	Board of Investment (BOI), Export Promotion Bureau (EPB), Bangladesh Export Processing Zones Authority (BEPZA)	MoCI, Foreign Investment Promotion Board (FIPB), Foreign Investment Implementation Authority (FIIA), Secretariat for Industrial Assistance (SIA)	Board of Investment (BOI), Trade Development Authority of Pakistan (TDAP)	Board of Investment (BOI), Engineering Development Board (EDB)
Industry associations	Bangladesh Garment Manufacturers and Exporters Association (BGMEA), Bangladesh Knitwear Manufacturers and Exporters Association (BKMEA), Bangladesh Textile Mills Association (BTMA)	Apparel Export Promotion Council (AEPC), Confederation of Indian Textile Industry (CITI), Clothing Manufacturers Association of India (CMAI), Confederation of Indian Apparel Exporters (CIAE)	Pakistan Readymade Garment Manufacturer and Exporter Association (PRGMEA), All Pakistan Textile Mill Association (APTMA), Pakistan Textile Exporters Association (PTEA)	Joint Apparel Association Forum (JAAF)
Trade unions: General	Bangladesh Centre for Workers' Solidarity (BCWS)	Hind Mazdoor Sabha (HMS), All India Trade Union Congress (AITUC), India National Trade Union Congress (INTUC)	All Pakistan Trade Union Federation (APTUF), National Trade Union Federation (NTUF)	Jathika Sevaka Sangamaya (JSS), National Workers Congress (NWC), Free Trade Zone Workers Union (FTZWU)
Trade unions: T&A-specific	National Garment Workers' Federation (NGWF), Bangladesh Independent Garment Workers Union Federation (BIGUF), Bangladesh Garment & Industrial Workers Federation (BGIWF)	Garment and Textile Workers Union (GATWU), Garment and Fashion Workers Union (GAFWU), Mazdoor Ekta Manch (MEM)	Pakistan National Textile Leather Garments & General Workers Federation (PNTLGGWF)	n.a.

Source: Updated from Frederick and Staritz 2012.

Note: FDI = foreign direct investment; T&A = textiles and apparel; n.a. = Not applicable.

Table 5A.3 Trade Agreements and GSP Benefits

Country	Regional group	Regional trade agreements	Bilateral/multilateral trade agreements	Generalized system of preferences (GSP)[a] benefits	WTO member
Bangladesh			Proposal by India	Australia, Canada, Japan, New Zealand, Norway, Russian Federation, Switzerland, Turkey, EU (EBA); LDC	Yes
India			Chile (PTA); Korea, Rep.; Singapore; Sri Lanka (2000); Japan; Malaysia (negotiations with EU)	Canada (withdrawn in 2013), Japan, New Zealand, Norway, Russia, Switzerland, Turkey, EU (GSP for apparel only; textiles omitted)	Yes
Sri Lanka	SAARC	SAFTA	India (2001), Pakistan (2005)	Canada, Japan, New Zealand, Norway, Russia, Switzerland, Turkey, EU (GSP+: mid-2005–2010; GSP 2010–present)	Yes
Pakistan			China, Malaysia, Sri Lanka (2005), the Islamic Republic of Iran (PTA), Mauritius (PTA)	Canada, Japan, New Zealand, Norway, Russia, Switzerland, Turkey, EU (GSP; since 2014 GSP+); United States	Yes
Vietnam		ASEAN-Japan, ASEAN-Australia-New Zealand, ASEAN-China, ASEAN-India, ASEAN-South Korea, Rep.	Vietnam-Japan EPA, Israel, Chile (TPP negotiations ongoing)	Canada, Japan, New Zealand, Norway, Russia, Switzerland, Turkey, EU (GSP)	Yes (2007)
Indonesia	ASEAN		Japan (effective since 2008); Pakistan (effective since 2013)	Canada (withdrawn in 2013), Japan, New Zealand, Norway, Russia, Switzerland, Turkey, EU (GSP)	Yes
Cambodia			—	Australia, Canada, Japan, New Zealand, Norway, Russia, Switzerland, Turkey, EU (EBA); LDC	Yes (2004)
China	—	ASEAN-China (Jan. 1, 2010)	Pakistan; New Zealand; Chile; Costa Rica; Hong Kong SAR; Macao, SAR; Peru; Singapore; Taiwan, China; Thailand	Canada (withdrawn in 2013), Japan, New Zealand, Norway, Switzerland (T&A suspended), Turkey	Yes (2001)

Source: updated from Frederick and Staritz 2012, table 3.11, p. 77.

Note: ASEAN = Association of South East Asian Nations; EBA = Everything but Arms; EPA = Economic Partnership Agreement; EU = European Union; FTA = free trade agreement; GSP+ = GSP that offers preferential market access to vulnerable developing countries; LDCs = least developed countries; PTA = Preferential Trade Agreement; SAARC = South Asian Association for Regional Cooperation; SAFTA = South Asian Free Trade Agreement; T&A = textiles and apparel; TPP = Trans-Pacific Partnership; UAE = United Arab Emirates; WTO = World Trade Organization; — = not available.

a. U.S. GSP not included, as apparel is excluded from the U.S. GSP. Further, the U.S. GSP program ended in July 2013 when Congress failed to renew it. Canada's GSP reform withdraws GSP benefits from 72 countries, including China, India, and Indonesia (effective January 2015).

Notes

1. See chapter 2 for details on data sources and key factors, including quality. In this chapter, we do not discuss quality since it is generally a firm-specific characteristic that is not easily influenced by state or national level policies.

2. One of the largest Sri Lankan apparel manufacturers states that it has no difficulty importing inputs in Bangladesh for their Export Oriented Unit (EOU). But in India, although its plant faces no problems importing trim, it does have difficulties importing synthetic fabric, which requires an import license and customs clearance procedures that are lengthy and complicated. Thus, it avoids producing apparel made out of synthetic fabric (National Stakeholders 2014).

3. Chapter 2 reports the average monthly wage in the apparel sector and the minimum wage per month. Although wages would also vary by type of product, this data are not available.

4. In India, industry associations have asked for exemption of excise and customs duty paid for liquid fuels used for particularly diesel generators (AEPC 2013a). In Pakistan, the government suggested that electricity units should switch to coal because it is cheaper than gas. According to the Secretary General of JAAF, a recently introduced reform in electricity tariffs in Sri Lanka will translate into a 15 percent increase for apparel manufacturers and severely impact textile manufacturers' washing and dyeing plants (*Sunday Observer* 2013).

5. A further issue is that mother vessels do not regularly come to ports in India, which requires filing orders on smaller ships that have to be reloaded in Colombo, Singapore, or Dubai, thereby increasing time and costs (National Stakeholders 2014).

6. www.ibtimes.com/despite-low-pay-poor-work-conditions-garment-factories -empowering-millions-bangladeshi-women-1563419.

Bibliography

ADB (Asian Development Bank). 2014. *Quarterly Economic Update: Bangladesh, March 2014*. ADB.

AEPC (Apparel Export Promotion Council). 2013a. "Interministerial Workshop on the Apparel Sector." Background Note, AEPC.

———. 2013b. "Disha: The Journey So Far." *Apparel India* 1 (5).

Aggarwal, A. 2005. "Performance of Export Processing Zones: A Comparative Analysis of India, Sri Lanka and Bangladesh." ICRIER Working Paper 155, Indian Council for Research on International Economic Relations.

———. 2007. "Impact of Special Economic Zones on Employment, Poverty and Human Development." ICRIER Working Paper 194, Indian Council for Research on International Economic Relations.

———. 2010. "Economic Impacts of SEZs: Theoretical Approaches and Analysis of Newly Notified SEZs in India." MPRA Paper 20902.

Ahmed, F., A. Greenleaf, and A. Sacks. 2014. "The Paradox of Export Growth in Areas of Weak Governance: The Case of the Ready Made Garment Sector in Bangladesh." *World Development* 56.

Anner, M., J. Bair, and J. Blasi. 2013. "Toward Joint Liability in Global Supply Chains: Addressing the Root Causes of Labor Violations in International Subcontracting Networks." *Comparative Labor Law & Policy Journal* 35 (1): 1–43.

Barrie, L. 2014. "August 14. Analysis: U.S. Apparel Imports Show Continuing China Competitiveness." just-style.com. http://www.just-style.com/analysis/us-apparel -imports-show-continuing-china-competitiveness_id122560.aspx.

BBS (Bangladesh Bureau of Statistics). 2013a. *Cottage Industry Survey 2011*. BBS.

———. 2013b. *Survey of Manufacturing Industries (SMI) 2012*. BBS. http://www.bbs.gov .bd/WebTestApplication/userfiles/Image/LatestReports/SMI-%202012.pdf.

———. (Various). *Bangladesh Household Income and Expenditure Survey (HIES)*. BBS.

BEPZA (Bangladesh Export Processing Zones Authority). 2013. *Annual Report 2010–2011*. BEPZA. http://www.epzbangladesh.org.bd/web_admin/web_tender_files/BEPZA _2010-2011.pdf.

Besley, T., and R. Burgess. 2004. "Can Labor Regulation Hinder Economic Performance? Evidence from India." *Quarterly Journal of Economics* 119 (1): 91–134.

Bhaskaran, R., D. Nathan, N. Phillips, and C. Upendranadh. 2010. "Home-Based Child Labour in Delhi's Garment Production: Contemporary Forms of Unfree Labour in Global Production." *Indian Journal of Labour Economics* 53 (4): 607–24.

Birnbaum, D. 2013. *Competitiveness of India's Apparel Export*. Apparel Export Promotion Council (APEC).

———. 2014a. "Bangladesh Industry Development Moving Backwards." just-style.com, April 16. http://www.just-style.com/comment/bangladesh-industry-development -moving-backwards_id121251.aspx.

———. 2014b. "Comment: Bangladesh's Garment Trend Lines Look Pretty Poor." just-style.com, June 8.

———. 2014c. *DRAFT: Bihar Apparel Industry Development Project*. Prepared for Final Report I. Bangkok, Thailand: World Bank.

Bloom, Nicholas, Benn Eifert, Aprajit Mahajan, David McKenzie, and John Roberts. 2012. "Does Management Matter? Evidence from India." *Quarterly Journal of Economics*, November.

Cirera, Xavier, and Rajith Lakshman. 2014. *The Impact of Export Processing Zones on Employment, Wages and Labour Conditions in Developing Countries, 3ie Systematic Review 10*. London: International Initiative for Impact Evaluation (3ie).

Clothesource. 2008. "The Great Apparel Sourcing Issues of 2008—and How to Deal with Them." *Just-Style Management Briefing* (March). Bromsgrove, UK: Aroq Limited.

Daher, Mike, and Joe Chmielewski. 2013. "Private Label Sourcing Strategies to Differentiate and Defend: Insights from the 2012–2013 Private Label Sourcing Survey." Deloitte Consulting LLP.

Donaldson, T. 2014. 2014: "Global Sourcing to Be More Costly as Worldwide Minimum Wages Continue to Rise." *Sourcing Journal*. https://www.sourcingjournalonline.com /minimum-wages-steadily-rising-low-cost-sourcing-countries-td/.

Emerging Textiles. 2014. *Labour Costs in Apparel Manufacturing Countries* (Monthly Report). www.emergingtextiles.com/?q=art&s=140129-labour-costs.

Euromonitor/Passport. 2014. *World Apparel Market Statistics: 1999–2013*. Retrieved March 24, 2014, from Euromonitor International.

FBIC (Fung Business Intelligence Center). 2007. "Apparel Production and Cluster Development in China." *Li & Fung Research Centre Industry Series* 10.

FBS (Government of Pakistan, Federal Bureau of Statistics). (Various). *Pakistan Labor Force Survey (LFS)*. FBS. http://www.pbs.gov.pk/labour-force-publications.

Flanagan, M. 2014a. The Flanarant: Can You Choose Your Productivity Philosophy? just-style.com, February 19.

———. 2014b. "The Flanarant: Garment Growth Unlikely under India's Modi." just-style .com, June 9. http://www.just-style.com/comment/garment-growth-unlikely-under -indias-modi_id121934.aspx.

Frederick, S., and G. Gereffi. 2011. "Upgrading and Restructuring in the Global Apparel Value Chain: Why China and Asia Are Outperforming Mexico and Central America." *International Journal of Technological Learning, Innovation and Development* 4 (1/2/3): 67–95.

Frederick, S., and C. Staritz. 2012. "Developments in the Global Apparel Industry after the MFA Phaseout." In *Sewing Sucess? Employment, Wages and Poverty following the End of the Multi-fibre Arrangement*, edited by G. Lopez-Acevedo and R. Robertson, 41–86. Washington, DC: World Bank.

FWF (Fair Wear Foundation). 2012. *India Country Study.* FWF.

Gereffi, G. 1994. "The Organization of Buyer-Driven Global Commodity Chains: How U.S. Retailers Shape Overseas Production Networks." In *Commodity Chains and Global Capitalism*, edited by G. Gereffi and M. Korzeniewicz, 95–122. Westport, CT: Praeger.

———. 1999. "International Trade and Industrial Upgrading in the Apparel Commodity Chain." *Journal of International Economics* 48: 37–70.

Gereffi, G., and S. Frederick. 2010. "The Global Apparel Value Chain, Trade and the Economic Crisis: Challenges and Opportunities for Developing Countries." Policy Research Working Paper 5281, World Bank, Washington, DC.

Gereffi, G., and O. Memedovic. 2003. *The Global Apparel Value Chain: What Prospects for Upgrading by Developing Countries.* Vienna, Austria: United Nations Industrial Development Organization (UNIDO).

Gifford, J., and S. Ansett. 2014. "10 Things that Have Changed since the Bangladesh Factory Collapse." *The Guardian*, April 2. http://www.theguardian.com/sustainable -business/bangladesh-factory-collapse-10-things-changed.

Global Apparel Buyers. 2014. Interviews with Global Apparel Buyers. Interviewer: S. Frederick.

Goto, K. 2014. "Vietnam: Upgrading from the Export to the Domestic Market." In *The Garment Industry in Low-Income Countries: An Entry Point of Industrialization*, edited by T. Fukunishi and T. Yamagata, 105–31. Basingstoke, UK: Palgrave Macmillan.

GSO (General Statistics Office) Vietnam. 2014. *Statistical Yearbook of Vietnam 2013.* Hanoi. GSO.

Haider, M. 2007. "Competitiveness of the Bangladesh Ready-Made Garment Industry in Major International Markets." *Asia-Pacific Trade and Investment Review* 3 (1): 3–27.

Hamdani, K. 2009. *Foreign Direct Investment Prospects for Pakistan.* Islamabad: Pakistan Institute of Development Economics.

Harrigan, J., and G. Barrows. 2009. "Testing the Theory of Trade Policy: Evidence from the Abrupt End of the Multifibre Arrangement." *Review of Economics and Statistics* 91 (2): 282–94.

Hirway, I. 2008. "Trade and Gender Inequalities in Labour Market: Case of Textile and Garment Industry in India." Paper presented at the International Seminar on Moving towards Gender Sensitization of Trade Policy, organized by UNCTAD (United Nations

Conference on Trade and Development), New Delhi, India. http://s3.amazonaws.com/zanran_storage/www.unctadindia.org/ContentPages/452292790.pdf.

ILO (International Labour Organization). 2010a. *ILO Better Work Vietnam Fact Sheet*. ILO.

———. 2010b. "Women Continue to Face Discrimination in the World of Work." Press Release. http://www.ilo.org/islamabad/info/public/pr/lang--en/WCMS_150228/index.htm.

———. 2013a. *Bangladesh Country Report: Trade and Employment*. Dhaka, Bangladesh: ILO.

———. 2013b. "Joint Action Plan to Promote Workplace Safety and Health Launched in Karachi." Press release: October 4, 2013.

———. 2014. "Wages and Working Hours in the Textiles, Clothing, Leather and Footwear Industries." Issue paper for discussion at the Global Dialogue Forum on Wages and Working Hours in the Textiles, Clothing, Leather and Footwear Industries, September 23–25, 2014.

India MOSPI-CSO (Ministry of Statistics and Programme Implementation, Central Statistics Office). 2014. *Annual Survey of Industries 2011–2012*. Volume I. New Delhi: MOSPI-CSO.

India MOSPI-NSSO (Ministry of Statistics and Programme Implementation, National Sample Survey Office). 2013. *Economic Characteristics of Unincorporated Non-agricultural Enterprises (Excluding Construction) in India*. New Delhi: MOSPI-NSSO.

———. (Various). *National Sample Survey (NSS): Employment and Unemployment Situation in India*. http://www.data.gov.in/dataset-group-name/national-sample-survey.

ITC (International Trade Centre). (Various). *Investment Map*. www.investmentmap.org.

JAAF (Joint Apparel Association Forum). 2011. *Sri Lanka Upgrades Infrastructure for Garment Exports*. http://www.jaafsl.com/news/515-sri-lanka-upgrades-infrastructure-for-garment-exports.

Jordan, Luke Simon, Bertine Kamphuis, and S.P. Setia. 2014. "A New Agenda: Improving the Competitiveness of the Textiles and Apparel Value Chain in India." Working Paper, World Bank, Washington, DC.

Kathuria, Sanjay, and M. M. Malouche. 2016. *Toward New Sources of Competitiveness in Bangladesh: A Bangladesh Diagnostic Trade Integration Study*. Washington, DC: World Bank.

Kelegama, S., and J. Wijayasiri. 2004. *Ready-Made Garment Industry in Sri Lanka: Facing the Global Challenge*. Colombo, Sri Lanka: Institute of Policy Studies.

KSA-AM (Kurt Salmon Associates-Apparel Magazine). 2007–2013. *Excellence in Global Sourcing Survey*. Kurt Salmon Associates and Apparel Magazine.

Lu, Sheng. 2014. "2014 U.S. Fashion Industry Benchmarking Study." Department of Textiles, Fashion Merchandising and Design, University of Rhode Island.

McKinsey & Company. 2011. *Bangladesh's Ready-Made Garments Landscape: The Challenge of Growth*. McKinsey & Company Apparel, Fashion & Luxury Practice.

———. 2013. *The Global Sourcing Map—Balancing Cost, Compliance, and Capacity: McKinsey's Apparel CPO Survey 2013*. McKinsey & Company Apparel, Fashion & Luxury Practice.

MINTEX (Government of Pakistan, Ministry of Textile Industry). 2012. *Yearbook 2010–11 and 2011–12*. Islamabad: MINTEX.

———. 2015. *Textiles Policy 2014–19*. Islamabad: MINTEX.

Muzzini, E., and G. Aparicio. 2013. *Bangladesh: The Path to Middle-Income Status from an Urban Perspective*. Washington, DC: World Bank. http://elibrary.worldbank.org/doi/book/10.1596/978-0-8213-9859-3.

Nabi, I., and N. Hamid. 2013. *Garments as a Driver of Economic Growth: Insights from Pakistan Case Studies*. London: International Growth Centre.

Nathan Associates. 2005. *Survey of U.S. Apparel Buyers: Sourcing from Sub-Saharan Africa in the Post-quota Era*. University of Sussex.

National Stakeholders. 2014. *Interviews with National Industry Stakeholders*. Interviewer: C. Staritz.

Natsuda, Kaoru, Kenta Goto, and John Thoburn. 2009. "Challenges to the Cambodian Garment Industry in the Global Garment Value Chain." RCAPS Working Paper 09-3, Ritsumeikan Center for Asia Pacific Studies, Ritsumeikan Asia Pacific University.

NBS (National Bureau of Statistics). 2007. *China's Annual Survey of Industrial Firms (ASIF) (1998–2008)*. Beijing: NBS.

NCAER (National Council of Applied Economic Research). 2009. *Assessing the Prospects for India's Textile and Clothing Sector*. New Delhi: NCAER.

OTEXA (U.S. International Trade Administration Office of Textiles and Apparel). 2014. *Market Reports/Tariffs: Textiles, Apparel, Footwear and Travel Goods*. Washington, DC: OTEXA.

Raihan, S., and M. A. Razzaque. 2007. "A Review of the Evolution of Trade and Industrial Policies in Bangladesh." In *Trade and Industrial Policy Environment in Bangladesh with Special Emphasis on Some Non-traditional Export Sectors*, edited by A. Razzaque and S. Raihan. Dhaka, Bangladesh: Pathak Samabesh.

Rama, M. 2014. *Breaking Barriers to Regional Integration in South Asia*. Manila: Asian Development Bank.

Saheed, H. 2009. "Prospects for the Textile and Garment Industry in Pakistan." *Textile Outlook International* 142: 55–102.

———. 2010. "Prospects for the Textile and Clothing Industry in Sri Lanka." *Textile Outlook International* 147: 79–119.

———. 2012a. "Prospects for the Textile and Clothing Industry in India." *Textile Outlook International* 156: 86–127.

———. 2012b. "Prospects for the Textile and Clothing Industry in Indonesia." *Textile Outlook International* 155: 70–109.

———. 2012c. "Prospects for the Textile and Clothing Industry in Vietnam." *Textile Outlook International* 159: 71–110.

———. 2013. "Prospects for the Textile and Clothing Industry in Cambodia." *Textile Outlook International* 161: 119–58.

———. 2014. "Prospects for the Textile and Clothing Industry in China." *Textile Outlook International* 168: 79–133.

Sahoo, P., G. Nataraj, and R. K. Dash. 2014. *Foreign Direct Investment in South Asia: Policy, Impact, Determinants and Challenges*. New Delhi: Springer.

Saleman, Y., and L. S. Jordan. 2013. *The Implementation of Industrial Parks: Some Lessons Learned in India*. Washington, DC: World Bank.

Sandhu, Kamran Yousef. 2011. "Challenges to Pakistan's Value Added Industry." Paper presented at the Third International Conference on Textile and Clothing, Institute of Textile and Industrial Science, Lahore. http://umt.edu.pk/ictc2011/Presentation.html.

Sri Lanka DCS (Department of Census and Statistics). 2014. *Annual Survey of Industries 2012*. Colombo: Sri Lanka DCS.

———. (Various). *Sri Lanka Labor Force Survey (LFS)*. Colombo: Sri Lanka DCS. http://www.statistics.gov.lk/page.asp?page=Labour%20Force.

Staritz, Cornelia. 2011. *Making the Cut? Low-Income Countries and the Global Clothing Value Chain in a Post-quota and Post-crisis World*: Washington, DC: World Bank.

Staritz, Cornelia, and Stacey Frederick. 2014. "Chapter 7: Sector Case Study—Apparel." In *Making Foreign Direct Investment Work for Sub-Saharan Africa: Local Spillovers and Competitiveness in Global Value Chains*, edited by T. Farole and D. Winkler, 209–44. Washington, DC: World Bank.

Statistics Indonesia. 2000–2011. *Annual Manufacturing Survey (Establishments with 20+ Workers)*. Badan Pusat Statistik (BPS). http://www.bps.go.id/eng/menutab.php?kat=2&tabel=1&id_subyek=09.

Sunday Observer. 2013. "Apparel Industry Will Overcome Challenges." *Sunday Observer*, May 5. http://www.sundayobserver.lk/2013/05/05/fin26.asp.

Tewari, M. 2008. *Deepening Intra-regional Trade and Investment in South Asia: The Case of the Textile and Clothing Industry*. India Council for Research on International Economic Relations (ICRIER).

———. 2009. *The Textiles and Clothing Industry Study on Intraregional Trade and Investment in South Asia*, 40–69. Mandaluyong City, the Philippines: Asian Development Bank (ADB).

Tewari, M., and M. Singh. 2010. *Benchmarking the International Competitiveness of the Indian Garment and Textile Industry*. New Delhi.

TEXMIN (Ministry of Textiles, India). 2015. *Annual Report 2014/15*. New Delhi: TEXMIN.

UNCTAD (United Nations Conference on Trade and Development). 2014. *Skill Development in the Bangladesh Garments Industry: The Role of TNCs*. New York and Geneva: United Nations.

UNCTADSTAT. 1970–2012. *Inward and Outward Foreign Direct Investment Flows, Annual, 1970–2012*. http://unctadstat.unctad.org/TableViewer/tableView.aspx.

UNIDO (United Nations Development Organization). 2013. "Industrial Statistics Database: INDSTAT4 (2013 edition)." Retrieved May 6, 2014, from UNIDO. http://www.unido.org/en/resources/statistics/statistical-databases/indstat4-2013-edition.html.

UNSD (United Nations Statistics Division). 2014a. "World Apparel (HS1992 61+62) Imports (1990–2012)." Retrieved March 3–6, 2014, from UNSD.

———. 2014b. "World Apparel Imports (1992–2012) by Product Categories." Retrieved May 13–15, 2014, from UNSD.

———. 2014c. "World Apparel Imports (2000, 2005, 2009, 2012), HS (six-digits)." Retrieved June 20, 2014, from UNSD.

———. 2014d. "World Fabric and Yarn/Thread Exports (1990–2012) by Product Categories." Retrieved April 1, 2014, from UNSD.

———. 2014e. "World Total and Apparel (HS1992) Imports (All Years)." Retrieved August 11, 2014, from UNSD.

———. 2015. "World Apparel Imports (2013) (HS92)." Retrieved January, 14 2015, from UNSD.

Wijayasiri, J., and J. Dissanayake. 2008. *Case Study 3: The Ending of the Multi-fiber Agreement and Innovation in Sri Lankan Textile and Clothing Industry.* Paris: Organisation for Economic Co-operation and Development.

World Bank. 2005. "End of MFA Quotas: Key Issues and Strategic Options for Bangladesh Readymade Garment Industry." Bangladesh Development Series Paper 2, World Bank, Dhaka, Bangladesh.

———. 2012. *World Bank Enterprise Survey: China.* Washington, DC: World Bank.

———. 2013a. *Beyond Low Wage Labor: Strengthening Bangladesh's Competitiveness.* Vol. 2 of *Bangladesh Diagnostic Trade Integration Study (DTIS).* Washington, DC: World Bank.

———. 2013b. "Value Chain Analysis for Polo Shirts." In Vol. 3 of *Bangladesh Diagnostic Trade Integration Study (DTIS).* Washington, DC: World Bank.

———. 2014a. *World Bank Enterprise Survey: India.* Washington, DC: World Bank.

———. 2014b. *World Development Indicators (WDI), Population (Total) in 2013.* Washington, DC: World Bank.

WTO (World Trade Organization). 2008. *Trade Policy Review: Pakistan Report by the WTO Secretariat.* Geneva: WTO.

———. 2013. *Tariff Download Facility, Applied MFN Tariffs.* Retrieved March 25, 2014, from WTO. http://tariffdata.wto.org/Default.aspx.

WTO (World Trade Organization), UNCTAD (United Nations Conference on Trade and Development) and ITC (International Trade Centre). 2014. *World Tariff Profiles 2014.* Geneva: WTO, UNCTAD, and ITC.

Yunus, M., and T. Yamagata. 2014. "Bangladesh: Market Force Supersedes Control." In *The Garment Industry in Low-Income Countries: An Entry Point of Industrialization*, edited by T. Fukunishi and T. Yamagata, 77–104. Basingstoke, UK: Palgrave Macmillan.

Yusuf, S. 2013. "Can Chinese FDI Accelerate Pakistan's Growth?" IGC Working Paper, London, UK: International Growth Centre (IGC).

Zhu, S., and J. Pickles. 2014. "Bring In, Go Up, Go West, Go Out: Upgrading, Regionalisation and Delocalisation in China's Apparel Production Networks." *Journal of Contemporary Asia* 44: 36–63.

Zohir, S. C. 2001a. *Gender Balance in the EPZ: A Socio-economic Study of Dhaka Export Processing Zone in Bangladesh.* Bangladesh Institute of Development Studies.

———. 2001b. "Social Impact of the Growth of Garment Industry in Bangladesh." *Bangladesh Development Studies* 27 (4): 41–80.

South Asian Country Fact Sheets

BANGLADESH

Current Status

Market share: Bangladesh has the largest apparel export industry of the four South Asian sample countries at $22.8 billion, and the largest market share at about 6.4 percent of global apparel exports. The apparel industry is also extremely important to the economy, accounting for 83 percent of total exports. The industry is dominated by locally owned firms, but foreign direct investment (FDI) played a central role in launching the industry, providing linkages to foreign buyers, technology, and knowledge transfer. The industry is considered a "growth supplier" (like Pakistan)—rather than a "stable supplier" (like India and Sri Lanka)—in that it has increased export value and global market share since the early 1990s.

Product diversity: It is a primary destination for basic commodity items produced in long runs, predominately made from cotton (including trousers, knit and woven shirts, and sweaters/sweatshirts). Firms mostly specialize in low-value and mid-market priced apparel and have not penetrated the high-end apparel market.

Working conditions: Wages and working conditions have long been a source of concern, as evidenced by the frequent strikes and labor unrest after the Rana Plaza disaster in April 2–13 (the single worst incident in the history of the apparel industry, which killed about 1,200 people) and other incidents such as the fire at Tazreen Fashions in November 2012.

Job Potential

How would Bangladesh fare if Chinese prices/wages rose by 10 percent under current policies? For the U.S. market, apparel employment would *rise* (thanks to higher labor demand and the anticipated increase in apparel exports), 4.22 percent for males and 4.39 percent for females. But for the EU market, apparel employment would *drop* by 0.74 percent for males and 0.77 percent for females.

How would this affect Bangladesh's labor pool? As firms demand more labor, apparel wages are likely to increase. A 1 percent increase in expected wages would raise the probability of women entering the labor force by 30.6 percent.

Top Policy Areas

Factors buyers care about (cost and non-cost): Production costs and quality have always been important and have become even more so given the stepped-up competition after the end of the Multifibre Arrangement (MFA) and the global economic crisis. *Stitches to Riches* highlights the following findings: Bangladesh is one of the lowest countries in terms of prices in nearly every major apparel product category. At present, this appears to make up for the issues in meeting buyers' desired criteria in the areas of compliance, quality, and reliability.

Bangladesh could benefit from the following policies:

- Improve productivity by adopting policies (such as additional incentives and transparency) to attract more FDI to ensure access to buyers and additional capital.
- Improve quality and product diversity by reducing import barriers to man-made fibers (through bonded warehouses, duty drawback, cash subsidy, and export processing zones (EPZs)).
- Improve compliance and reliability by ensuring that social policies are enforced (such as better safety conditions in EPZs) and encouraging firms to relocate to EPZs.

INDIA

Current Status

Market share: India ranks second in in terms of value ($12.5 billion) and global market share (3.5 percent), although unlike Bangladesh and Sri Lanka, apparel's share of total country exports is quite low at 5 percent. FDI has played a limited role (less than 1 percent) as a share of overall investment in the textile and apparel industry and as a share of the country's overall FDI inflows. It is considered a "stable supplier" (like Sri Lanka)—rather than a "growth supplier" (like Bangladesh and Pakistan)—in that it has increased export value but its global market share is stable or declining, and growth rates are lower than the world average.

Product diversity: Overall, like Pakistan, it has a more diversified export structure than Bangladesh and Sri Lanka, thanks to a well-developed fiber (cotton), textile, and apparel manufacturing base, with the textile industry larger than the apparel industry in terms of export value. It primarily exports cotton products, including woven and knit tops, skirts, men's bottoms, and embellished and embroidered apparel.

Working conditions: Workers in the formal sector generally enjoy better working conditions and wages than those in the informal sector, where compliance is limited and where most apparel workers are actually employed.

Job Potential

How would India fare if Chinese prices/wages rose by 10 percent under current policies? For the U.S. market, apparel employment would *rise* (thanks to higher labor demand and the anticipated increase in apparel exports), 3.32 percent for males and 2.51 percent for females. For the EU market, apparel employment would *rise* by 4.30 percent for males and 3.26 for females.

How would India's labor pool be affected? As firms demand more labor, apparel wages are likely to increase. A 1 percent increase in expected wages would raise the probability of women entering the labor force by 18.9 percent.

Top Policy Areas

Factors buyers care about (cost and non-cost): Production costs and quality have always been important and have become even more so given the stepped-up competition after the end of the MFA and the global economic crisis. *Stitches to Riches* highlights the following findings: India has mid-range unit values (as does China), despite buyers' perceptions of its having comparatively higher prices. Where they differ, however, is across all other criteria, with India ranking among the bottom in productivity, product diversity, and lead times.

The following policies could help India increase apparel exports:

- Improve product diversity by reducing tariffs and import barriers to ease access to man-made fibers (such as more transparency for duty drawback schemes and bonded warehouses, and removing anti-dumping duties on man-made fibers). Also lower excise taxes or provide other incentives to develop a domestic man-made fiber industry.
- Improve productivity by helping firms enter the formal sector and take advantage of economies of scale with less complex labor policies. Also promote FDI for apparel by adopting clear and transparent policies on foreign ownership (already in place for textiles) and within export processing zones (EPZs).
- Improve market diversity by taking advantage of access to emerging markets.
- Shorten lead times by using industrial parks to provide better infrastructure in a concentrated way.

SRI LANKA

Current Status

Market share: Sri Lanka ranks third in terms of value ($4.4 billion) and global market share (1.2 percent), although apparel has a relatively high share of total country exports at 45 percent. Similar to Bangladesh, FDI played a central role in initiating the industry in Sri Lanka, but today the industry is dominated by joint ventures and domestically owned. It is considered a "stable supplier" (like India)—rather than a "growth supplier" (like Bangladesh and Pakistan)—in that it has increased export value but its global market share is stable or declining, and growth rates are lower than the world average.

Product diversity: Its export profile differs from that of other South Asian countries because the country is a source of intimate apparel, trousers, and swimwear, and exports are equally divided between cotton and man-made fiber products. Its exports are more niche and fashion-oriented items rather than volume products.

Working conditions: These are generally better than in the other South Asian countries.

Job Potential

How would Sri Lanka do if Chinese prices/wages rose by 10 percent under current policies? For the U.S. market, apparel employment would *rise* (thanks to higher labor demand and the anticipated increase in apparel exports), 0.09 percent for males and 0.08 percent for females. For the EU market, apparel employment would *rise* by 8.55 percent for males and 7.87 percent for females.

How would Sri Lanka's labor pool be affected? As firms demand more labor, apparel wages are likely to increase. A 1 percent increase in expected wages would raise the probability of women entering the labor force by 89.2 percent.

Top Policy Areas

Factors buyers care about (cost and non-cost): Production costs and quality have always been important and have become even more so given the stepped-up competition after the end of the MFA and the global economic crisis. *Stitches to Riches* highlights the following findings: Sri Lanka's apparel prices are higher than competitors in all major product categories (driven at least partly by relatively high and rising labor costs). It also needs to improve on lead times and product range and availability. But it is viewed positively in other areas (notably compliance and political stability).

Sri Lanka could benefit from the following policies:

- Diversify end markets and export destinations for existing products (such as active wear and intimate apparel) by entering into more trade agreements and adopting clear investment policies to demonstrate political stability and attract FDI.
- Diversify by expanding into new products such as formal wear and high-end outerwear that require higher levels of skill. Also position itself as a regional apparel and textile trade hub to take advantage of infrastructure and location.
- Relieve labor shortages by promoting industrial relocation (such as tapping into the more remote and war-torn areas in the North and East) and attracting more female workers (who benefit from working in factories located close to their villages).
- Capitalize on its skills advantage by encouraging firms to expand into new products such as formal wear and high-end outwear.

PAKISTAN

Current Status

Market share: Pakistan ranks fourth in terms of value ($4.2 billion) with the same global market share (1.2 percent) as Sri Lanka, though apparel's share of total exports is lower at 19 percent. FDI has not played an important role; in the apparel sector, the share of foreign-owned firms is estimated to be less than 2 percent, and only slightly higher in the textile sector. It is considered a "growth supplier" (like Bangladesh)—rather than a "stable supplier" (like India and Sri Lanka)—in that it has increased export value and global market share since the early 1990s.

Product diversity: It specializes in basic cotton woven denim and chino trousers, low-priced knitwear such as polo shirts and t-shirts, and fleece sweatshirts.

Working conditions: They are better in the formal industry than in the large cottage sector, but short-term or temporary contracts are widely used, particularly for women, and the factory fire in Karachi in September 2012 highlighted poor safety standards.

Job Potential

How would Pakistan do if Chinese prices/wages rose by 10 percent under current policies? For the U.S. market, apparel employment would *rise* (thanks to higher labor demand and the anticipated increase in apparel exports), 8.93 percent for males and 8.50 percent for females. For the EU market, apparel employment would *drop* by 0.21 percent for males and 0.20 for females.

How would Pakistan's labor pool be affected? As firms demand more labor, apparel wages are likely to increase. A 1 percent increase in expected wages would raise the probability of women entering the labor force by 16.3 percent.

Top Policy Areas

Factors buyers care about (cost and non-cost): Production costs and quality have always been important and have become even more so given the stepped-up competition after the end of the MFA and the global economic crisis. *Stitches to Riches* highlights the following findings: Pakistan offers low prices in most product categories, but it lags behind competitors in reliability and political stability.

Pakistan could benefit from the following policies:

- Increase product diversity by reducing barriers on imports so as to ease access to man-made fibers (such as duty and tax remission for exports, and export processing zones (EPZs)).
- Attract FDI by adopting policies to reduce red tape and increase transparency to close the gap with South Asian countries whose textile and apparel industries are located primarily on the coast.
- Diversify markets by taking advantage of market access to emerging markets.
- Shorten lead times by improving road infrastructure to facilitate access to ports for exporting firms.

- Shorten lead times by clustering strategies to provide key infrastructure and common facilities.
- Enhance perceptions of stability; many buyers will not travel to Pakistan, so domestic firms often travel to Dubai to meet them, which makes sourcing complicated.

www.ingramcontent.com/pod-product-compliance
Lightning Source LLC
Chambersburg PA
CBHW041700210326
41598CB00007B/479